THE SETTLEMENT AFTER THE
WAR IN SOUTH AFRICA.

THE SETTLEMENT
AFTER THE WAR
IN SOUTH AFRICA

BY

M. J. FARRELLY, LL.D.

KENNIKAT PRESS
Port Washington, N. Y./London

THE SETTLEMENT AFTER THE WAR IN SOUTH AFRICA

First published in 1900
Reissued in 1971 by Kennikat Press
Library of Congress Catalog Card No: 78-118468
ISBN 0-8046-1217-X

Manufactured by Taylor Publishing Company   Dallas, Texas

CONTENTS.

APPENDICES.

THE WAR AND ITS ISSUES: FROM VARIOUS STANDPOINTS.

INTRODUCTION.

It is now the greater part of four years since I first came to South Africa with the intention of carefully studying at first hand its various problems—political, racial, economical and legal. I had determined on a year's travel, deciding on South Africa instead of Australia or America on account of the fact that for many years past I have known as personal friends or acquaintances most South Africans of British or Dutch descent who have studied law at the Inns of Court in London—a connection which I have found of the utmost value and interest in my travels, as South Africa, whether Dutch or British, has been for a long time, and seems likely to continue to be, ruled largely by lawyers.

My purpose was to write an impartially worded statement of the various burning questions, some of the developments of which have now fixed on South Africa the eyes of the civilised world—Boer and Uitlander in the Transvaal—Imperial or Republican factor, Dutch or British predominance in all South Africa—black and white—missionary and anti-missionary — Indian and anti-Indian — capitalist and labourer at the diamond fields of Kimberley and on the Gold Reef of the Witwatersrand—Roman-Dutch and British law in all South Africa.

With such an object in view I have visited every State and Colony and territory south of the Zambesi River, and I have had the privilege of discussing most pending political questions—of so much greater magnitude since then than I quite realised at the beginning as possible—with nearly every leading public man in South Africa, from the High Commissioner, and other imperial governors and administrators of British territories and British agents in the Transvaal, to the present and late Ministers of the two Colonies of the Cape and of Natal; from the presidents and executives and volksraads of the Republics of the Vaal and of the Orange River to leaders of the Bond in Cape Town, to leaders of the Uitlanders of Johannesburg and to Reform prisoners in Pretoria jail. In this way I have steadily adhered to the method of inquiry which I mapped out before I reached South Africa, and which I stated in the first of a short series of letters which I contributed to a leading London journal, beginning in November, 1896.

As I have stated, my inquiry was not confined to the purely political question of British or Dutch predominance in South Africa now engrossing all minds. In pursuance of my original design, I collected their views on the exploitation of minerals from directors of " De Beers " in Kimberley, as well as from Socialists in Pretoria; from Johannesburg millionaires and from workmen in the gold mines. On land tenure I have conversed with Boer commandants holding cattle runs of twelve thousand acres as well as with the Bijwoner, living on an overlord's land with a less certain than the most precarious of feudal tenures. I have inquired into the prospects of missionary enterprise, visiting the chief missions of all the Churches in Basutoland (the greatest of the armed Kaffir reserves) and have compared, later on, the methods of civilising the Kaffir adopted by the Société Évangélique de Paris in Morija with those followed at the monastery of the German Trappists in Natal. I have noted the doubts as to native adaptability to Christianity presented to me by white trader and Kaffir chief. On the momentous problem for the European race of the right way to deal with the Kaffir—the *origo malorum* between British and Dutch—Kaffir reserve or Kaffir dispersion—the land for the black or for the white—and generally the relation of the Kaffir to the dominant race, in the towns and on the veld, on the farm and in the mine, I have ascertained the theories of European mine owners, of Boer stock farmers, of British agriculturists; of missionaries who champion the Kaffir almost to the verge of claiming for him social and political equality; as well as of home-born and Colonial British who approve of the Kaffir's exclusion from the foot-path in Johannesburg. As far as possible I have contrasted with these theories what the Zulu and the Basuto, the Swazi and the Matabele have to say to one on those matters, and on the incomprehensible ways of Boer and Briton and white men in general; although the task of penetrating into the recesses of the Kaffir mind, I am assured, by life-long observers, is one which no European can ever feel even hopeful of having achieved. On the utility of permitting or encouraging Indian immigration I have been favoured with views so widely divergent as, in Rhodesia, those of the Chamber of Commerce of Buluwayo, and in Durban, those of the Association of Indians (Mohammedan and Hindu) of Natal.

The legal problems of South Africa—questions of legislation and administration—I have had the privilege of discussing with all the Chief Justices and most of the Judges of the High Courts, as well as with past and present Attorneys-General and State Attorneys of the Cape, of Natal, of Rhodesia, of Griqualand West, of the Transvaal and of the Orange Free State; and also with the Resident of Basutoland, with Native Commissioners, and other magistrates administering the law affecting natives in the Kaffir reserves and in territory occupied by Europeans. No one in Europe who has not made a special study of this aspect of the South African public field can form an adequate conception of the number and complexity of these problems, dealing with such unfamiliar topics as the degree to which legislation should admit natives to civil or political rights, similar to those possessed by Europeans; the recognition to be accorded to native usages; the regulation of Asiatic immigration; the effect of systems of land tenure, native and European, on the supply of labour for agriculture, for the mines, for industries and generally on the economical progress of the country: the special, and, to European eyes, the anomalous laws enacted to protect the production of diamonds and gold; the restriction of the supply of alcohol to the natives; the prohibition of the supply to them of arms.

The very titles of these enactments and of the officials to enforce them, strike strangely on the ear; the Curfew L aws the Glen Grey Act, the Faction Fight Acts, the Native Commissioners, the Protector of Indians. Above all, fruitful of endless and persistent and fierce controversy among lawyers and laymen alike, are the famous enactments styled the I.D.B. Acts, which, contrary to usual principles of jurisprudence, reverse the burden of proof for all persons, European or native, by making it incumbent on the possessor of rough diamonds to prove his innocence.

Legislative power has been vested in authorities of every kind, and promulgated in every form, from enactments by British Colonial Parliaments of the Cape and Natal, to resolutions of a Chartered Company and of a Legislative Council in Rhodesia; from Volksraad besluits in the Transvaal to proclamations of the High Commissioner in the native reserves.

In another book I hope to publish the result of these inquiries. It is true that I have adhered to this method of investigation long past the period which I had originally believed would be sufficient. This, however, was the result of a discovery—made by other Europe-born inquirers in South Africa—that, however admirable a method of induction is the collection of opinion on both sides of every controversy, a year is not a sufficient time in which to test the value of opinions or the reliability of assurances. Within the first year I carried out my plan of travel almost in full. If, however, I had written my conclusions in November 1897, I should now be compelled to very gravely modify them. For—to take the problem overshadowing South Africa even then, now so tragically solved—I had come to the conclusion that there would be no war between the British and Dutch. I had accepted the assurances given to me, from the Orange River to the Limpopo, by men in the highest station in the Republics, that no war party and no war spirit existed; and

I had agreed with the view of Mr. Bryce, whose book on South Africa I had followed with attention, that infinite patience and the slow touch of time would heal.

This view, indeed, was repeatedly expressed to me within the past twelve months—when I had long ceased to hold it —by public men of such political experience as past and present Ministers of the Crown in Cape Colony and Natal, and by men of such opportunities of gauging the most sensitive barometer of peace and war as the Committee of the Johannesburg Stock Exchange.

However, at the end of my appointed time, a pressure of professional work (chiefly reaching me as advisory counsel to the Transvaal Republic on the legal questions arising under the Conventions with the Imperial Government) decided me to prolong my stay in South Africa for another year.

Since then, the increasing strain of the ever-darkening political scene, fraught with such sequence of blood and tears to all who live in South Africa and to all citizens of the Empire—a situation which, so far off as November, 1898, I saw and proclaimed could have no ending but war—has held me as a spectator, and, to some slight degree, a most unwilling actor in the drama, which I had come only to witness.

That I have warned, with all the force I could command, the Governments of the two Republics against the fatal course into which they were led by counsellors of their own race, I have no reason to regret; although much, that my warning was in vain.

CAPE TOWN,
  July, 1900.

THE SETTLEMENT AFTER THE WAR IN SOUTH AFRICA.

CHAPTER I.

METHOD OF INVESTIGATION.

IN a dispatch which I sent to a London journal from Johannesburg, dated the 21st November, 1896, I wrote:—

"To investigate the more important facts of the political situation in the Transvaal and South Africa was the task which I set before me some months ago. Fuller information as to the reality of the relations between British and Dutch in South Africa is obviously a necessity of the hour, in view of the influence exercised by home opinion on European expansion in that quarter of the world. The plan of inquiry which, after a good deal of consideration, seemed to me the most likely to be useful, was to ascertain the opinions of leading public men in the Transvaal, the Free State, and the Cape Colony on all those points relating to South African political affairs on which home opinion appeared specially to require information, and which at the same time are of the first importance. This information has been freely given to me, and I shall in consequence be able, where controversy exists, to present the views of both sides. I decided also to see as far as possible all aspects of life in the Transvaal and South Africa—on the farms and in the veldt, as well as at the mines and in the towns. It is, of course, not to be forgotten that some controversies about South African affairs cannot be decided by any investigation into facts. Often the dispute is not about facts, but about general theories of life and action. Take, for instance, the question of the arming of natives, as the Basutos were armed with European weapons with which they defeated a General of the Imperial forces forty years ago, which they have refused to surrender to a colonial demand, and which they still retain. Diametrically opposite conclusions will be reached by theorists who think that the white man has no right to be in South Africa —a not altogether unheard-of section at home—and those who hold that European immigration stands in need of no apology. No investigation into facts can alter this divergence of view. Similarly, on the question of vote or no vote for the natives, or on that of British or Dutch supremacy— if supremacy and not fusion there must be—or on that of Imperial expansion or Imperial abandonment of our dependencies, not so much, if at all, do the facts of the situation, as the political preferences or other prejudices of the disputant, determine his opinion and action. To save time and useless trouble, I therefore decided to take some things, fruitful enough of controversy, as granted. I take it as granted that Europeans have a right to immigrate to South Africa or any other region of the earth in which they can live in health. I assume that the native races have certain rights, at least those of being treated with humanity and justice, however far they may fall short of fitness for equality of political privileges. I assume that the British and Dutch speaking settlers are equally entitled to be here; they are manifestly destined to stay here. I shall not waste time in arguing for the proposition that the British Government has no occasion to apologise for its existence in South Africa, and is justified in doing its best to develop territory in its possession for the advantage of the citizens of the Empire and of civilisation generally. Finally, I take it that a general agreement among South Africans as to a particular policy or as to the existence of a particular state of things is more likely to be correct than conclusions arrived at by home-staying politicians or others who have never come into contact with the social conditions about which they theorise.

"It may occur to some that this enumeration is unnecessary. But if recent criticism of the conduct of South African affairs be scrutinised it will be seen that exactly contrary assumptions underlie much that has been written. Unfortunately, too, the history of South Africa displays at large the grave and lasting consequences of blunders of British policy, due only partly to ignorance of the actualities of the situation, but much more attributable to fixed theories of political ethics or professedly religious principle as to the rights of the Kaffir, the respective claims of the British and Dutch, the right or duty of the Imperial Government to abandon or remain in South Africa. And the holders of these, like most other theories, are practically proof against argument based on facts. Not, however, that theory, political, philanthropic or religious, is alone to blame. The see-saw of party government—most unhappily allowed to affect Imperial policy as regards the Colonies, although supposed to be excluded from affecting Imperial foreign policy—has enabled the incessant veering of home opinion to shape the direction of South African politics. But it is nearly always some fact, proof, theory or other (often, no doubt, shielding itself behind misrepresentation of facts) which has periodically convulsed home opinion, and so contributed quite as much to direct Imperial action as the presence or absence of information as to the value of gold reefs, or the utility of Colonies as feeders of trade, or the material advantages or material dangers of new fields for emigration.

"The first discovery to be made by anyone who endeavours to get at the outlines of the problem, is that the political situation in the Transvaal cannot be separated from that in the Cape Colony, in the Orange Free State, and in Natal. Politics in the Transvaal are so intimately interwoven with those of the neighbouring Republic and those of the old Colony—of which both the Republics are historically off-shoots—that they are incomprehensible if taken separately. A mixed European population, starting from the old Colony—originally Hollander, French, Huguenot, and British—spreads over all these States. In the towns, English is spoken; in the country—with the exception of the English-speaking Eastern province of the Cape—Dutch. But the population is practically bilingual, in the sense that nearly every one can speak the two languages, although English is for the town, and Dutch for the country and for speaking to the Kaffir. The two Republics were severed from British dominion within living memory—the Transvaal in 1852, and the Free State in 1854. The connection between the Republics and the Colonies is not comparable to the case even of such close neighbours as Switzerland and Italy. It can only be compared—and even then the comparison falls short of the reality—to the connections arising from the interchange of population between the different sections of the United Kingdom. Family ties link together the whole population—Dutch speaking and English speaking—from Table Mountain in the Cape to the Limpopo in the Transvaal. A common history and tradition, a common religion, and a common use of the two languages, weld them into a community. Even the persons who play on the public stage in one section of the territory are borrowed from another. The present President of the South African Republic was born a British subject in the Cape Colony; the Chief Justice is an immigrant from the Colony. The President of the Orange Free State who held office longest, bore a title conferred by the Queen. The present Chief Justice is a brother of the Chief Justice of Cape Colony. The highest officials of both Republics have been repeatedly chosen from the Colony. Dingaan's Day—the Transvaal public festival commemorated on the 16th December—celebrated the defeat by the Boer emigrants from the Cape of a Zulu chief in the now British colony of Natal. Not one public act of importance can be done by the Transvaal Government or the Cape Government without its effect passing from one end to the other of this contiguous territory of the Republics and the Colonies, and affecting all this mixed European population. The diversion of Transvaal trade to Delagoa Bay touches immediately the Cape Boer. As showing the community of sentiment and interest which pervades this mixed population, out of many instances, those of Majuba Hill and the Jameson Raid are sufficient. They affected and were affected by the politics of the Cape Colony only one degree less immediately than those of the Republics. In fact, South Africa presents much of the situation which New Amsterdam presented before the complete fusion of British and Dutch produced the New York of the War of Independence.

" British and Dutch are here in South Africa to stay. The self-governing Colonies and the British Government are as much in possession as are the Republics. In the interest of European civilisation, harmonious co-operation between British and Dutch is plainly desirable; the common interest of both sections (equally concerned in the maintenance of internal peace and security, order and efficiency of administration) points in the same way. Some perception of this common interest is shown by the existence of a certain body of sentiment in favour of a confederation of the Colonies and of the Republics. The presence of a common danger is a permanent stimulus to that sentiment. The black man never fails to realise, and by his action to suggest to the white man, the underlying solidarity of interest, if not of sentiment of all Europeans. When Boer and Briton were supposed to be in conflict as a consequence of the Jameson Raid the Matabele marked his sense of the occasion by rising in revolt at Bulawayo. The fact, however, that a political combination is desirable is unhappily no proof that rulers and people will cause it to be formed. Washington thought in 1787 that disruption was more likely to result from the jealousies of the States than federation from their perception of a common interest. This, too, although among many links of union between the States were to be counted the use of a common language, the existence of similar Republican constitutions, and the memory of common perils endured and victories gained. It is clear that there were forces making for union in America not to be found in South Africa. But this is not all. The alternatives before the American States were those of federation on the one hand, and separate State existence on the other. The issue was a single one. In

South Africa, the possibilities of the future are more numerous. Will the future bring confederation or separate development? If confederation, is it to be under the shield of the British Empire, or as the union of a group of States independent of the Empire? And, lastly, whether the States be confederated or isolated, subject to the British Empire, or independent, what section of the population, British or Dutch speaking, seems likely to predominate in political power and in language? The mind of the people in South Africa must largely furnish the ultimate determinant of the future. It will be a fatal error to suppose that so-called "practical" considerations (meaning those of immediate pecuniary gain) must necessarily decide their future action. Of all facts, the most stubborn and creative are the ingrained beliefs and prejudices of a people—which are usually attributable to quite other causes than a regard for their material interests. A generalisation which is correct enough when applied to operators on the Stock Exchange fails to explain the action of a generation of Huguenots who lost all in fleeing from France.

"On the other hand, the set of home opinion must play a large part. Dominant British opinion was certainly behind the King in his attempt to tax the American colonies.

"In South Africa, Imperialist and Republican, British-born and Boer, colonists of every nationality seem to agree with impressive unanimity that one great cause—if not the greatest—of such cleavage of British and Dutch as exists has always been an apprehension of Imperial enforcement of a mistaken policy as regards the natives. The Englishman at home who creates public opinion is understood to be liable to be swayed by a section who proclaim the black man as a brother and a citizen, capable of exercising and absolutely entitled to full political citizen's rights and entire social equality. Two centuries of experience have led the Dutch-speaking colonists to believe that tutelage, and not equality, is the black man's portion of justice. His belief is that shared by Sir Theophilus Shepstone, and announced as a rule for future British administration in the proclamation of 1877, which annexed the Transvaal. 'Equal justice does not and should not involve the granting of equal rights, such as the exercise of the right of voting, to savages, or their becoming members of a legislative body, or their being entitled to other civil privileges which are incompatible with their uncivilised condition.' It is true that the institution of responsible government in the Colonies has lessened the prospect of Imperial interference in the matter, as the Cape Glen Grey Act shows. But there are in practice limits to the self-government of a self-governing dependency, and to the extent to which it can disregard current British opinion. The creation of the coloured vote in Cape Colony has not reassured the Boer. This subject, therefore, is one for careful inquiry, as immediately bearing on the prospects between Briton and Boer, and of confederation between the States. It may be convenient if I mention here the other subjects on which I have sought information from men of all parties through South Africa.

"As far as bearing on present conditions and prospects, the history of the European in South Africa, and particularly of the circumstances which have formed the character of the Boer, must be considered. The present condition of parties in the Transvaal particularly, and in the Free State and Cape Colony; their grounds of divergence, racial and religious, and their policies I have made the subject of special inquiry; as also the policy of the Transvaal Government, internal and external, and the policy of foreign powers, including Germany, as regards the Republics and South Africa. The views of eminent lawyers, including the Chief Justices of the Republics, on the question of the existence or non-existence of the suzerainty over the Transvaal proclaimed by the Convention of Pretoria of 1881, will be of interest. Leading men on both sides of the internal controversy have given with considerable care their views as to the validity of the claims of the Uitlanders, and on all the matters of legislation and administration raised on their behalf. The relation of all the coloured races, including the immigrant Indians and Chinese, to the white population constitute, as has already been stated, a matter of the gravest interest; and I have been favoured with the opinion of the arbitrator appointed by the British and Transvaal Governments to decide upon the claims of the Indians to be admitted to the Transvaal. The views of the various political parties as to the right policy for the British Government, the Colonies and the Republics respectively in South African affairs have also been a matter for inquiry. In my following letters I shall deal with these subjects. Where divergence of views exists I shall state as fairly as I can the case presented by the authorities on both sides. Finally, I shall state the conclusions at which I have arrived."

In an interview published in the *Pretoria Press* of the 6th December, 1896, I said :—

"The last point to which I should wish to refer is the prospect of a lasting peace between the two divisions of the European race in South Africa, the English and the Dutch sections of the population. I do not wish to put forward my opinion as a final conclusion, but I think that if there should be a frank recognition on either side, that the other side is entitled to be here, and a spirit of reasonable compromise, there is no reason why a *modus vivendi* should not be arrived at. Not perhaps in the present, but almost certainly in the future, the pressure of the Kaffir and the other non-European populations would be likely to lead to the coalition and the ultimate fusion of the white people. The fact that a certain course of action is a reasonable one and for the benefit of all parties is no proof, however, that it is going to be adopted."

These last remarks have unfortunately proved prophetic, but this citation from the interview will show the spirit in which I had entered into my inquiries and in which they were conducted to the end.

CHAPTER II

THE NECESSITY OF FINALITY IN THE SETTLEMENT.

THE one conclusion which is borne in upon the mind of anyone of any European nationality who has considered the complex problems of the South African situation is the necessity of a final settlement, once for all, of the question— In whose hands is political power to be committed? On the answer to this question depends the whole future of the race in South Africa. This is obvious; but much more depends on the solution. On it depend the safeguarding of the integrity of the British Empire and the fulfilment of its high mission in the world. On the solution depends the preservation of all that the great Raj means for all the subject races of the world, for Kaffir, for Hindu, for Malay; as well as for the European colonist who has been so strangely impelled to annex within the brief period of a few generations the whole surface of the habitable globe. The object with which I write, therefore, is to show that, above and beyond the rights and wrongs of the particular issue to which Boer and Briton in South Africa are committed, finality in the settlement should be the dominating thought in the minds of the statesmen who will have to decide when the cannon is silent; finality imperatively required to further the mission in the world of the European race, a mission so strongly realised now in England and in the Empire by those who, a few years ago, would have looked upon the vision as an idle dream; to promote the fusion of the European race in South Africa in furtherance of the higher mission of the race the world over; to ensure the elevation ultimately, and in the present the just treatment of the subordinate races; a burden not of the white man's selection. These are the objects to be borne in mind by those who endeavour to influence the final settlement of the present struggle, in South Africa for British Imperial or Boer Republican prodominance. That the continued existence of the Empire turns on the inclusion or the exclusion of South Africa from its sphere of influence any impartial student of the situation must feel convinced. But that nothing must be left to the settlement of time alone in this struggle between Imperial British and Republican Dutch supremacy, is the one great political fact which I purpose to make clear.

The integrity of the British Empire, it is a truism to say, rests on its moral as much as or even more than on its material foundation. It may be thought unnecessary—but it is not—to recall a truth falling in the category of those so well known that people think they may be safely neglected. Its moral foundation centres in its prestige. Its material foundation in the extent of its territory, in its strength in armaments, in its numbers of men trained to arms, in its possession of gold, in the dimensions of its trade.

Prestige is a word not in very good repute in England; a foreign word not perfectly acclimatised. Nevertheless, it deserves naturalisation, for, dispassionately considered, it represents the reputation of the Empire and of its governing classes within as well as without its own borders for, primarily, military power in men and munitions of war, in valour and in tactical skill; but quite as much for sanity, for intelligence, for a sense of justice in administration, and for gratitude to its public servants. Macaulay points out most truly how the chief foundation in India of the permanence of British rule is due to the conviction in the mind of every Indian, of Rajput, of Sikh, of Gurkha, of Bengali, of the absolute reliance which they can place on the plighted British word. Every sworder of John Company knew that his daily ration of rice would be paid to him as his veteran's pension as safely as the salary of the viceroy; although the

veteran warrior were lying helpless in the most forgotten of
remote villages. Whereas, notwithstanding the promise of
mountains of gold from the native ruler, the certain fate of
the veteran warrior no longer fit to wield his weapon was to
be thrown out on the roadside to furnish a meal for the
vultures. In the word "prestige" must be included
reputation for qualities such as this, the Empire's gratitude
and its sense of justice.

The present war in South Africa and all the preceding
race strife between British and Dutch is attributable to the
fact that the reputation of the Imperial Government, not
alone with the Dutch, but with the British descended
colonist, with the Kaffir and with the Indian immigrant, has
been precisely the reverse of its reputation in India. No
firmness, no consistency; alternately negrophilist and anti-
Kaffir; alternately expansionist and Manchester School.
Nothing more fixed than the certainty of Imperial change;
unless indeed it were the cruelty of Imperial ingratitude.

How then will the reputation of the Imperial power for
the qualities of good government be affected by any uncertainty in the final settlement?

It is to be remembered that not alone the peoples of
Europe, but the people of the United States of America will
be judges on the Imperial action in the settlement of South
Africa. And not alone these, but the self-governing people
of Canada, of Australia and New Zealand, and the vast
subject population of India and of the far East; above all,
in this matter of the settlement, the British colonist in
South Africa and those of Dutch descent, who are hanging
with anxious attention upon the Imperial decision, and are
considering now, and will decide at the end, what estimate
they should form of the likelihood of the Imperial sceptre
remaining in the hands of the composite nation, Celt and
Teuton and Scandinavian, in the Islands of the Northern
Sea.

Let us glance at the other, the material foundations of
the Empire. How will they be affected by the prospect
whether the settlement in South Africa is to be permanent

or temporary; whether a chance is to remain of an alien and hostile power rising in arms and excluding the Empire from South African territory? It is admitted that it is essential to the maintenance of the British Empire in its integrity that the sea route to India and Australia should be kept open. If a hostile power were to dominate South Africa the maintenance of that route would be clearly impossible. The sinking of a single ship in the Suez Canal would block the road to India. If India and Australia were severed from the Empire, the defection or the annexation of Canada would clearly be a matter of a very short time. A speck on the map would represent British territory after such defections; after such an annihilation of the life-work of Clive and Hastings, of Wolfe, of Pitt and Nelson and Wellington, of Havelock and Lawrence, and of the contemporary administrators and generals who from Kandahar to Cairo, from Simla to Cape Town, from Khartoum to Bloemfontein and Pretoria, have carried on the work of their predecessors as servants of the Empire.

Looking at South Africa exclusively, the newer age would see the gold and the diamonds of the Witwatersrand and Kimberley, the most productive fields in the world, in the hands of a hostile power. The recent policy and action of the two Dutch-speaking Republics have given proof, if proof were wanted, that gold and diamonds are equivalent to the possession of cannon and rifles, and provisions and all munition of war, and the services of veteran strategists and skilled artillerists. And even the most home-looking of theorists could not fail to see that, in regard to trade, the loss of South African predominance would mean the necessary downfall of the commercial prosperity of the British Isles. The trade route to Central Africa, to preserve which so many British statesmen have striven (even the Colonial Minister of Majuba Hill), would be lost for ever. The fruits of the annexation of Egypt and of the conquest of the Soudan would be destroyed.

But the moral foundation of the Empire is the most important. Stronger than steel is the sword of the spirit. The

Empire rules India by the mind rather than by the cannon. What will be the effect of Imperial vacillation, want of intelligence, want of appreciation of the facts of the external world, on the minds of the people of India? and on the minds of the people of Canada, Australia and New Zealand? and on the minds of the people of the American Commonwealth, tending now so closely to friendly co-operation with the Empire in the common world work of the race?

Now the arguments used in England, in the controversy at present proceeding there as to the settlement in South Africa, mainly turn on the contention, raised by a small minority, that none of these important consequences bearing upon the integrity of the Empire depends in the least on the solution of the South African crisis. It is contended that the question of Dutch or British supremacy may be solved one way or the other without affecting the future of the Empire; without impairing its prestige in India or in the Colonies, in Europe or in the American commonwealth; without cutting off its sea route to India and Australia, or the over-land route through Africa to the Soudan and Egypt.

To some minds, and I confess to mine, the most complete answer to this contention is to be found in the universal conviction of the British Colonies, not merely in Africa, but in Australia, New Zealand and in Canada, that the issue of Dutch or British supremacy in South Africa means life or death to the Empire. To many it seems worse than idle for a section in England, whose experience has never reached the outlying territories of the Empire, to set up their opinion on a matter of this kind against the universal consciousness of the people in the self-governing colonies, who are convinced, and who have sealed their conviction with their blood, that the whole future of the Empire, its material and moral foundation, turns on the assertion and the firm establishment once for all of Imperial supremacy in South Africa. Securus judicat orbis terrarum.

With this conviction I have been compelled by the logic of facts to agree; and my task in these pages is to show the reasons why I think this conviction should be shared by all citizens of the Empire. I propose first to consider the general outline of the history of British and Dutch relations in South Africa, and the conclusions as to the right Imperial policy now to be adopted to be deduced from that history. But before considering this part of the subject there are two considerations I wish to lay stress upon.

The first is, that the Empire is exceedingly modern; it has not lasted for ever; there is no vast store of political experience, such as in popular imagination exists, to draw upon. What has existed only one hundred and fifty years need not last for ever.

The restless activity of the island-born Elizabethan sailors, though fully a century later in their enterprises than the Portuguese under Prince Henry the Navigator, has caused in most British minds an illusion of greater antiquity in the Empire than history warrants. The Battle of Plassey in 1757 marks practically the beginning of our present world-wide dominion. The victories of Drake and Raleigh, the colonisations of Penn and Baltimore, were obliterated as far as the Empire was concerned when, one hundred and twenty-five years ago, a mad king controlled the destinies of England, and by an assertion of almost Russian autocracy—"Mettre le roi hors de page"—cut off the American colonies from the British community, whose laws and language and religion and social forms they inherit; a tie so much stronger than at one time was believed the happier developments of later years have shown. This, of course, is only true as to the material foundation and the extent of the territory of the Empire. The Empire is exceedingly modern in the extent of its territory; nearly as modern as the United States of America.

Now, strange though it may seem to home-staying Britons, this modernness—with its suggestion of the Empire being merely temporary—is fully present to the minds of many leading South Africans, more especially those of Dutch descent. At a Queen's jubilee banquet in Johannesburg in June 1897, I heard an unquestionably loyal speaker of Dutch descent refer to the inevitable dissolution of the

Empire; to what he took to be the inevitable time when a separate and independent South African nation would take its place in the world. In a recent missive to the Governments of Europe an official of a Dutch Republic referred to the Empire as a Colossus with feet of clay. A comet, not a fixed star, is the conception of our world-wide dominion, cherished not alone by some of our good cousins on the Continent of Europe, but by some citizens of the Empire.

This is a conception which most citizens of the Empire do not share. Rather the drawing together of the English-speaking peoples is their ideal goal. And to some of us, who are students of the Law of Nations, rather the political incorporation of the whole of the dominant race of Europe is the event towards which we move, than any repetition of the sundering of the community of the race; which, beginning in the disruption of the Empire of the Cæsars, ended in the disruption of the Empire of the Hapsburgs.* But it should never be left out of the mind of the statesmen who direct immediate Imperial action—although happily not ultimate Imperial destiny—that their firmness, their sense of justice, their gratitude for service to the Empire, their tenacity of purpose, their approximation to or receding from the Hapsburg grip, are being carefully scrutinised by millions the world over—some with anxiety lest they fall below their Imperial station; others with hope, nay, with a sure belief, that they will fall.

The other consideration I wish to present is that the preservation of the heritage of the British Empire—the most glorious instrument of justice the world has yet seen —is not the private property of individual British citizens to be accepted or abandoned as a "damnosa hereditas," at

---

* Since these lines were written, and for the first time since the last Crusade, and more completely than in the Crusades, the Great Powers of the European race stand united in arms against a non-European foe. The massacres in China have brought about that united European intervention which some observers have long foreseen as inevitable. (In an article on the United States Chinese Exclusion Act, published in the American *Law Review* of October 1894, I referred to this prospect of general European intervention.)

the suggestion of their individual interests. It is a trust
for the whole human race.

I have referred to the brief period of time within which
the British Empire has been built up; but the process has
been only a part, although a mighty part, of a much greater
movement. It is difficult to realise how few of the European
race have clearly conceived the brevity of the term within
which the whole of the earth has fallen under the control
of European ideas, of law, of limits of social conduct, to
some degree of religion and everywhere of European military
power. At the present moment the supreme law in all that
vast section of Africa which stretches from the Zambesi to
the Lion's Head takes as its highest authority—highest
though not most immediate—the decrees of a Pretorian
Prefect of the Roman Empire in York; and yet here, least
of all in the community of Christendom, is the solidarity of
the European race the world over recognised. That the
dispersion of the race over the whole globe and its being
placed in a position of guidance over subject populations is
an accident few can believe. But, apart from this, of the
deepening of the perception of duty towards these races,
of the spirit which, in regard to one section of Europeans, is
called Imperialism, and the acceptance of the white man's
burden, there can be no doubt. Here, in South Africa, one
is the more struck by the rude recrudescence of 16th century
nationalist particularism, an unfortunate result of the disruption almost completed in that age of the organised
community of Europe—a disruption which has given rise
to so many things besides the individualist form of the
present Law of Nations. Now, to many minds, it is clear
that this revolt of Dutch sentiment in South Africa against
the dominant spirit of the European world furnishes the proof
of its destiny of failure. But it is none the less essential
that that strange perversion of thought among some Englishmen, which leads them to look on devotion to the integrity
of the Empire as an exhibition of national selfishness, should
be banished from the minds of those on whom the high
function of directing Imperial action has fallen.

CHAPTER III.

HISTORY OF THE BRITISH AND DUTCH IN SOUTH AFRICA.

THE necessity of revictualling the Dutch ships engaged in the East India trade, and the adoption by Louis XIV. of a policy of religious conformity in France, were the causes of the complexion borne by the original white population in South Africa. Soldiers, sailors and farmers in the service of the Dutch East India Company, and French Huguenots, have combined, with a large German contingent, to form the Dutch-speaking people.* Strange to say, the territory of the Cape was, long before the Dutch occupation of 1652, declared a British possession by certain English captains. But the annexation of 1620 was not confirmed by the Government of James I., no more than the annexation of Spitzbergen by other bold mariners; and when the Huguenots came to the Cape after the Revocation of the Edict of Nantes in 1685, the Dutch Company held undisputed possession of the tiny colony at the Castle on the Peninsula. As was to be expected in such a small community, the Huguenot mind has played a greater part at the Cape than in England, or Ireland, or Holland, whither the bulk of the refugees fled. The intensity of the Huguenots' convictions, reaching to fanaticism, seems the true origin of the present religious fervour of the average Boer. Notwithstanding a careful and

* I am reminded by Chief Justice Kotz' of the Transvaal that, for some unexplained reason, writers on South Africa ignore the very large German strain in the Dutch-speaking people; although names so well known as that of President Kruger are obviously German. In 1806, the time of the second British occupation, about one-third of the names were German.

systematic exclusion of undesirable members from permanent residence, the other colonists of the Dutch Company, however determined and valiant, cannot have been characterised by an extraordinary depth of religious conviction. In fact, the servants of the Company were largely recruited from desperate and broken men of every European nationality. But dominating, overshadowing, affecting all that has happened till this year of 1900, was an event of 1658, before the Huguenots had come. A number of slaves, captured from Portuguese slave ships, were handed over to the New Colony, being sold on credit to the farmers. All the same, let us not forget that philanthropy which abolished, also established, negro slavery. The captive West African was bought by Christian missionaries to prevent his being eaten, or boats being floated in his blood.

The British Empire's acquisition of a real footing in India in the second half of the 18th century, and the anti-republican zeal of the last Stadtholder of the house of Orange-Nassau, determined the presence of the British section of the population. Since the original temporary cession after the French Revolution—" les provisoires sont les plus permanents "—made by the exiled Stadtholder, writing from Kew, and more especially since the definite cession of the Cape and Ceylon and Guiana from the Kingdom of Holland to the Imperial Crown in 1814, a cession based on payment of several millions of British money, the stream of British immigration has been steady. Except in one instance, it has not been of very great volume, or setting towards the country rather than the town. This exception was the State-aided immigration of 1820, when the eastern province of Cape Colony was colonised from England. As a result, the Eastern Province is the only district where the farming population speaks English. In the rest of the Colony, and generally through South Africa, English is spoken in the towns and Dutch in the country.

The characteristics of the present Boer population of the two Republics are mainly due to their life in the Colony before the Great Trek of 1836. Their religion, their government, their language, their military organisation, all formed part of their life in the Colony. Even the nomadic life of trekking had its origin there, though their subsequent flight from British rule, continued for over a generation, deepened the habit and gave it a political purpose.

The language is a simplified modification of the Hollander tongue of the 17th century. French was forcibly suppressed early in the 18th century; otherwise it is probable that, as the Huguenots were the great religious and intellectual force in the little community, the language would now be French as well as so many of the family names. Their religion is Calvinist, of the Dutch variety; here, as elsewhere, disciplining the mind by the stress of fatalism, which moulded English Roundhead and Scottish Covenanter as well as the Lowland Burgher who fought with Alva. Their strength in fight is made tenfold by the conviction that the sword of the Lord smites for His saints. President Kruger's speech in Pretoria in December 1896, ascribing his burghers' victories to the direct interposition of Heaven, and warning his marksmen not to boast of their skill with the rifle, and his address in Kroonstad in March 1900, ascribing the reverse of the anniversary of Majuba Day, and the capture of General Cronje, to their boastful celebrations of Majuba, give an epitome of the orthodox Boer's view of success in war. At the same time, a struggle for existence prolonged over generations, against beasts and men, lions and leopards, Bushman's poisoned arrow and Zulu's assegai, have developed courage, resource and self-reliance. More than this, military discipline, not to be acquired in isolated border combats, has been impressed on the farmer's mind by a system, reaching back for centuries, of universal compulsory military service. Every male from eighteen to sixty is under the military command of the Field-Cornet of his district. In times of extreme danger the age limit begins at sixteen, and has no fixed time for ending. The steel-bow tenancy of the northern farmers on the Scottish borders is the nearest British parallel.

But, notwithstanding his democratic church and democratic military duties, and, until very recently, a general condition of equality in respect to economical position, what has been evolved is not a peasant *égalitaire*, but a peasant aristocrat. The subjection of the negro, whether by force or other inducement, and the relegation to an inferior and alien race of nearly all manual labour, have produced in the Boer a distaste for such labour—a distaste, no doubt, intensified by climatic influence—and has contributed to form as well an extreme independence of demeanour, quite dissociated from any reliance on an abstract liberty of the citizen. His people are the chosen race of the Bible, which is his guide; and it is part of the design of Providence that the black man should toil.

Lastly, the Government of the Colony, both Dutch and British, was conducted in many points in such an ill-judged manner, having regard to the bent of the popular mind, as to produce an ingrained hostility to Government interference. In all things political, autocrat; in all things commercial, monopolistic, such was the government of the Dutch East India Company. Strong Government and military obedience the Boer was ready to support, and to enforce when urgent necessity plainly showed such to be unavoidable. But for ordinary purposes and every-day life as little of Government as possible. And to prevent military usurpation they came to prefer to elect by popular vote even their military commanders, from Field-Cornet to Commandant-General. To this impatience of anything they consider as unnecessary official meddling, their heritage of revolt in their blood and their memory largely contributed. Their ancestors—fugitive adventurers of every European nationality, Hollanders who carved a Republic from the territory of Philip II., French who fled from their fair land sooner than obey their King; the descendants, hereditary revolters, impatient of restraint, religiously fanatic and religiously war-like, peasant aristocrats by Divine decree, Roundheads turned Virginia planters, Frenchmen and Germans who speak Dutch.

Such was their character in the old Colony.

Next comes the event—the result of that character and of

the circumstances of the time—the event which created one British Colony and two Boer Republics, the Great Trek. The Great Trek of 1836 was a strange sight.

"Masses of the people, including some of the very best men in the country, abandoned or sold for little or nothing some of the choicest lands in South Africa, and left the Colony avowedly to get rid of English rule and to form independent communities anywhere and at any distance in the interior."

What caused this flight? The answer to this question will set in a clear light many of the perils and difficulties of the present and past political situation in the Transvaal and South Africa, and will carry a lesson for guides of British public opinion.

The remote causes are, of course, to be found deep in the past life of Dutch and Huguenot and British. The immediate cause was the well-meaning but utterly misguided policy of the Imperial Government. Missionaries and party see-saw divide the blame. This policy may be described as negrophile and anti-Boer as regards the relations of black and white, and as alternately rash and timid as regards territorial expansion. The British Government has frequently, and at one time invariably, assumed the truth of missionary allegations, and held that, in all quarrels between Boer and Kaffir, the Boer was always wrong; going at one time to the fantastic and monstrous extreme of endeavouring to subject Dutch-speaking white men to the coercive criminal jurisdiction of Griqua chiefs. The British Government, according to whether an Imperialist or Little Englander party happened to be in power, has swung again and again with bewildering inconsistency from a policy of extending the territory of the Empire at vast expenditure of blood and treasure, to a policy of abandoning territory with precipitation and with an astonishing disregard of obligations to friends and allies.

The manifesto of Pieter Retief, one of the Boer leaders, dated 22nd January, 1837, sets forth the main causes of the Great Trek. The abolition by the British Government of the apprentice labour system—long applied to the blacks, and of the Dutch system of compelling them to reside in definite locations—had flooded the Colony with wandering plunderers —"turbulent and dishonest vagrants," as Retief calls them. The manner in which the Imperial abolition of slavery had been carried out had inflicted severe loss on the farmers. Only a fraction of the real value of the slaves was allotted by the Imperial Parliament; and this fraction was reduced to a nominal sum by the extraordinary condition that payment would only be made in London, a condition which compelled the farmer to sell his claim for a trivial amount to an agent. The British policy of recognising the "independence" and "sovereignty" of Kaffir savages on the Colonial borders had rendered the farmers on the border districts liable to constant risk of pillage and murder, which the British Government either could not or would not check, while it actively interfered to prevent the farmers avenging themselves. The missionary anti-Boer agitation in England and the predominance of the London Missionary Society's agent (a Dr. Phillips), in the direction of British policy at Cape Town, had convinced the farmers that no fair play was to be expected from any British Government. The revolutionary doctrine of the political equality of white and black, denounced with entire accuracy by the first British Governor of the Cape as an invention of the French Revolution, and subsequently to be repudiated by the first British Governor of the Transvaal, had been, on missionary instigation, adopted as a Christian theory of Government by the Imperial authorities. The Dutch-speaking farmer, who had to live among the blacks so placed on political equality, regarded this policy as not only irreligious and unscriptural, but as destructive of order, and "proper relations between master and servant," and as a standing danger to life and property.

On the border all these evils pressed most heavily; so from the border districts of Beaufort, Graaf Reinet, Somerset, Albany, and Uitenhage, set off this exodus of the chosen people, 98 per cent. of the whole coming from those districts. The emigrant farmers with their wives, and children, and servants, their house-waggons and long teams of oxen, and, above all, with their rifles and their Bibles, set their faces to the wilderness.

" We solemnly declare that we leave this country with a desire to enjoy a quieter life than we have hitherto led. We will not molest any people or deprive them of the smallest property ; but, if attacked, we shall consider ourselves fully justified in defending our persons and effects to the utmost of our ability against every enemy. We complain of the unjustifiable odium which has been cast upon us by interested and dishonest persons under the name of religion, whose testimony is believed in England to the exclusion of all evidence in our favour ; and we can see, as the results of this prejudice, nothing but the total ruin of the country. We quit this Colony under the full assurance that the English Government has nothing more to require of us, and will allow us to govern ourselves without its interference in future. We are leaving the fruitful land of our birth, in which we have suffered enormous losses and continual vexation ; but we go with a firm reliance on an all-seeing, just, and merciful God, whom we shall always fear and humbly endeavour to obey."

On a summer day in December 1896, I have taken down from the lips of a " Voortrekker" of 1836—at that time in Graaf Reinet a boy of 10—an enumeration of the causes of the Great Trek identical with those in the manifesto of Retief; although he told me he had no recollection of that manifesto. But, as typical of the Boer even of to-day, I append other reasons he assigned, and to which, in characteristic fashion, his wife assented. The first was that the Colony was becoming too crowded. The next was that the trek fever had seized on the people, as in 1868 it drove the Boers over the Kalahari desert to escape from death to a subjection to a German military administration. The last was that the Great Trek was designed by Providence, so that savage places of the earth might be peopled by Christian men.

The territorial results of this movement of a few thousand Boers have already been referred to. But the effect on the mind of the Boer has been no less marked. As a friendly chronicler put it, "Having been on trek for 44 years, the trek has eaten itself into their hearts. They are still on trek." * But it is not merely the trek fever—moving for,

* Mr. W. A. Aylward.

moving's sake. It has been consecrated by time and proved efficiency as a political remedy for oppression. And British territory now hems them in and prevents their trekking further. The love of isolation has matured in the heart of the Boer; he feels crowded if a single habitation can he seen anywhere within the sweep of the horizon. His house, as he would wish it to be, and as it still is in most cases, reminds one of a ship on the open sea; with the blue arch of the sky above, and the green and grey circle of the veld around, broken by nothing but the slopes of the kopje, blue in the distance.

It is difficult within brief limits to trace even in outline the events which followed the Great Trek. Only those bearing immediately on present problems can be touched, and the fewest words must suffice. The emigrant farmers leaving the Colony came upon a coast region on the Eastern slope swept bare of inhabitants by the murderous legions of Tshaka, the Zulu chief, who had perfected a new military organisation. This land was a *res nullius*. Tshaka merely exterminated; he did not occupy. The farmers first tried peaceful methods. The treacherous Zulu Dingaan, successor to Tshaka, beguiled their leaders with their words, and then massacred Retief and his companions at his kraal at which they were his guests. The farmers then tried war, and broke the power of Dingaan on December 16th, hence the Transvaal State festival, and founded the Republic of Natal. Here they were met by Colonial proclamations calling them British subjects. A British enactment of 1836 assumed jurisdiction for the Cape Courts over offences by white persons in Africa, south of latitude 25°, the latitude of Delagoa Bay. Finally, in 1845, after many shiftings of policy, the Imperial Government authorised the annexation of Natal—after the Boers had attempted to form an alliance with Holland—an offer which the King of Holland repudiated. Fleeing again from British rule, the Boers retired to the interior beyond the Drakensberg range, and again set up their Republican Government and their Dutch-speaking Volksraad. Yet again pursued by proclamations of their British allegiance, they fought and lost the battle of Boomplatz in 1848, and their territory from the Orange River to the Vaal was annexed to the British Crown as the Orange River Sovereignty. All the Boers north of the Vaal River—the territory of the present Transvaal—were left unsubdued, but still were designated British subjects and rebels by proclamation, and a price was set on the head of their leader, Pretorius the elder.

So far the advance movement against the Boers was in favour, notwithstanding some waverings, with the Imperial Government. The pendulum now began to swing in the opposite direction. The reaction began as a countermove to the subtle and ungrateful policy of Moshesh, the Basuto chief, really a creature of the previous negrophilist policy of the British administration. Moshesh was a petty Basuto chief, who had taken advantage of the destruction of his Zulu enemies by the Boers and of Imperial negrophilist policy to gather around him in the mountains now called Basutoland the broken remnants of many clans. These, with British sanction, he armed with European weapons, and became a power in the land. To consolidate his power he proceeded to intrigue against the British who had created him—herein as ungrateful as any European prince or democracy. He proposed an armed union with Pretorius and the proscribed emigrants beyond the Vaal River, and a forcible intervention in the Orange River Sovereignty.

The Imperial pendulum swung. After having for six years (from 1846 to 1852) protested that the emigrant farmers were under indissoluble allegiance to the British Crown, and would never be allowed to set up their Republican Volksraad, a complete change of front followed the unmasking of the Basuto. "The minutes of a meeting at Sand River"—commonly called the Sand River Convention— signed by British delegates, originally appointed to assess a fine on the Basutos, and delegates of the Transvaal rebels in January 1852, guarantee in the fullest manner on the part of the British Government to the Boers north of the Vaal River the right to manage their own affairs and to govern

themselves according to their own laws, without any interference on the part of the British Government.

The Imperial troops were then sent against the Basuto
chief, and were signally defeated at the battle of Berea, in
December 1852; Moshesh, at the head of thirty thousand
well-armed Basutos, driving back the British General Cath-
cart. What followed? A step, the effects of which exist in
South Africa to-day, to the astonishment of British and
Dutch alike; an unconditional surrender by the Imperial
Government.

The war against the Basuto was abandoned. But much
more than this. The home Government actually decided,
under the influence of a cold fit of "non-expansion" and
economy, accelerated by defeat in war, to follow up the
release of the Boers in the Transvaal, who asked for the
release, by the abandonment of the Boers and others in
the Orange River Sovereignty, who protested against the
desertion. The abandonment took place in total disregard
of the declared wishes of the Assembly. Delegates were
sent to England to protest. The Imperial Commissioner
shook off these too loyal subjects, and agreed with the anti-
British party to establish the Orange Free State. This
decision of the Imperial Government is embodied in the Convention of Bloemfontein of February 1854.

In the twenty years which elapsed from 1854 few events
peculiar to South Africa materially modified the situation.
The world-wide extension of means of communication, the
increasing perception of the importance of markets, had a
certain influence on British Imperial policy, but had not
created European rivalry. New conditions, however, arose
after this time. The discoveries in Central Africa came to
their culmination in the work of the expedition under
Sir Henry Stanley. The establishment of trading posts
by the King of the Belgians on the suggestion of that
explorer—after British authorities of the Colonial Office had
cautiously declined his offer—directed the minds of other
European States to Africa—once again to supply "something
new." "Ex Africa semper aliquid novi." The entry by

Germany into the industrial arena of the world market—one
of the results of its consolidation under Prussian influence—
and the rivalry of France in the same field, due to the
wonderful recuperating power of its people, ended in a
general European agreement on the subjugation of Africa,
embodied in the Act of the Berlin Congress. The "Scramble
for Africa" ensued; ancient Portuguese claims were revived,
and, within a decade, every power of Western Europe, except
Austria, was to be found with territorial claims over some
portion of the land inhabited by the black man.

In Imperial policy expansion became once more in the
ascendant. Under the Colonial Secretaryship of Lord Carnarvon—guided by and inspired by Mr. Froude—a design of
South African Confederation, rather than of direct Imperial
authority, was formed in 1874. One new condition had
meanwhile arisen in its favour. The grant of responsible
Government and local autonomy to the Cape Colony promised
considerably to restrain interference by home enthusiasts in
the conduct of native affairs.

Meantime, since 1854, the history of the two sparsely
populated Republics was one of incessant struggle with the
Basuto, the Griqua, and the other Kaffir powers which Imperial policy had allowed to be set up on their borders.
Internecine conflicts between the Boers themselves were not
unknown. The Transvaal was for the time rent into separate
republics; and a forcible annexation of the Orange Free State
was actually attempted by President Pretorious (the younger)
of the Transvaal—the same Pretorius being subsequently
elected President of the Free State. With the exception of
the Kaffir troubles, the progress in prosperity of the two
Republics was unmistakable, though few in Europe before
1877—outside of British circles—were interested either in
the constitution or the geographical position of these minor
experiments in Republican Government. Much, however,
might be said of the wise rule of Sir John Brand, President
of the Free State for a quarter of a century, and of the
ambitious dreams of President Burgers of the Transvaal—the
first to invoke aid from the Hollanders in men and money.

For a long time prior to 1877 certain Colonial statesmen, such as Sir George Grey and Sir Richard Southey, looked on the abandonment of the territory of the Republics as a colossal blunder of the Imperial Government. A vast South African dominion under the British flag, stretching from Cape Town to the Zambesi, was their ideal. They regarded the Boer system, says a friend of the Boers, as embodying " stagnation; waste of public land, which they looked on as the true treasury of Colonial Empire, and a retardation of the only progress they had faith in, which to their minds was of itself a crime." The accession to power of Lord Carnarvon, and the acceptance of the views of Mr. Froude, gave the Grey policy a forward impulse ; and Sir Theophilus Shepstone's annexation of the Transvaal in 1877 was one of the results.

The inevitable swing of the Imperial pendulum was, of course, to come. After Majuba Hill, when a British force was defeated by the Boers, the Transvaal was retroceded. The story of the retrocession is sufficiently familiar to obviate the necessity of repetition. Two observations will be sufficient for the present. In the first place, the parallel to the Imperial retreat before the Kaffir after the Basuto victory of Berea in 1852 is obvious. If the Transvaal was to be retroceded, it was unfortunate for British prestige that it was not surrendered before Majuba Hill. The South African deduction—for Boer and Basuto—was necessarily that the best way to get good terms from the British Empire is to fight. Again, the Government of Mr. Gladstone appears to have been under the impression that the territory of the Transvaal was too worthless to fight about.

In 1884 the States of South Africa consisted of two British Colonies (the Cape and Natal) ; two Boer Republics —the South African Republic and the Orange Free State ; and various native States under direct Imperial Government, such as Basutoland, Griqualand West, and others. It is worth noting that Basutoland was not declared British until the Basutos had been defeated in war by the Free State, when Sir Philip Wodehouse interfered ; and that all these nominally British territories are really Kaffir reserves. Also, that the propriety of the annexation of the Kimberley diamond fields was disputed by the Orange Free State; and that the operations of the Chartered Company were to end in cutting off the Boers from the interior. One of the ever-recurring fits of Imperial hesitation—the inner history of which will be interesting when it is published— allowed Germany to annex a vast tract of South-West Africa; all of which had been for years within the sphere of influence of the Cape Colony, and the chief, if not only port of which is still British. The agreement of the Imperial Government to submit British claims in Delagoa Bay to the arbitration of a French President had removed the British flag from that harbour, while, however, a right of pre-emption was retained.

This brief survey brings us down to the origin—the immediate cause—of the recent political situation in the Transvaal. An absolutely new complexion was put upon affairs by the opening of the goldfields and the discovery of gold in the Transvaal in 1887. No other political event of magnitude has since occurred; other than the British annexation of Zululand and Amatongaland.

The financial situation of the restored Republic is understood to have induced the throwing open of the goldfields, prospecting having been hitherto prohibited by the Volksraad of the farmer State. The inevitable inrush of British and other European gold-seekers changed the whole political conditions of the Transvaal—before that time every white man was welcome to be a burgher—indeed was placed on the Field-Cornet's list without application—and the introduction of many millions of European capital concentrated on its affairs the attention of the civilised world; an attention which political agitation from 1892 to the outbreak of the war had not caused to relax. The problem before the war obviously arose from the fact that the original Boer population retained all political power, having enacted new laws for that express purpose. The Boer leaders directed all the internal and external affairs of the mixed community, except in so far as the British Government retained a power of supervision over treaties with foreign States— a supervision regulated by the London Convention of 1884.

The Government of the Transvaal Republic is and was in the hands of about 15,000 Boer electors, representing about 60,000 to 80,000, people in all. These electors chose the President, the Commandant-General, the Volksraad. The total white population—the bulk of whom immigrated within the last twelve years—has been calculated at from 200,000 to 300,000, including the Boers. The native population is estimated at about 350,000. The area of the land— fertile, and rich in minerals—is about that of the United Kingdom. The gold output of £11,000,000 a year before the war had placed the Transvaal third if not second in the list of gold-producing countries; and its vast stores of coal and iron were practically untouched. The State, which in 1877 felt a debt of £215,000 a heavy burden (which it had no immediate means of paying), was in possession of a revenue of nearly £4,500,000, drawn almost exclusively from the gold mines.

In a letter from Pretoria in December 1896, I wrote :— " The upholders of the Boer Government justify their resolve to retain power in their hands on the ground that by this means alone can the Boer's independence and his right to govern his Republic in his own way be effectively maintained : and that in this way alone can his right in the land and in all which it produces be made predominant, as it justly should be. ' A crowd,' they say, ' of adventurers seeking money has met here from all quarters of the globe. The gold they extract was here, in our possession in our own land, before they came. We have not compelled their coming, nor is this their abiding place. They will return to their homes in a few years ; and strangers are never allowed to share in the government of their temporary dwelling-place. We do not know what they would do with political power if we gave it to them ; but to judge from their actions in the past and their present denunciations they would use it to oust us, of whose ways they do not approve. We are

the men who have fought for our freedom, and have wrested
this country from Moselekatse and his cruel Matabele hordes.
The strangers have fought no one; they came merely to
reap where we have sown.'

"It will be my task to set forth the claims of the
Uitlanders, and the reply of the Boers over all the main
points at issue.   Meanwhile, one striking feature of the
situation must be noted.   The Boer himself stands not where
he was; here, as everywhere, the old order changeth.   The
power of gold, called forth by the Boer Government, has
done more than assemble the Uitlanders of Johannesburg; it
has created the Boer of Pretoria—the townsman Boer, a
contradiction in terms.

"The main characteristics of the mind of the Boer, while
still on his wide-spreading farm, away in the dreamy hills,
with his Bible and his rifle, remain unchanged.   But in the
towns it is different, and the town Boer governs while the
country Boer reigns.

"The old order changeth.   The Boers have been divided
into social classes; and the mind of some of those classes
has sadly altered its outlook on the world.   Gold was the
great engine of both changes; education, altered purpose,
and altered social functions following.   The stoppage of the
trek ranks next; land, in vast farms, is no longer to be had
for the asking by any burgher.   Settled peace, and its
attendant ills, play a great part in the change.   And, lastly,
the shrinking of the world—the closing of the ranks of the
Family of Nations through steam and the telegraph—has
left sure if slow traces.

"Where formerly the Boers were a single class, with like
duties, equality of fortune, and a sentiment of equality, there
are now politicians and administrators, lawyers, engineers,
speculators in the mines, shares, and land values, as well as
farmers.   Even among the farmers a class has arisen ominous
as any—the landless rustic—the bijwoner, the bye-dweller."

CHAPTER IV.

BRITISH RIGHTS IN SOUTH AFRICA.

UNDERLYING much Continental criticism of British methods
in South Africa, and more especially of the Imperial negotiations with reference to the claims of the Uitlanders and
to the interpretation of the Conventions with the Republics,
is an assumption, taken directly from that section of the
South African press which upholds the Republican propaganda, that there is some superior right, inherent or acquired,
in the Dutch Republics over the Imperial Government to
existence or authority in South Africa; and similarly some
superior right in the Dutch and French Huguenot and
German descended individual colonist over the British
descended or British-born colonist. Is there any foundation
for this assumption?

In the preceding historical sketch I have stated, as fairly
as I could, the impression an unbiassed reading of South
African history is likely to make on one in no way hostile
to the Dutch sentiment or people. It discloses a long
list of mistakes of Imperial policy. To these I shall refer
again. But does it uphold the Boer propagandist assumption
that there is some superior right to South African territory,
and to the government of all or any portion of its inhabitants,
in the Republics rather than in the Imperial Government?
Or does it establish the more striking assumption that
colonists bearing Dutch, German, and Huguenot names
have any higher claim to live their lives in South Africa
under ordinary civilised conditions, including the condition
of political liberty, than those of British descent?

Let us first consider the right of the Imperial Government. The origin of its present title to the Cape Peninsula, and to a further stretch towards the interior (about one-third of the present Cape Colony) is based on a formal Treaty of Cession of 1814, between the Kingdom of Holland and the British Government, ceding the Cape Colony and other Dutch possessions to the Imperial Crown for the sum of £6,000,000. On cession, therefore, not conquest, the title rests. It is further to be noted that the original occupation of the Cape was undertaken in 1796 at the request and in the name of the last Stadtholder of the House of Orange, a fugitive in England. The annexation of 1806 was a warlike operation against the Batavian Republic, an ally of France, which, together with France, had engaged in war against the British. Nevertheless, in the negotiations at the general settlement of Europe following the overthrow of the First Napoleon in 1814, the British right to retain the possession of the Cape and to the portion of Cape Colony already referred to, was not based on a military occupation already effected. A purchase was negotiated, embodied in the Convention of 1814 with the Kingdom of Holland, then newly established, the Stadtholder having been transformed into a King. The original title to the Peninsula, therefore, which should clearly be borne in mind, is not conquest, but peaceful cession, on terms of mutual advantage to both the contracting Powers. The parallel which some Continental writers have found in the conquest and partition of Poland does not therefore seem very evident. The Peninsula, be it remembered, not the rest of the Cape Colony, which, with the exception of a small portion, bounded on the east by the Fish River, has never been under Dutch, but always under British Government.

But there are other titles of the Imperial Government in South Africa. Immense sums have been spent in Kaffir wars —a long series from the first date of British occupation until a few years ago. The wars of the Kei River created the Cape Colony as it is now known. The crushing of the Zulu, at a cost of £6,000,000, freed the Transvaal and the Orange Free

State in 1879 from ever present danger. Similarly, the occupation of Bechuanaland, at a cost of £2,000,000 in 1884, the pacification and firm government of the Basuto—the Gun War alone of 1883 cost £3,000,000—the reduction of the Matabele and the Mashona, have left the population in the Dutch-speaking States free from the Kaffir menace which threatened them for generations. Indeed, it is only too evident that the subduing of the Kaffir with a view to the maintenance of peace between the two sections of Europeans must be described as premature. If it had not been effected, the military energies of the Boer must necessarily have been occupied in defending his life against native risings, instead of in the war on the British Colonies. The blood of British soldiers has been for a hundred years shed like rain in repressing these attacks. Gaika and Galeka, Pondo and Griqua, Basuto and Zulu, Swazi and Matabele, and Mashona, have all taken their toll of blood from the forces of the Imperial Power.

Then, again, the peaceful subjugation and the restraining from attack of the Kaffir tribes is to be considered. In the present war 60,000 armed Basutos, thirsting for revenge for the loss of their land annexed to the Orange Free State, under the unequivocal designation of the " Conquered Territory," have been restrained from interfering by an Imperial Administrator. The Imperial Governor of Natal keeps in check a horde of 100,000 armed Zulus, who have petitioned for his permission, as their Supreme Chief, to take part in the present war. At a signal from the Imperial representative in Bechuanaland tens of thousands of Bechuanas would swarm over the western border of the Transvaal. One word from the High Commissioner would precipitate the Swazi on the eastern border.

These services in outlay of gold, in expenditure of blood, in labour of administration now affect, and always have affected, the safety and the prosperity of every European community, Dutch or British, in the Colonies, the Territories, or the Republics in all South Africa. The Imperial

Government has, indeed, thought the maintenance of peace and the upholding of civilisation to be worth the bones of many a Pomeranian Grenadier. Every sovereign expended, every soldier's life lost, has represented a direct gain to every European inhabitant, inside as well as outside, the Republics of the Vaal and the Orange River.

Again, the enormous British immigration into South Africa during the hundred years of British rule is to be remembered. The eastern province of Cape Colony is the English province *par excellence.* It is the result of an organised immigration of British farmers, brought about under the direct auspices of, and at an enormous cost to, the Imperial Government. In what respect is the title of these immigrants and their descendants to live in South Africa and hear their language spoken, less than the right of descendants of subjects of the Dutch Crown, now living in territory transferred by treaty to the Empire? There was no Dutch-speaking or other European population in that region when the British went there. Similar considerations obviously apply to the British immigration to Natal, colonised by British subjects in 1820, long before the Boers trekked to the Hinterland in 1836. And with as much force do they apply to the British colonisation of the vast territory northward to Rhodesia. What prior Boer title exists in these regions? Where, then, is the justification for the ideal of a Dutch-speaking Republic ruling South Africa from Bulawayo to Simonstown?

Greatest of the services to all South Africa are those rendered by the naval forces of the Imperial Power. It is indisputable that the peace of South Africa and the independence of its States are guarded by the Imperial navy. Without that protection no one believes that the territory of South Africa would be left free for a single year from annexation by a Great Power. The German annexation in 1884 of the comparatively barren tract of south-west Africa is a sufficient proof—if proof were wanted—that, in the European scramble for Africa, the richest portion of the whole continent in diamonds and gold would not have been forgotten.

It is, therefore, understating the case to say that all this expenditure of treasure, of lives, of labour, for a hundred years, and with no prospect of cessation in the present or in the future, show how intolerable is the assumption that the Dutch-speaking Republics, as States, have any superior right in the territory of South Africa over that of the Imperial Government.

Let us next consider the right of the British colonist as an individual, apart from his necessary participation in the right of the Imperial Government. The suggestion constantly appears in the writings of our continental critics that the British colonist is, somehow, an intruder in South Africa; that he has no right to be there except on sufferance by the Dutch. He has no right to hear his language spoken or have it taught to his children; he is, in fact, in every sense of the word, an alien. There is one sufficient answer. What has been said as to the action of the Imperial Power proves the right of British citizens the world over to emigrate to South Africa, and to live there on terms of equality with prior European immigrants. But the right of the British colonist in South Africa, derived from his participation in the right of the Empire of which he is a part, has been greatly increased by his own action during the century of British occupation. The blood of British colonists has been lavishly shed during the long series of Kaffir wars. The fighting has by no means been left to the professional soldier; the colonial-born British have always been as used to arms as their Dutch fellow-colonists, and their courage has been as undoubted. But no Dutch expenditure of capital or of labour can be mentioned as even distantly approximating to the lavish expenditure of money, of skill in industry, in agriculture, all over the South African territory, in the Colonies as well as the Republics. It is to attempt to prove the indisputable to argue as to what the capital and labour of British colonists have done, not alone in the Cape and Natal, and in Rhodesia, but in the territory of the Republics.

Where would be the wealth of Johannesburg, and where indeed the armaments of Pretoria, but for the capital and labour of British colonists ? *

* A leading journalist of Cape Town tells me that when a British colonial of South Africa reads what he describes as my icy analysis, his fingers tingle to grip his rifle as his charter of right. There is much in this feeling of irrepressible indignation at the assumption of a superior Boer title, with which every citizen of the Empire must sympathise ; but I have intentionally refrained from importing heat into the consideration of this particular aspect of the situation in South Africa, as my aim is not to denounce, but to convince.

CHAPTER V.

THE BOER CHARACTER.

IN November 1896 I wrote from Johannesburg, as quoted in a preceding chapter :—

" Of all facts, the most stubborn and creative are the ingrained beliefs and prejudices of a people—which are usually attributable to quite other causes than a regard for their material interests. A generalisation which is correct enough, when applied to operators on the Stock Exchange, fails to explain the action of a generation of Huguenots who lost all in fleeing from France."

One of the results of my four years' investigation has been to confirm my belief in the proposition of the truth of which I was convinced at the beginning.

The foundation cause of the whole antagonism between British and Dutch in South Africa, either in social or in political life; the foundation cause of the opposition of the Republics to the Imperial Government; the foundation cause of the present war, is to be found in the mind of the Boer people; and that mind is, and has been for generations, maintained in an attitude of profoundest distrust of the British Government and of the British colonist.

The immediate cause of the present war is a different matter, which I shall consider later. In the explosion of a mine the immediate cause may be described as the finger which presses the button completing the electric connection; but the wire must have been laid and the explosives placed before any explosion would have been possible. In South Africa the wires have been laid and the explosives placed in position by the inherited Boer distrust of the British

Government, of the British colonist, of all that was or is in their own phrase, " Engelsch gezind "—" English minded."

The Boer people's distrust of the British Government and of the British people in South Africa is the result, partly of their character, whether original or acquired ; partly of their degree of information as to past and present facts of British power and British purpose; and partly of the history of Boer dealings with the British. This distrust exists, and, as a British Imperial representative told me in Pretoria, is to be felt, palpable as a stone wall. It is accompanied by apprehension, rising on occasion to hatred ; and, however disagreeable the contemplation of the fact may be to loyal citizens of the Empire, is accompanied also with contempt.

The Boer character is that of the ordinary Hollander Dutch of the 16th century, stubborn and brave ; and of the French Huguenot of the same time, religious in the 16th-century sense of that term, with a not inconsiderable High German strain superadded. There are additional characteristics; the result of two centuries and a-half of their environment in South Africa. Boer ignorance of facts as to the power and purpose of the Empire, which ignorance need not surprise us so much when we reflect that it is shared by so many of our good cousins on the Continent of Europe, plays a great part. Not the least force to contribute to the deepening and strengthening of the rooted distrust in the Boer mind of British Government and British colonist have been past Imperial mistakes of omission and commission.

I have found a Boer leader, holding high office in the Orange Free State, who was not aware that the trek-ox and the ox-waggon were not an original invention of South Africa, but were a tolerably accurate reproduction of a similar feature in Hollander rural life. Similarly, I found educated Dutch South Africans who have not realised that the basic elements of the Boer character in war or in peace are a tolerably faithful reproduction of ordinary Lowlander characteristics of the 16th century in Europe, which have survived by isolation. That character above all is conservative, resisting change. *Stare super antiquas vias*, that is the most striking feature of the Boer mind.   They are stubborn and brave, which is equivalent to saying that they descend from the Dutch who broke their dykes to let in the sea ; and who still remember on the 1st April their Ducal-Spanish persecutor, and who still recall how

> " Op den eersten April
> Verloor Alva zyn Briel."

And, too, that they are descended from the French Huguenots, who at Moncontour met the shock of the veteran soldiers of the League, and at Ivry followed to victory the white plume of Navarre. Yet, again, that they descend from the sturdy *landsknecht* who followed the fortunes of Ulrich von Hutten, and from the rustic leveller in the Peasant Wars, who beat back with his pike the proudest of the German chivalry.   Their character is intensely clannish ; there is no room for the stranger except as a transitory guest.   Here, again, the 16th century of Europe is reproduced. The equality fantasy of that century as regards the non-European races, the experience of 250 years in South Africa has induced them to discard; but, unfortunately, part of their 16th-century heritage is to be found in their repudiation of the right to equality of the European stranger.   " He belongs to the other Commune—what is he doing here ? "

Super-added to this 16th-century foundation are acquired characteristics, the result of the life of Hollander and French Huguenot and German for the hundred years which lasted before the establishment of the Imperial rule.   The Boer's demeanour towards the Kaffir is precisely the reverse of that favoured by the amiable theorists who for so long a period directed the policy of Exeter Hall.   The Boer's dislike of Government and of taxation appears, primarily, to be traceable to past misgovernment of the Dutch East India Company. " In all things political, purely despotic; in all things commercial, purely monopolistic."   Old Testament texts are also at hand to show that only the alien should be taxed. Isolation in the veldt, and the illusion of being free from all protection or direction—not realising that the sea was kept by the Great Sea Power—contributed to this intense dislike. Dr. Johnson's favourite definition of excise best represents the Boer's conception of assessments for public purposes. Again, among modifying influences on their character must be counted their ignorance of facts of the world, especially of external political facts. Primarily this appears to be due to their isolation in the remote veldt in the first instance; but, of late years, quite as much to misleading " Afrikander," Hollander and German propagandists, who, consciously or unconsciously, transmitted to them their misleading conceptions of British purpose and British power.

Of no immediate political importance, more especially as regards the present political problem, but still indirectly affecting it as bearing upon the judgment of Europe-born visitors, must be noted the fact that not alone the clanship but the hospitality of the wandering Arab are closely paralleled in the ordinary life of the Boer of the veldt. This hospitality has sometimes misled the British inquirer into forgetting that its presence is perfectly compatible with the Arab's diplomacy.

CHAPTER VI.

A CENTURY OF IMPERIAL VACILLATION.

A CENTURY'S vacillation of the Imperial policy from 1800 to 1900, and a century's illustration of apparent Imperial ingratitude, have left profound traces on the Boer mind. Few in England have realised how great that vacillation has been, and how striking have been the instances of Imperial abandonment of their servants in high office, and of subjects found to be too loyal.

It is quite a commonplace of belief among British South Africans that the Empire must be a providential institution; as otherwise, its existence would have become impossible long ago.

Let us consider some of the most striking instances of the swinging of the Imperial pendulum. A proclamation of the first British Governor of the Cape, who took possession in 1795 at the suggestion of the exiled Stadtholder, proclaimed, with great accuracy, that the doctrine of the political equality of the Black and White races, of European and non-European, was an invention of the rashly experimenting minds who controlled a French Revolutionary Assembly. That an observer so near to the event should have fully appreciated the momentous nature of the decree of the French Constituent Assembly conferring the franchise on the blacks in the French islands of the West Indies, is perhaps a matter for some surprise. One result is to be seen at the present day in the travesty of civilised government, that alternately shocks and amuses the visitor to the so-called Black Republic of Hayti, where the barbarous rites of

Voodoo are defended by citation of purely European theories of religious liberty, and interference with even cannibal sacrifice is protested against as equal in atrocity to the massacre of St. Bartholomew; and where gratitude for their liberation from slavery takes shape in enactments prohibiting a white man from ownership of an inch of land in Hayti.

This is the first theory of the Imperial Government. What was their next? The humanitarian impulse directed by such leaders in England as Wilberforce had clothed, with a quasi-religious sanction, the French Revolutionary doctrine of the political equality of the negro; a new attitude was taken up by the Imperial Government. An anti-Boer pronative policy, directed by the London Missionary Society of South Africa and other missionary bodies, finally received Imperial sanction by the liberation of the slaves in 1833. But it did not end there. It gave political votes to the negroes in the Cape in 1870, and their vote now is a most appreciable factor in the election of Members to the Cape Parliament. Here, however, also there is no finality. I have already cited the Proclamation in 1877 of Sir Theophilus Shepstone, annexing the Transvaal to British territory, and repudiating any concession of political or social equality of savages.

Let us take another instance of shiftings of the Imperial policy. At the suggestion of the agents of the Missionary Societies the Imperial Government adopted, some seventy years ago, an astounding policy, which was no less than that of surrounding the Cape Colony with a ring of independent native States; and actually pursued this perverse idea to the extent of attempting to enforce the subjection of Dutch Voortrekkers to the criminal jurisdiction of a Griqua chief. What followed? This insane idea was abandoned on Dutch resistance; and, more than that, the whole policy of creating independent native States was abandoned as precipitately as it had been undertaken.

Take again, the astounding series of changes of policy with regard to the Basutos and Basuto territory. For twenty

years after 1830 the Imperial Administrators gave every
encouragement to the formation of an independent armed
Kaffir community in the mountains now called Basutoland,
a State practically created between 1830 and 1870 by the
skill of the Kaffir chief, Moshesh, aided by the diplomatic
guidance of the French missionaries of the Société Evan-
gélique, of Paris, whose first leader, it is instructive to learn,
had fought in the barricades in 1830, during the Three
Glorious Days of July.   In 1852 the Imperial Government
thought that the armed Basutos would become a danger, and
sent General Cathcart, with an army, to subdue and disarm
them.   The British General being defeated by Moshesh at
the Battle of Berea, the Imperial Government abandoned
their intention of subduing the Basutos.   Indeed, they went
further ; finding the Basuto War rather troublesome, they
abandoned the whole Orange River Sovereignty in 1854,
notwithstanding the protest of the Legislative Assembly at
Bloemfontein.   More changes were still to come.   During
the war between the Basutos and the Orange Free State the
Imperial Governor, Sir Philip Wodehouse, actually stopped
the transmission of ammunition through British territory to
the Free State, in violation of the Convention of Bloemfontein of 1854, and proclaimed his neutrality in war.   It is
most interesting to find that an Acting Military Governor of
Natal, though no lawyer, pointed out, with entire legal
accuracy, that, quite apart from the Convention of Bloemfontein, ·a Proclamation of neutrality on war between
Europeans and non-Europeans was a thing absolutely
unknown to International law, which has no application to
relations of peace or war, except among States of European
descent.   Yet another set of alterations of policy.   To induce
the Basutos to supply labour for the construction of the
Cape railways in 1870, rifles were given to them in payment
by the British authorities.   In 1882 the disastrous so-called
" Gun War " was started, with the object of disarming them
—a war memorable from the fact that General Gordon
admitted that he owed his life to the generosity of the
Basuto chief, Masupha, whose people were attacked while

Gordon was actually parleying with Masupha in the chief's kraal.*

The Basutos having made an unexpectedly firm resistance to the disarmament, this policy too was abandoned, and the territory in 1884 was handed back by the Cape Government to the Imperial authorities, by whom it is now administered as a Kaffir Reserve.

Take again the alternate hot and cold fits with regard to expansion and non-expansion of territory in South Africa. Look at the single instance of Natal. In 1844 the Imperial Government emphatically refused to sanction the various British occupations in Natal dating from 1820. In 1845 this policy was abandoned, and previous specific orders were recalled. Whatever may have been the motive, whether or not fears were entertained of a Boer Republic of Natalia obtaining possession of a port on the Indian Ocean, in the Harbour of Durban, and forming an alliance with Holland, the fact remains another instance of Imperial change.

Look again at the inconsistent attitude of the Home Government with reference to the recognition or non-recognition of the independence of the Boer emigrants from the Cape Colony. Before the Great Trek of 1836, an Attorney-General in the Cape sees no objection of the Boer farmers withdrawing themselves from British jurisdiction. Later on proclamations are issued denying the right of the Boer farmers to expatriate themselves, or to get free from the jurisdiction of the British Crown. Not merely proclamations but arms were used. Natal is annexed in 1845; the Boer leader, Pretorius, is defeated in the Battle of Boomplaats in 1849 by Sir Harry Smith; a price is set on the head of Pretorius, who fled north of the Vaal River. Then this design of preventing Boer independence is abandoned. The Sand River Convention of 1852 promises independence to

* In December 1896 I rode from Maseru to Thaba Bosigo, the Mountain of Darkness, to visit Masupha, and spoke to him about Gordon's visit. The veteran warrior had been rain-making, having alternately appealed to the shades of his ancestors on the sea-sand covered top of the Mount of Darkness, and at the French Missionary Church at the foot of his kraal to the higher powers of the other race.

the Transvaal. The Convention of Bloemfontein forces
independence on the unwilling Assembly of the Orange
River Sovereignty. But the end is by no means here.
Within a few years the Imperial Governor, Sir George Grey,
threatens the cancellation of the Conventions of Bloemfon-
tein and of the Sand River if union between the two
Republics be attempted. In 1866 Governor Sir Philip
Wodehouse officially suggests the cancellation of the Con-
ventions. In 1868 he takes the Basutos under his protec-
tion after they had been defeated by the Boers of the Free
State. In 1877 Sir Theophilus Shepstone annexes the
Transvaal. In 1881, after the defeat of Majuba Hill,
Mr. Gladstone retrocedes the Transvaal.

From 1845 to 1854, with some waverings and intervals,
the non-expansionist theory is emphatically asserted by the
Imperial Government. In 1822 it is definitely abandoned,
of course with the inevitable wavering; as, for instance, in
1884, with reference to the territory now called German
South-West Africa, annexed by Prince Bismarck, after the
British Colonial Office had neglected to occupy it in response
to his inquiry. But still, since then, we have generally
had nothing but annexations: No Man's Land, Bechuanaland, Zulu and Mashonaland, Matabeleland, and Rhodesia.
Amatongaland on the eastern coast.

British rights in 1870 was emphatically asserted with
regard to Delagoa Bay. To save a few thousand pounds, for
which Portugal was willing to sell at that time Delagoa
Bay, the British Colonial Office preferred to abandon the
claim for arbitration, which experience might have told
them was sure to be unfavourable to any British claim; and
accordingly in 1874 the award of Marshal McMahon,
President of the French Republic, assigned the bay and
territory to the Portuguese. What wonder then that the
conviction remains in the Boer mind that nothing is fixed
but Imperial change? Most striking of all, most deeply
permanent in its result, has been their remembrance of a
contrast between Governor Wolseley's speech in the Transvaal during the British occupation and Prime Minister

Gladstone's retrocession. "As long as the sun shines in the heavens the Transvaal will remain British territory." "You may as well expect the Vaal River to run back to its source as the act of annexation to be reversed." Such was General Wolseley's confident declaration.

It would take too long to give, in anything like sufficient detail, the instances of apparent Imperial ingratitude in the treatment by the Imperial Government of their own high officials and of their Colonial supporters. With the abandonment of Sir George Grey, the recall and the cancellation of the policy of Sir Bartle Frere, both Governors and High Commissioners; the supercession of Sir Theophilus Shepstone, the Imperial Commissioner who annexed the Transvaal; a supercession occurring long before the retroceding of the country, all these steps have left a deep impression on the Boer mind. And, as regards the body of the loyal colonists, it is a commonplace to hear that it does not pay to be loyal. British colonists, who settled on the Orange River Sovereignty while it was British territory, were abandoned in 1854, contrary to the declared wishes, contrary to the protest of the Legislative Assembly at Bloemfontein, contrary to the arguments and entreaties of the deputation of the Assembly sent to Westminster to protest. The Imperial Governor, who carried out the expulsion of the territory from the Empire, even went the length of describing the too loyal protestors as disaffected persons; in the Transvaal, British colonists who had settled during British occupation, investing all their capital in reliance on General Wolseley's declaration of the permanence of British rule, found themselves abandoned after the defeat of Majuba Hill.

CHAPTER VII.

BOER DISTRUST OF BRITISH.

DISTRUST, apprehension, depreciation; these, I have said, constitute the resultant present attitude and frame of mind of Boers to British. As it is now, and as it has been for generations past. As I have shown, their distrust is due partly to memory of Imperial vacillation, partly to memory of Imperial ingratitude to faithful servants and loyal subjects. It is due, however, to other causes as well; chief among these must be reckoned the long association of the Boer with Kaffir wiles. Nowhere more than with the Kaffir chiefs of South Africa is appreciated the conception of language as an instrument given to man to conceal his thoughts. Again, the distrust is based partly on ignorance of the Imperial Government's real motives.

The Boer apprehension of injury from the Imperial power at times culminates in hatred. Again, a multitude of causes have called this feeling into being. The memory of past injuries, or of deeds which Boers regard as injuries, plays a great part. For there were some real injuries, although others are fictitious. The Boer dislike of Government and of taxation has already been referred to, and the Boer dislike of being interfered with in treatment of the Kaffir, and the Boer dislike of being crowded out by strangers. The total result is an ever-present apprehension of injury from the action of the Imperial power.

Of past injuries some, as I have said, were real. For instance, the method of carrying out the abolition of slavery in South Africa at the order of the Imperial Government in

1834, an order issued without the slightest regard to South African feeling under the influence of the Wilberforce agitation, this method left much to be desired. An absurdly inadequate sum of about a million and a half was allocated to South African slave-owners, and the payment of this sum was rendered a simple farce by the preposterous condition which required the payment to be made in London alone ; the results of this condition being necessarily that the task of receiving payment had to be assigned to speculative agents, with the result that the greater part of the compensation did not reach the owners despoiled, and even in some cases that their claim for compensation was abandoned.

Then, again, among other real grievances, must be mentioned the persistent negrophilist interference of the Imperial Government between Boer and Kaffir in the border wars. As the manifesto of Piet Retief recites, no protection was given to border farmers against the inroads of marauding savages. When the Boer farmer betook him to rifle and horse and repelled these invasions, the Imperial Government, under the impulse of an uninstructed public opinion in England, and of negrophilist missionaries in South Africa, interfered and prevented the farmer from reaping the fruits of his victory, replacing the blameless Kaffir in the *status quo ante bellum*.

Then, again, it must be admitted that the failure of the Imperial Government to carry out its promise given, through Sir Theophilus Shepstone, to grant Home Rule to the Transvaal, did constitute a real grievance.

But of the past injuries which rankle most in the Boer mind, and which have been seen to have real foundation, must be reckoned the extraordinary demeanour of various military Governors ruling in the name of the Empire. For instance, the demeanour of Sir Owen Lanyon, Governor of the Transvaal, is still daily recalled by the Boer ; a man who refused to shake hands with members of the Volksraad—an intolerable insult to proud peasants who regarded themselves as of the Lord's Elect.

Among injuries in the past inflicted on the Boer by

Imperial action are some which rankle greatly as grievances, but which any partial observer can only conclude, in view of the spirit of hostility which the present war and all the preparation for it have revealed, to be only apparent. The action of the Imperial Government was really justifiable. First among these was the annexation of Basutoland by Sir Philip Wodehouse intervening to prevent the Orange Free State from annexing Basutoland, after fourteen years' desultory warfare with the Basuto, to whose fury the Orange River Sovereignty had been abandoned by an economical Manchester School Ministry in Westminster. Really justifiable Sir Philip Wodehouse's intervention appears to have been, in the light of later facts and of the present war. At that time the strip of territory between the Basutoland mountains, the range of the Molutis and the Drakensberg, stretched No Man's Land to the sea. One hears still in Basutoland of dreams in the early sixties of French annexation by Napoleon the Third, from the Caledon River to the coast. The French missionaries, who were first to enter that loveliest of the lands of South Africa, and whose work of exploration has left such permanent traces as the name of Mont aux Sources, which they give to the highest snow-clad peak, of nearly 12,000 feet, in the whole sub-continent, could not have viewed with other than satisfaction such an extension of the Empire which was peace. But one is told that the "Entente Cordiale" prevented the realisation of the dream.*

Seeing that the occupation of Basutoland by the Orange Free Street would most probably have entailed as a consequence Boer occupation of the sea-coast from the slopes of the Drakensberg, and in view of the war spirit now so unhappily evidenced among Boer peoples, Sir Philip Wodehouse's policy of intervention and annexation, to protect the integrity of the Empire, has been amply justified by time.

A German attempt to annex the same coast—under title of concessions by a Kaffir chief of much later date (in

* Riding through Basutoland one can still find a trader who can speak only French and Sesuto, as I did one day in January 1897.

1884), I am reminded by a leading member of the Cape Parliament—was defeated by the action of the late Cape Ministry.

The annexation of the Diamond Fields of Kimberley figures as another and the greatest item in the Boer accusations of rapacity and bad faith against the Imperial Government. It is said that on titles granted by Griqua chiefs, subsequently held invalid by a British High Court, the diamond fields of Kimberley were declared a British possession. This argument was one with which, at one time, I was considerably impressed; but the case on the other side has now proved to be much stronger than at one time it seemed, when it was based merely on the cession of the Diamond Fields, negotiated with Sir John Brand, the President of the Orange Free State, and the payment to the Orange Free State of a sum in compensation of £90,000. When we have witnessed the use to which the possession and control of the Gold Fields of the Witwatersrand has been put by the Boer Republics—how gold has been transmuted into artillery and rifles and the services of skilled generals from Algiers, such as the late Comte de Villebois-Mareuil—one cannot say that the sole justification of the Imperial annexing of the Diamond Fields is to be found in the difficulties which a small pastoral state would find in policing the cosmopolitan population of Du Toit's Pan.

Among the purely fictitious injuries of the past in the relations of the Boer and Imperial Governments must be counted the famous executions of Slachter's Nek in 1815. Certain farmers, who had resisted arrest, and fired on and killed officers of the law, were tried for murder and rebellion, and were executed under a combination of singularly cruel and pathetic circumstances, including that of ropes breaking at the first attempt at their execution. One could hardly admit that even real harshness attributable to the Imperial British authorities of such a far-off time, if fully established, could militate against or outweigh the accumulation of British rights in South Africa for the last century. Not so long before in Newgate, in London, an Englishwoman, whose husband was seized by the press-gang of the Naval authorities, and who, to save herself from starvation, stole a loaf of bread, was hanged, an act denounced in the House of Commons as a foul judicial murder. Such were the manners of the age ; and not in British territory alone, as Victor Hugo's story of Jean Valjean sufficiently shows. But the utter injustice of citing the execution of Slachter's Nek as a proof of British cruelty or of British tyranny over the Dutch, is rendered manifest by the single consideration that the trial was held, the sentence delivered and the sentence executed by Dutch officials—judge, jury, and executive officials being all Dutch. Many more examples of high-handed administration could be cited from the records of the Dutch Administration of the Cape during the hundred and fifty years of Dutch rule in the Peninsula. Revolt of Dutch farmers and trek into the wilderness were by no means unknown during the rule of the Dutch East India Company, nor yet appeal and remonstrance to the States-General at the Hague.

CHAPTER VIII.

BOER DEPRECIATION OF BRITISH CHARACTER AND POWER.

The Boer depreciation of British character as exhibited by both the Imperial Government and the British colonist springs from quite a combination of causes, some of which have already been referred to. For Imperial indecision in the past nothing but contempt is felt by the stubborn Hollander and Huguenot race, which knows its own mind. Anything but respect has been the result of the spectacles they witnessed of Imperial ingratitude to public servants, and to British and Dutch loyalists in the Orange River Sovereignty in 1854, and in the Transvaal Province in 1885.*

The Boers, people and Government, well remember that the Imperial Government threw over Sir George Grey, recalled Sir Bartle Frere, and dismissed Sir Theophilus Shepstone. There is nothing very astonishing, therefore, in the fact that they expected that the British Parliament would also abandon Sir Alfred Milner.

The effect on the Boer mind of the plentiful lack of information on the part of the British Government of facts of life and of the world, palpable to all who have lived in South Africa, for instance, that the position to which Kaffirs are entitled in justice is not one of equality, has not raised their estimate of British intelligence. Ignorance of fact

---

* In January 1897 I had an interesting conversation at his farm in the Conquered Territory, a district of the Free State, with a son of the last British resident of Bloemfontein who had settled down as a burgher of the Orange Free State, and who had become in every respect a typical burgher.

they interpret as lack of intellectual acumen. The humanitarian wave of sentiment, which for the last hundred years has so dominated British home opinion, they do not share in the least, no more than the English of the eighteenth or of the seventeenth or the sixteenth century. In fact, counsellors are not wanted to tell them that the spirit, which dates from the French Encyclopædists and from Bentham and Wilberforce and McKenzie in England at the beginning of the nineteenth century, is only affectation of superior virtue at the expense of other people; and that, like the Cromwellian Puritan's interference with bear-baiting, which was prompted by the desire not to save pain to the bear, but to prevent the man being amused, so British interference with the domestic discipline of the Kaffir was intended rather, under the pretext of virtue, to annoy the Boer and to weaken his power in the land.

Again, the non-expansionist theories affected by various parties in succession in England, prompting Imperial Governments in one generation after another to declare their unalterable resolve not to move further into the interior, have not greatly impressed the Boer with respect for British intelligence and consistency—theories expounded first by missionaries, who tried to build up independent Kaffir "sovereignties," later on by Manchester School economists, who had not yet realised that trade follows the flag; and, last of all, by the so-called Little Englanders, whose theory that the Empire must always be wrong no Boer thinks of reciprocating by a contention that the Republics must always be in error. The Boer, however, is furnished with various explanations of these theories, all of them very unflattering to British intelligence. A high Imperial administrator was the first to point out to me that the Boers regard the missionary's interference as due to the missionary's perception of his private pecuniary interest. Where the Kaffir tribe was left undisturbed, and the Kaffir chief ruled as king, the missionary sat by his side, sharing his authority and emoluments as mayor of the palace. The Manchester School economist they regarded as an example of the painful effects of want of intelligence and of rash dealing with facts 6,000 miles away, beyond the ken of the distant experimenter. Little Englanderism they regard as either lack of patriotism—for every Boer believes himself bound to take the side of his own people—or else fear of expense and increase of taxation; or else party interest seeking a high-minded excuse to turn the other political party out of office ; or else what our Continental cousins believe to be our national weakness—the affectation of superior virtue.

Much has been said in South Africa, of recent years, of the advantages and of the dangers of magnanimity. The High Commissioner in a recent speech in Capetown has vindicated the wisdom and the statesmanship of exhibiting, during and after the war, the British quality of magnanimity. That quality is genuine as we know. The British are one of the very few peoples who do not personally hate their enemies in war or their rivals in commerce. They have adopted and fully exercise the precept of their greatest predecessors in the political organisation of the European race. No Roman administrator has more fully acted on the precept—*Parcere subjectis, et debellare superbos.* Now, the Boer way of regarding actions of the Imperial Government claimed as exhibitions of magnanimity is very instructive. It is quite untrue that they do not appreciate magnanimity. But, as lawyers say, they join issue on the facts. What has been represented as magnanimity they do not regard as magnanimity at all. For instance, take the retrocession of the Transvaal after the British defeat at Majuba Hill. They regarded it, and still regard it, as Lord Randolph Churchill held in his book on South Africa, as a measure adopted after full consideration of political and economical advantages. They remind you that no gold reefs had been discovered in the Transvaal at that time; that Prime Minister Gladstone had cited the official description twenty-six years previously of the British Commissioner who negotiated the Sand River Convention, that the Transvaal was a howling wilderness. The Imperial Government knew that President Brand had intimated that he would be unable to restrain his burghers

of the Orange Free State from siding with the Transvaal, if
the war were prolonged ; and the Imperial Government did
not care to spend tens of thousands of lives of British
soldiers, and tens of millions of British money, in reducing
to subjection a howling wilderness of barren and worthless
and wind-swept veldt.   A Republican Chief Justice pointed
out to me how absurd on this account it was for the Imperial
Government to expect abject protestations of gratitude for
this exhibition of magnanimity—magnanimity merely in
pretence.   The pretence was an aggravation of the original
crime of annexing the Transvaal.   Now, Lord Kimberley's
recent speech shows that this Boer contention all along (that
the intimation of Sir John Brand, President of the Orange
Free State, as to the action of his burghers really did weigh
with at least one of the members of the Gladstone Cabinet
and that one the Colonial Minister, in deciding on the
retrocession of the Transvaal without avenging Majuba Hill)
was not without foundation.

Then, again, one phase of British public life, which we
see is really due to the spirit of justice which animates our
people at home, presents itself in a totally different light to
the Boer in South Africa.   The Opposition in the House of
Commons or in the House of Lords criticise the conduct of
the war as carried out by the Government in power.   This
the Boers do not regard as unpatriotic, although they regard
the publication of the debate as unpatriotic.   But that any
citizen of the British Empire should take sides against the
Imperial Government during that war does not appear to the
Boer to constitute any ground for admiring the British
character.   Whatever their party differences, war unites the
Boers and silences faction.   Above all things, however, the
chief grounds of the Boer depreciation of the Imperial
Government, and of the British people at home and in South
Africa, is to be found in their estimate of the military
capacity both of the Imperial troops and of the British
civilian population.

The actual defeats of British forces for the last half
century by Kaffir and by Boer have never been forgotten,

and are every day recalled. The battle of Berea in 1852; the defeat of Majuba Hill in 1881; the series of defeats which made up the Basutoland Gun War from 1882 to 1885; the surrender of Doornkop in 1896 of troops commanded by officers of the Imperial army, had quite prepared the Boers for their initial victories in the present war, and they were not in the least surprised to have driven back again and again seven generals of the Imperial forces. Magersfontein, and Stormberg, and Colenso, and Spionkop, seemed to them the only natural sequence of their past experiences, unbroken, save by Elandslaagte, until the tide of war turned on the anniversary of the "winter day that withered hope and pride;" the anniversary, on the 27th February, 1900, of Majuba Hill, whose memory now is erased by Paardeberg.

Let me sum up the Boer estimate of the Imperial British army; for Colonial troops they have always had a different estimate. The Boers regard the rank and file of the Imperial army as brave but unintelligent. Their Young Afrikander counsellors have read French as well as English literature, and quote Napoleon's description of the British army and people, "A nation of lions led by jackasses."

The officers of the Imperial army have never stood high in their estimation. They do not understand why, owing to absurdly inadequate pay and a preposterous scale of mess and amusements expenditure, the possession of wealth and social position is practically essential, with the possible exception of one in a hundred thousand cases, to rank in the army and to command in the field ; and they do not think that this method of organising an army is either fair to the average citizen or to the rank and file considered individually, and above all is unpatriotic, as jeopardising the safety of the State itself. They cannot understand how the British people or Parliament are insane enough to tolerate such a method of national suicide. Were such a system attempted among the Boers there would be a general rebellion, and the Government would be overturned in a day. Although not part of their Huguenot heritage, the Boers act in the organisation of their military forces strictly on the French principle of Napoleon—" La carrière ouverte aux talents."

General Joubert's explanation to Sir Evelyn Wood in the negotiations after Majuba of the Boers' reasons for picking off the British officers—not merely that they were the eyes of their corps, but that they were wealthy aristocratic professional soldiers, whereas with the British rank and file the Boer had no grievance—is sufficiently instructive. As regards the undoubted courage of British officers, the Boers regard its exhibition as not truly patriotic, being a mere seeking of personal distinction; and they do not think that a desire to gain a cross or other marks of bravery is in the least a justification for a servant of the State exposing himself to unnecessary danger, more especially when his death may involve that of the troops under his command. Boer criticism is often directed to the refusal of Imperial officers to take colonial advice; they ascribe this refusal to professional pride, to silly ideas of superiority over colonists on social grounds, and to professional jealousy of volunteer soldiers. They tell one many stories of what they regard as singular inefficiency, walking into traps which would deceive no Boer. At the same time, the Boers greatly resent what they describe as the overbearing demeanour of Imperial officers to the common British soldier, with whom, on the other hand, the Boer, from commandant to the youngest recruit on commando, is inclined to fraternise. In fact, as some of our candid though friendly critics from the German army have pointed out to us, they hold the theory of the German critics, that officers of the Imperial army do not appear to take up the army as a serious profession, but rather as an appanage of their social rank, or as a social distinction; that they are more interested in displaying gorgeous uniforms on parade, or in figuring as carpet-soldiers in drawing-rooms than in studying tactics; and that they are much more interested in polo than in Kriegspiel. Boer leaders have frequently commented also on what they describe as nepotism in the appointments to the British War Office and in the Imperial army, and, indeed, in the British Foreign

Office and Colonial Office as well. It is quite true that there is no nepotism in their military appointments. These go by merit alone.

Their low estimate of the military capacity of the British civilian population is equally marked. The rawest Boer boy from the veldt smiles at the ignorance of rifles and horses shown by wandering British visitors and tourists, and shown too by the Uitlanders on the Witwatersrand. The Boers have not the wider vision to see that this military incapacity of the British civilian population is the result of industrialism, of the division of labour; and very largely too of British reliance on the Navy; and most of all of the fact that, for generations, the ordinary British civilian has had no occasion to draw the sword on British soil. In England, especially, no battle has been fought since the march of the Young Pretender to Derby in 1745.

It is needless to say that I am not to be taken as approving of every detail of the Boer indictment of the British Army organisation, as it exists at present; although, apparently, to judge by the criticism of our Continental friends, and more especially by similar criticism made by Colonial troops from South Africa, there is foundation of fact justifying their view. What I am concerned with is the mental attitude of the Boer people in its relation to causing the war. Therefore, I would point out, what, most of all, has caused the Boer depreciation of Imperial military power is their false estimate, shared by many of our Continental friends, of the reserve force, of the real military strength, of the Empire when its existence is seen by its citizens to be in danger.

Until the present war, and the striking exhibition of patriotism which it has evoked from the people of the United Kingdom, and until that heart-stirring rally of the Colonies, which has impressed the world, the Boers, both people and Governments, really thought that the little red Army List enumerated the whole force of the Empire.*

---

* Even so enlightened a man and so gallant a soldier as General Joubert apparently thought so, as letters of his published in the French and German press at the outbreak of the war seem to show. The highest

The Boers, Governments and people, genuinely believed that Mammon-worship had killed patriotism in England. They too hastily took the formula—"A nation of shop-keepers"—as an accurate guide to the likely action of the British people at home. "Shopkeepers intent on nothing but money." Many members of both the Governments of the Republics have been educated in London, and judged the people of England and of the United Kingdom from the denizens of the East End; and even these they mis-judged.

Again, too, they agreed with such a high authority as Mr. John Morley, that in any great war Canada or Australia, so far from rallying to the help of the Empire, would "cut the painter." Mr. Goldwin Smith's prophecies of the annexation of Canada by the United States of America were quite familiar to them. They believed that the hold of the Empire on India was of the most precarious kind, and that the 300,000,000 of people were merely waiting for an opportunity of revolt. Hollander, German, French, all their Continental friends really believed these theories; and impressed them on the mind of the Boer in the Volksraads and on the veldt. Above and beyond all things, they were certain that the courage of the Imperial Government itself was gone; that they were afraid of Russia in India, afraid of Dutch rebellion in the Cape, afraid of French-Canadian secession; afraid of French intervention in Egypt—one even spoke to me of a fancied French annexation of the Channel Islands, whose inhabitants, as loyal as any in the whole sweep of the Empire, describe themselves as having conquered England and beaten France—afraid of every Power in the civilised world; even of Italy taking Malta and Spain seizing Gibraltar.

The Boers have had a rude awakening.

---

officials of the Governments at Pretoria and Bloemfontein listened to you with polite and patient incredulity when you endeavoured to show how mistaken was this theory, and upon what an immense reserve fund of patriotism and determination, in the highest and in the lowest social ranks, in the castle as well as in the slum, the Empire could draw.

NOTE.—What the views of the educated Boer—the young Afrikander—were is fairly paralleled by those ascribed to many French people, in the following extract from an article by Baron Pierre de Coubertin, in the *Fortnightly Review* for May 1900.

Referring to the might of the Empire, and the average Frenchman's estimate of it, the writer states:—

" There is nothing in the world so hard to bring home to a Frenchman's mind as the nature of that power. He persists in judging Anglo-Saxon society by his own 'Napoleonic' and 'centralising' ideas. He cannot be made to see that all these countries scattered over the surface of the globe can form a whole; he is always expecting a break up, and is firmly persuaded that the smallest event might serve to bring it about. He believes, on the authority of a few worthy globe-trotters, who, in the words of the Psalmist, have eyes but they see not, that the native populations of the different English Colonies are oppressed and longing to revolt. Already his prophetic vision sees Ireland, India, Burmah, Jamaica, Australia, New Zealand, the Cape, Egypt, Canada, proclaiming their *independence*, as if that magic word expressed the highest hopes of all these countries. You cannot get it into his head that they are all loyal to England, because they are happy under her rule and because there is something quite wonderful in her power of organisation and administration."

CHAPTER IX.

THE POLICY OF PRESIDENT KRUGER.

In the historical sketch which I have given of the relations between the British and the Dutch in South Africa, I have endeavoured, as I have already stated, to place a view of the political position as it would strike any citizen of the Empire, who came to the consideration of the problem without any bias against the aspirations, or the past history, of the Dutch-speaking people.

"Measures, not men"—that was, and is, and always shall be a favourite popular fallacy. Let me quote from a great political philosopher: "With small men no great things are done." The policy of President Kruger has not been in the least the policy of a small man. But he has not attained to the vision of the first Bonaparte. One cannot do everything oneself; the most obsequious instrument is usually the most completely useless.

The plight of the Pretorian English after the retrocession of the Transvaal was truly piteous. They had invested their all in the British territory of the Transvaal province, relying on the declaration of the Imperial Governor: "As long as the sun shines, as long as rivers run, the Transvaal remains British territory." They saw how that promise, without fault of the promiser, had been kept. They buried the British flag in Pretoria with the prophetic epitaph "Resurgam." Wherefore the appreciation by the Pretorian English of Imperial faith and honour and gratitude has always been extreme. And as regards the conquering Boer, it is enough to say that the Pretorian as to the Johannesburger is as wine unto water, in their divergence from fraternisation with anything that is Dutch.

The Triumvirate of the Boers — Kruger, Pretorious, Joubert—were indeed triumphant. Immediately after the retrocession the divergent policies of Kruger, elected President, and of Joubert, elected Commandant-General, became evident.

In a preceding chapter I have endeavoured to explain the lines on which parties were divided. Exactly as among the 17th-century English, the lines ran on principles of Church government; it would seem an exaggeration to say religious principle. The Doppers were the Roundheads among the Boers of the day. They represent what Edmund Burke calls the dissidence of dissent, the Protestantism of the Protestant religion. A Dop is a round cap; the Dopper was the Roundhead. The Dopper objects to music in the church; and in the contest between the policies of Paul Kruger and Piet Joubert he made his co-sectary the victor.

No one who has met the old President Kruger can doubt in the least that he is a most striking historical character; one who will stand out for centuries to come, and will wield in legend and story a great power on the minds of men. One is in doubt whether to reflect on the historic parallel of that English commander of mercenaries, who, the great Aguto, figures in the records of the Republic of Florence, and sleeps in his English village home as Sir John Hawkwood; or on recent ingenious romances wherein a 19th-century humanitarian survival finds himself surrounded with new, undreamt of, and paralysing conditions, in a time and a generation which had far forgotten the influences, and passed from the conditions which had determined his mental development.

For the President is a Lowland Hollander of the 17th century in mind, whatever may be on one side his High German descent. Stubborn, brave, stoical, he cut off his own thumb with a knife when it was shattered by a rifle bullet. He believes absolutely in the divine destiny of his people, and transfers to them all the promises of the Lord of the Old Testament, who led His chosen people out of the wilderness. The sword of the Lord and of Gideon still smites for the chosen people; and, if one is surprised to find what a lack of sense of historic continuity is manifested in this hermit, crab-like assumption of an ancient and cast-off tenement, let us remember that our worthy Independents, who stood up against the Man of Blood, and smote him at Brentford and Naseby—that sergeant " Bind-their-kings-in-chains-and-their-nobles-in-links-of-iron " who plied his sword in Ireton's army—were afflicted by a similar lack of perception of historical perspective. The President really believes, and always has believed, that the Boers are the chosen people of the Old Testament, to whom the children of Ham should be servants, and that they are promised the annexing of the Promised Land. Some, who doubt the President's sincerity, do not know the fact that he was one of the first Voortrekkers born in the Cape Colony; one who, in 1836 as a boy of thirteen, followed in the steps and adhered to the Proclamation of Piet Retief.

President Kruger's policy, in pursuance of the mission which his election imposed on him—for all that power, whether that of President, or Landdrost, or Field-Cornet, is from on high no Boer, at least no Boer of the President's generation, can doubt—was clearly, from the first, to establish the power of the chosen race; or, transmuting this phrase into language understood by English-speaking people of the Empire and of the United States of America, to establish a great Dutch-speaking Afrikander Power—the United States of South Africa.

The first necessity for the accomplishment of this policy was necessarily to secure the power of the President himself. With the keen vision of a Cardinal Richelieu (whom a Transvaal official recently reminded the Uitlanders of Johannesburg bore the name so familiar in South Africa as that of Du Plessis); with the relentless purpose of a Prince Bismarck, the President evidently made up his mind that, to accomplish this providential mission, certain steps were necessary; and these steps he took without hesitation, with firmness, inspired by his 17th-century conception of patriotic ardour and religious purpose.

The next step was to do everything which was possible to eliminate Imperial control of the destinies of the Republic. The expelled Orange Free State, expelled from the Empire against its will, had absolute power, under the Treaty of Bloemfontein of 1854, to conclude treaties with foreign Powers, without any Imperial sanction or possibility of veto. The President designed to secure similar freedom for the Republic north of the Vaal River.

The next desirable thing which he clearly contemplated in the interests of his burghers, who always desired land for the occupation of their increasing population, was to secure the expansion of their territory to the north, and thereby to allow the trek to secure opportunities of limitless continuation.

Next to this to secure a scaport. The nucleus of the United States of South Africa would be greatly assisted in obtaining world-wide recognition of its status as a sovereign State, if its warships should sail the seas, and its flag was to be seen from Hamburg to Marseilles, and from Naples to Trieste.

Most of all, however, and most urgently was needed the acquisition of gold for the Treasury of the Republic. When the Imperial Commissioner annexed the Transvaal in 1877 the treasury was empty. The Boer has an aversion to pay taxes so strong that it may be almost described as constitutional. How was the gold to be procured ?

Because, unless some weakness hardly to be hoped for even in the most vacillating Government at Westminster, it could hardly be expected that the Imperial Government would peaceably submit to being driven into the sea, not to mention the colonist of British descent, whose knowledge of his rights and determination to maintain them were but too well known. Without gold, no war preparations could be contemplated.

It is quite easy to prepare for war if you have gold, with

which to obtain cannon and rifles, and ammunition, and skilled strategists, veterans in stricken fields and expert artillerists. There is no necessity, if things go well, of declaring war until the British Empire is at war with another Great Power.

In furtherance of this policy, too, the President's obvious duty was to seek the support of the sister Republic of the Orange Free State; and, above all things, if diplomacy or preferential trade advantages, or promises (no matter how lavish) of political domination could secure it, the support of one of the Great Powers of Europe.

This policy the President steadily carried out, with qualities of determination and foresight which must wring an unwilling admiration from the most loyal citizen of the Empire.

It was a mere incident in the consolidation of his personal power, but still absolutely essential, that he should eliminate any Transvaalers whose power and authority in the Republic rested on their own weight with the burghers, and not on their nomination by the President, and who were likely to endeavour to carry out a policy of independent initiative, which possibly might conflict with the President's designs.

In pursuance of the policy of eliminating Imperial control, a deputation was sent to England at the end of 1883 with the object of obtaining certain modifications of the Convention of Pretoria of 1881, which embodied the result of the Majuba Hill negotiation. The Convention of Pretoria contained many restrictions on the liberty of the Government of the Republic, both as regards their internal action with reference to the Kaffir and the foreign negotiations of the Republic with the Great Powers of Europe. The deputation, of which President Kruger was a member, succeeded in obtaining from Lord Derby, then Colonial Minister, many modifications of the Convention, in their direction of giving a freer hand to the Government of the Republic. I shall revert to this subject at greater length later on in connection with the Suzerainty Controversy of October 1897. Suffice it here to note that the deputation succeeded in procuring the abrogation of the right of the Imperial Government to move its troops through the territory of the Republic, and procured also the practical abolition of the right of the British Agent to interfere on behalf of the natives, and removed from the hands of the Imperial Foreign Office the function of negotiating all agreements between the Republic and Foreign Powers. But the crowning triumph for the negotiators of the New Convention of London of 1884 was that the obnoxious word Suzerainty was omitted by Lord Derby from the New Convention; and that the only control over the foreign affairs of the Republic retained was a veto on treaties which, to be valid, should be exercised within six months.

Now, as regards the expansion of the territory of the Republic which the President regarded as necessary to its prosperity, it is to be noted that, while the Conventions of Pretoria and London contained provisions prohibiting the conclusion of treaties between native chiefs on the east or the west of the Republic without the sanction of the Imperial power, no such restriction is imposed on the trek to the north. The motives of these restrictions are clear enough, when one considers the traditional policy of the Imperial Government with regard to the Boers obtaining a foothold on the Indian Ocean; and, on the other hand, the perception by the Colonial Office (even under the secretary-ship of Lord Derby) of the desirability of maintaining the trade route to the interior of Africa. Still, expansion to the north was expressly permitted to the Republic.

This right to the north continued until the policy of Mr. Cecil Rhodes, ending in the occupation of Mashona land and Matabeleland, put an end to all prospect of the expansion of the President's territory north of the Limpopo.

The Bechuanaland Expedition of 1884, under Sir Charles Warren, costing the Imperial Government some millions, put an end to expansion on the west by suppressing the new Boer Republics of Stellaland and Goshen, which President

Kruger had proposed to annex to the Transvaal. The importance of this step, from the Imperial point of view, may be seen, when it is considered that such expansion would necessarily have ended in the joining of the Transvaal territory in the west to the eastern border of German South-West Africa; and, consequently, the cutting off of the British trade route to Central Africa, which even Lord Derby—whose interest in African affairs, I was told by a member of the Transvaal Deputation of 1883, could be expressed in the wonder why the African elephant was not domesticated—was desirous of maintaining. If such a junction had been effected, there could obviously have been no Cape to Cairo route.

The policy of Mr. Cecil Rhodes having completely hindered any peaceable expansion of the Transvaal territory, and warlike expansion being out of the question for the time being, the President made the next best bargain he could—that is to say, he entered into negotiations with the Imperial Government to obtain their sanction to an outlet on the sea. Between the Transvaal and the Indian Ocean, and between the Portuguese of Delagoa Bay and the British Colony of Natal, stretched a narrow strip of land called Amatongaland, in the occupation of some Kaffir chiefs, and not yet annexed by any European Power. Now, the Conventions of both Pretoria and London of 1881 and 1884 expressly provide that no treaties could be made by the Transvaal with native chiefs to the east or west of the Republic without the express consent of the Imperial Government. In return, therefore, for his promise to support the British Chartered Company in their establishing of law and order in Rhodesia, the President obtained the consent of the Imperial Government, embodied in the Swaziland Convention of 1890, to his taking over, in full sovereignty, a strip of land reaching from the eastern border of the Transvaal to the Indian Ocean at Kosi Bay. The Convention stipulated that the strip of land was for the construction of a railway, which had to be completed within three years. In 1894 a new Convention of Swaziland was

negotiated, chiefly for the purpose of obtaining the annexation of Swaziland to the Transvaal; but the President, with
a strange lack of his usual foresight, omitted to include in
its provisions a continuation of the agreement with the
Imperial Government relative to the strip of land in
sovereignty and the railway to Kosi Bay. It is understood
that he intended to have it embodied in a separate Convention. Nevertheless, the promise of the Republic to aid the
British Chartered Company in Rhodesia was repeated in the
Swaziland Convention of 1894. Soon after this period, as
the term of three years had expired, the Imperial Government took a step, seemingly of very slight importance,
consisting in the annexation to the Imperial Crown of the
worthless slip of territory of Amatongaland; whereupon
the two Dutch Republics were completely hemmed in by
British territory, and the President's dream of his port on the
Indian Ocean became no longer realisable by peaceable
means.

It must be noted that the President had not a unanimous
Volksraad with him in this desire of his to acquire a seaport. Several members and high officials held that the
possession would be a weakness in case of war with any
great Power.*

The President, nevertheless, undoubtedly considered this
loss of his opportunity of constructing a harbour as a great
grievance, for which he held Mr. Rhodes chiefly responsible.

* The progress of the present war would seem to bear out the correctness of the latter view, one which was very forcibly impressed on me by
that able lawyer, Dr. Coster, whose service to the Republic he had adopted
ended in his gallant death, leading a corps of his Hollander fellow-
countrymen at Elandslaagte. In October of last year at Delagoa Bay
I noticed the striking anxiety of the officers of Her Majesty's warships
that the rumours of an intention of a Republican commando to seize
Kosi Bay should be confirmed, an anxiety which one gallant officer of
H.M.S. *Philomel* expressed to me with considerable emphasis. It seems
indisputable that the possession of Delagoa Bay in the hands of a neutral
power, and thereby the impossibility of the British fleet blockading the
harbour, has been of distinct advantage to the Dutch Republics in
enabling them to keep up their supplies. If either Delagoa Bay or Kosi
Bay had been in Dutch hands, a rigorous blockade of the coast would
certainly have been carried out, and all ships carrying supplies for the
Boer armies would have been seized as prizes of war.

The President's design of replenishing his Treasury was indeed, as all the world knows, completely successful. The earlier law of the Transvaal prohibited prospecting for gold anywhere in the Republican territory; as the burghers, who set such store upon their isolation on the veldt, quite realised that an influx of miners would put an end to their pastoral quiet, and their exclusive possession of land. For similar reasons, as the Imperial Government desires to maintain Basutoland as a Kaffir reserve, prospecting for minerals is prohibited there; and apart from other risks from native hostility any prospector would be promptly deported across the Caledon River. During the presence in London, in 1883, of the deputation to Lord Derby for the negotiation of the New Convention of 1884, the President invited capitalists from all the world to develop the mineral resources of the Transvaal, promising them every protection—a promise reiterated in the most emphatic terms in an official letter from the Secretary of the Deputation, dated 13th December, 1883, published in the press at the time.

Having obtained from Lord Derby the right of conducting diplomatic negotiations independently of the British Foreign Office, the President promptly proceeded to make use of his power. Immediately negotiations were entered into with Germany and Holland, Prince Bismarck, who had previously declined any direct negotiations, immediately recognising the altered international status of the Republic. To this branch of the subject I shall refer again, in considering the policy of the German Imperial Government in South Africa generally.

The President, in pursuance of his policy of obtaining the support of Foreign Powers, entered into the closest relation with Holland and the Hollander people. He appointed as his representative in Europe the Hollander Baron Beelaerts van Blokland, residing at the Hague. The President also secured the services of the most able of all his public servants, a member of the Bar of Holland, Dr. W. J. Leyds (at present the Minister Plenipotentiary of the Republic in Europe), and many other Hollanders for every branch of the public service. In pursuance of the same policy a Netherlands Company was, after years of negotiation, which is sufficiently familiar in connection with the recently published award of the Berne Arbitrators, placed in possession and control of the railways of the Transvaal leading to the Portuguese harbour of Delagoa Bay. Considerable dissatisfaction was always expressed by those of Dutch South African descent at this exclusion of themselves from the public service ; but, as has already been pointed out, it was apparently necessary to enable the President to consolidate his own power so as to carry out his wider political designs. Dutch Afrikanders, as were called those educated men from the Colonies of the Cape and Natal, would stand more on their own feet, and would depend less on the President's nomination. Even the able lawyer above referred to, who acted as secretary of the London Deputation, and whose own standing with the burghers was considerable, did not remain long in the President's confidence. Dr. Jorissen, State Attorney of the Republic, the negotiator of the Majuba Hill Convention, was dismissed while on leave of absence in England. Precisely as Cardinal Richelieu crushed the recalcitrant nobles, and precisely as Louis XI. surrounded himself with his corps of Scottish archers, or Louis XIV. with his Swiss guards, so did the President surround himself with an army of skilled officials, who could possibly have no leverage on the minds of his burghers with which to thwart his far-seeing policy. For this reason, quite as much as from the fact that few of the burghers of the Transvaal were sufficiently educated to discharge the duties of any Government office, must be ascribed the President's preference for the service of immigrants from Holland.

Before referring at greater length to the transmuting of the gold of the Rand—won from the Reef by the capital and toil of the British and other European immigrants who had flocked to the newly-created town of Johannesburg at the President's invitation — into cannon and forts and experienced soldiers, it will be necessary for me to direct attention to another portion of the political field in South Africa. For it must never be forgotten that, as I have stated in the first chapter, the whole of the political field in South Africa — from Cape Town to Kimberley, from Kimberley to Durban, from Bloemfontein to Pretoria—all constitutes one vast chess-board. No single move can be taken at any one point without the fortunes of the whole field being affected.

CHAPTER X.

THE YOUNG AFRIKANDER PROPAGANDA: 1881.

" The winter day that withered hope and pride."

(1.) Majuba and the Foundation of the Bond : The Platform.—(2.) Majuba
and the Dutch Journals: The Press.—(3.) Majuba and Stellen-
bosch : The School.—(4.) Majuba and the Dutch Reformed Church :
The Pulpit.

THE vision of a separate Dutch-speaking nationality, exclusively governed by Dutch hands, and conforming itself to
traditional Dutch methods, seems always to have been fixed
in the minds of the Boer Voortrekkers in the Republics.
The danger to the British Empire involved in any such
establishing of an alien Power in South Africa, and the
danger of leaving a nucleus of hostility in the Republics on
the British borders, was distinctly foreseen and pointed out
by such British Imperial Governors as Sir George Grey, Sir
Philip Wodehouse, Sir Bartle Frere, and Sir Theophilus
Shepstone. Their treatment at the hands of the Imperial
Government has already been referred to. But, until the
retrocession of the Transvaal, very little indeed had been
done in furtherance of that ideal. President Burgers, of the
Transvaal, a Hollander immigrant, endeavoured in the early
'seventies to take some steps towards the realisation of the
ideal. He had great schemes for the making of Pretoria
a centre for the creation of an all-embracing South African
Republic in the future—schemes which extended so far as
the formation of a railway to Delagoa Bay and the establishing of a great university in Pretoria. But his support from
the burghers was rather lukewarm. Independence they

liked very well, and isolation in the veldt, and not being
interfered with by the British; but far-reaching schemes of
railways and universities and other such gorgeous palaces
of fancy, which involved in the immediate present the
payment of taxes by tax-hating burghers, seem not to have
appealed to them.   For other reasons also—chiefly his want
of harmony with their religious beliefs—President Burgers
fell into disfavour with the Boers, who even went the length
of abandoning their President when, immediately before the
annexation of the Transvaal, he was leading them in war
against Sekukuni, a Kaffir chief.   So President Burgers was
deposed by Sir Theophilus Shepstone, who found the treasury
in Pretoria completely empty; the teachers, with whose aid
President Burgers desired to found his university of Pretoria,
took to other occupations; and the President's iron rails
for his projected railway to Lourenço Marques lay rusting
at Delagoa Bay.

Then occurred that event which has shaped the whole
movement of South African politics for the last twenty years
—the retrocession of the Transvaal, after the unavenged
defeat of Majuba Hill.   Perhaps, if the genius of President
Kruger, his skill and resource, and his procuring the exploitation of the gold mines by European capitalists and miners,
had not been there to utilise it—that terrific shock to South
African confidence in the resolution, the good faith, the consistency, or even the sense of self-preservation, to be expected
from an Imperial Government in Westminster—no such
world-moving consequences would have occurred.   But President Kruger was there, and the gold lying hid in the Rand
was procured in many millions.

Before referring to the birth of the so-called Young
Afrikander Propaganda, which spread over South Africa
immediately after the retrocession of the Transvaal, let me
indicate the manner in which, I think, any fair-minded
citizen of the Empire should view the formation of this idea
of an independent Afrikander nation, and the steps taken to
realise it.   I do not think I can express it better than by a
quotation from a letter addressed to me in Johannesburg, in

October 1896, by a leading resident in Johannesburg,* who, like most colonists of British descent, is a strong Imperialist. He says :—

" To say one word that would interfere with the prospects of harmonious co-operation between the British and the Dutch would be criminal. The means to bring about such co-operation are, it seems to me, to be achieved only by England making such a demonstration of her determination to remain the supreme and ruling power in South Africa as would make any thought of attempting to oust her jurisdiction the phantasm only of the lightest of feather-brained politicians.

" There is no doubt that many of the Dutch population please themselves with thoughts and ambitions of establishing an independent Afrikander nation. This ambition is no doubt creditable from their point of view, but it is absolutely inconsistent with British interests, not only in South Africa, but throughout the Continent of Europe, and, if I may venture to say so, with the due and orderly spread of civilisation amongst the native tribes."

The policy of the Gladstone Cabinet, in its deciding to retrocede the Transvaal after the defeat of Majuba Hill, has practically dominated the whole of South African politics for the last twenty years. That policy was announced by Mr. Gladstone as one of magnanimity ; and so it was undoubtedly regarded by the people of the United Kingdom. So it was not regarded by anyone, British or Dutch, in South Africa. I have already referred to the interpretation put on the retrocession given to me by a Republican Chief Justice. When that is the view of the retrocession held by a man of the highest education, what must be the estimate of every Boer of the veldt ?

Four great movements of a propaganda through the Cape Colony and the Republics began on the perception by the Boers, in the Colony and in the Republics, that the Imperial Government was prepared to submit to defeat. The platform, the press, the school, and the pulpit, all, by combined action, proceeded to impress on the public mind that, in view of the weakness and indecision of the Imperial Government, it was not merely possible, but certain, that a new Afrikander

* Mr. H. S. Caldecott, now Chairman of the Uitlander Committee of Natal.

nation, absolutely independent of the Imperial Crown, could be created.

Now, it does not seem of the highest importance, although much controversy has turned on this point, whether forcible expulsion of the Imperial power or pacific negotiation was looked upon as the more feasible method. The goal, held steadily in view, was the establishing of an independent nation ruling all South Africa, from the Zambesi to the sea. Of course, the advantages of the defence of that independence to be obtained from the navy of the greatest sea-Power in the world were quite obvious; therefore, it was always put forward, as part of the Afrikander policy, to grant the British Empire the possession of Simonstown, in the Cape Peninsula, as a coaling station for warships for India and Australia. Indeed, a contribution to the Imperial navy was admitted by all Afrikander propagandists to be only fair, in view of the services the Imperial navy would render in policing the coast and warding off foreign attack. Even in the Republics many were always to be found to advocate such a subvention in aid of the Imperial navy.

The origin of the Bond, as was called the political organisation formed in the British Colony of the Cape, formed recently the subject of an interesting correspondence, beginning with a letter from Mr. Theophilus Schreiner, brother of the late Cape Prime Minister. This letter is of such interest that I reproduce it here :—

Mr. Reitz's Manifesto.

To the Editor of the " Cape Times."

SIR,—My attention has only just now been drawn to the manifesto of Mr. Reitz, State Secretary of the Transvaal, to the Orange Free State burghers, as published in the *Cape Argus*, 19th inst.

In this shameful and shameless document Sir Alfred Milner, Mr. Chamberlain, the British Cabinet, the Queen of England, and the British nation are declared to be murderers, robbers, breakers of treaties, and the responsibility for the present war between the Republics and England is sought to be laid on their shoulders in a wealth of scurrilous and mendacious statement.

I feel impelled to write the following lines, not to discuss matters

which have passed beyond the pale of argument, but to throw a little
personal historic light on the question as to who is responsible for the
present war, which may serve to show that not England, nor England's
Queen, nor England's Government are the real originators of the same.

I met Mr. Reitz, then a judge of the Orange Free State, in Bloemfontein between seventeen and eighteen years ago, shortly after the
retrocession of the Transvaal and when he was busy establishing the
Afrikander Bond. It must be patent to every one that, at that time at
all events, England and its Government had no intention of taking away
the independence of the Transvaal, for she had just "magnanimously"
granted the same; no intention of making war on the Republics, for she
had just made peace; no intention to seize the Rand gold-fields, for they
were not yet discovered. At that time then I met Mr. Reitz, and he did
his best to get me to become a member of his Afrikander Bond, but after
studying its constitution and programme, I refused to do so, whereupon
the following colloquy in substance took place, which has been indelibly
imprinted on my mind ever since.

REITZ : " Why do you refuse ? Is the object of getting the people to
take an interest in political matters not a good one ? "

MYSELF : " Yes, it is; but I seem to see plainly here, between the
lines of this constitution, much more ultimately aimed at than that."

REITZ : " What ? "

MYSELF : " I see quite clearly that the ultimate object aimed at is the
overthrow of the British power, and the expulsion of the British flag from
South Africa."

REITZ (with his pleasant conscious smile, as of one whose secret
thought and purpose had been discovered, and who was not altogether
dipleased that such was the case) : " Well, what if it is so ? "

MYSELF : " You don't suppose, do you, that that flag is going to
disappear from South Africa without a tremendous struggle and fight ? "

REITZ (with the same pleasant, self-satisfied, and yet semi-apologetic
smile): " Well, I suppose not; but even so, what of that ? "

MYSELF : " Only this, that when that struggle takes place you and I
will be on opposite sides, and, what is more, the God who was on the side
of the Transvaal in the late war, because it had right on its side, will be
on the side of England, because He must view with abhorrence any
plotting and scheming to overthrow her power and position in South
Africa, which have been ordained by Him."

REITZ : " We'll see."

Thus the conversation ended ; but during the seventeen years that
have elapsed I have watched the propaganda for the overthrow of British
power in South Africa being ceaselessly spread by every possible means—
the press, the pulpit, the platform, the schools, the colleges, the legislature
—until it has culminated in the present war, of which Mr. Reitz and his
co-workers are the origin and the cause. Believe me, sir, the day on

which F. W. Reitz sat down to pen his ultimatum to Great Britain was the proudest and happiest moment of his life, and one which had for long years been looked forward to by him with eager longing and expectation.

He and his co-workers have for years past plotted, worked, prepared for this war, and the only matters in connection with it in which they are disappointed are, firstly, that they would rather the war had come several years later, so that their anti-British propaganda might more fully have permeated the country; secondly, that they would have liked to declare war against England at a time when she should be involved in some great struggle with a foreign Power instead of at a time when she is free to give all her attention to South Africa; and, lastly, they are disappointed at finding out that English soldiers can fight.

It *is* true that an active factor in bringing about this war has been the existence of the gold-fields of the Rand, not, however, as asserted, because England covets them and is determined to seize them, but because the wealth drained from them has enabled the Republics to become military powers of a strength far out of proportion to their population, and thus has led F. W. Reitz & Co. to think that their dream of a Pan-Afrikander Republic and the ousting of the British flag may become a reality. Hence their declaration of war against England rather than grant just political rights to the inhabitants, whom that same wealth has led to settle down in the Transvaal, and whose presence and numbers, however useful to the Dutch Republics towards the production of wealth to be used for the setting forward of their political aims, might, if they became possessors of the franchise, prove damaging to the success of the scheme of the great Pan-Afrikander Republic. Although I have been obliged, in this record of an historic reminiscence, to mention the Afrikander Bond, I do not wish to be supposed to be attacking that body as it exists in the Cape Colony at the present time, or to accuse it of backing Mr. Reitz up in his declaration of war against the British Empire. Its leaders claim that they and it are loyal to England. So be it. My object is to show that, not the British Government, but the Republics, led by Kruger, Reitz, Steyn, and their co-workers, have been steadily marching on towards this war, and consciously plotting for it, ever since the "magnanimous" retrocession of the Transvaal by England, and even before the Witwatersrand Gold-fields were discovered.

I am, etc.,

THEO. SCHREINER.

Riversdale, October 31. [1899.]

A pamphlet recently published in Cape Town, entitled "The Birth of the Bond," consisting in a reprint of a pamphlet entitled "De Transvaalsche Oorlog" ("The Transvaal War"), issued, in 1881, by a Dutch paper called

De Patriot, contains the following statements among many others of a like kind.

The Preface of the translation runs as follows :—

" This is a translation of a pamphlet published in Dutch in the first half of the year 1882, shortly after the surrender of the Transvaal to the Boers. The title of the original is ' De Transvaalsche Oorlog ' (' The Transvaal War'), and its contents have been faithfully reproduced, excepting that a portion has been omitted to avoid repetition.

" It consists of a series of leading articles, originally published in *De Patriot,* then the most vigorous of the Bond organs. It is believed they have never before been translated into English, and consequently they will prove a revelation to British colonists and to the British public at home of the hatred, as bitter as it was ungrateful, which at that time was cherished by Afrikanders in this Colony, as well as in the Republics, against the English people, and against everything English, and which has been vigorously fomented ever since by the most shameless mis-representations.

" Here, too, the reader may view the Afrikander Bond at its very beginning, and mark the lines on which it was projected, and which have been exactly followed out in its ill-omened career. We see that it was designed to be a preparation for an Afrikander ' nation,' a confederation totally independent of Great Britain. With this key all the moves of the Bond and of the Republics fall into their places—the enmity practised towards English colonists, the diligent propagation of the Dutch language, the underground war against Imperial influence, the dogged refusal to make concessions to the Uitlanders, the accumulation of war material, the fostering of the manufacture of explosives, the consolidation of the two Republics, the assumption of absolute independence, and the declaration of war at the earliest moment it was thought safe.

" Fortunately the grand conspiracy has failed, but we earnestly desire that our countrymen should realise the danger from which South Africa has had a narrow escape; and there can be no better means to this end than the universal perusal of the following pages." *

The Transvaal War.

The moral pressure was too strong : England was forced to give back the stolen Transvaal. If the Transvaalers had indeed stayed quiet, as nearly all advised them to do, then England's injustice would have been successful; she would have been confirmed in her robbery, and would also easily have absorbed the Free State. Now all her thieving is over, and

---

* The translation is published at the *Journal* Office, Grahamstown Cape Colony, and is dated February 1900.

probably she will never repeat it. Might has run its race against right, and lost, and will never be able to renew the conflict on such favourable terms. And our faith in the righteous is all the stronger, that England will be yet more severely punished, if she dares to begin again with her policy of robbery and murder.

England's power has been repeatedly beaten and humbled. The little respect which an Afrikander still had for British troops and cannon is utterly done away. And England has learned so much respect for us Afrikanders that she will take care not to be so ready to make war with us again. Think of it; no English soldier had the honour to set his foot on Transvaal ground. Those that were in the Transvaal already had to sit still in the forts like mice in a trap, and those that were to go and relieve them got their sound beating in the Natal territory.

The Transvaalers have now got what they wanted, and what they for four years vainly solicited from England, namely, the revocation of the annexation, the giving back of their land, and the restoration of the South African Republic.

The Free State shall now also remain a free State, and England must now keep her claws off from the Transvaal long enough for us Afrikanders to recover strength a little and pull things to rights.

The Afrikanders have now a little time and opportunity to develop themselves as a people. We had all been fearing that the Jingoes would simply overwhelm us.

The Transvaalers are now restored to credit, in their own eyes and in the eyes of all the world. Now all Europe and America are alive to the rights of our affairs, and it will be dangerous for England to go on with her accustomed plundering.

The Afrikanders, especially the young ones, have now got an aversion to foreign languages and customs, and particularly to the English, and an ambition is awakened within them for their own people and their own language. The Englishman has made himself hated, language and all. And this is well; for the contrary evil had already made great progress.

The English sovereignty over South Africa has now gone back at least half a century. Good: we are heartily glad of it.

THE FORMATION OF THE AFRIKANDER BOND.

This is another matter which we must now carry through. Now or never. We have seen how necessary it is that the Afrikanders should have a general union or body, so as to be able to work together. This was never more necessary than now. Even the *Volksblad*, which formerly was not favourable to such a Bond, and even now objects to its being empowered to watch the press, finds the establishment of the Bond not only advisable but pressingly needful. It remarks : " All doubt as to the pressing necessity of taking this matter in hand vanishes now that we see that branches of the London South African Union are being formed at the

Cape, so as to give powerful assistance to the English merchants. If there must be a conflict between English and Dutch here, then let the Dutch take care that they are ready for it."

The Free State *Express* of 7th April last publishes the draft of such a Bond, similar to what we have several times proposed in *The Patriot*, but worked out more in detail by some friends at Bloemfontein. Here follows its constitution :—

The object of the Afrikander Bond is the establishment of a South African nationality through the cultivation of a true love of this our fatherland.

The Bond must grow up out of the heart of the people : the rules can come on after. This is now our time to establish the Bond, while a national consciousness has been awakened through the Transvaal war. And the Bond must be our preparation for the future confederation of all the States and Colonies of South Africa. The English Government keeps talking of a Confederation under the British flag. That will never happen (daar kom niks van nie). We can assure them of that. We have often said it; there is just one hindrance to Confederation, and that is the English flag. Let them take that away, and within a year the Confederation under the free Afrikander flag would be established.

But so long as the English flag remains here, the Afrikander Bond must be our Confederation. And the British will after a while realise that Froude's advice is the best for them; they must be content with Simon's Bay as a naval and military station on the road to India and give over all the rest of South Africa to the Afrikanders.

If an Englishman is willing to become an Afrikander and acknowledge our land and people and language, then we will acknowledge him as our countryman and heartily support him, or one of any other nationality on the same terms.

THE ANTI-BRITISH CAMPAIGN—NO TRADING WITH THE BRITISH.

We must form trading associations with Europe and the United States of America. There is now good opportunity for this, as there has recently been started a direct line of steamers between Germany, Holland, Belgium, and South Africa, and it is said there is to be a separate line to run from Belgium to the Cape. There is also now so much interest in South Africa awakened in Europe, and such sympathy felt for our Boer nationality, that it will be easy to establish the desired trade connections.

The Amsterdam *Handelsblad* (*Journal of Trade*) remarks : —

" The future of England lies in India, and the future of Holland in South Africa. When our capitalists vigorously develop this trade, and for example form a syndicate to buy Delagoa Bay from Portugal, then a railway from Cape Town to Bloemfontein, Potchefstroom, Pretoria, Delagoa Bay will be a lucrative investment. And when in course of time the Dutch language shall universally prevail in South Africa, this most extensive territory will become a North America for Holland and enable us to balance the Anglo-Saxon race."

The Boer stores which we must establish must be Dutch or Afrikander through and through, not any English. No English signboard, no English advertisements in English newspapers, no English bookkeepers; no, all Dutch or Afrikander. Just as English stores help to uphold English newspapers, English schools, English social life in a town, so on the contrary our Boer stores must work to prevent the English element from prevailing, and must uphold the Afrikander spirit in the place, as against the English spirit.

Yes, England is, as Bilderdyk, the Dutch poet, has rightly called her, "a gang of robbers," and those islanders live only by plunder; their ships plunder on every shore; their vultures fly over mountain and valley, and light upon every carcase; they gather and glean whatever they can; therefore it is that they have so many colonies, and therefore they raked in the Transvaal. And now we must endeavour, instead of their being able to plunder more in our land, to cut it off so that they shall have less, and if possible nothing to prey on in our land. And then we shall whether we are not quickly rid of these vultures. Where there is no carcase, there you see no vultures. The trade is still under the English flag; thus England cannot hinder us from starting such associations in the Colony and Natal, and the Free State and Transvaal are of course free to do so. But the English rob us not only with their stores, but particularly with their banks. We give an extract from the Amsterdam *Handelsblad* of March 13th, from which anyone, and our Transvaal friends above all, may see how an English bank dared to serve us. "The only bank in the Transvaal was in English hands. It had advanced money on the Seccocoeni war. Suddenly it demanded payment, and refused all further credit. That was the cause of the talk later on (says Mr. Moodie) about the empty State chest, and the few pence that the Queen's treasurer found as a balance of ready money." And how are we to prevent such an evil? Why, in the same manner as with the stores, by helping ourselves.

Let us start a National Bank, with branches in all towns and villages of our land.

PREPARATIONS FOR WAR.

To start manufactures of the munitions of war is another lesson which we must learn from the events of last year, particularly from the late wars in the Transvaal and Basutoland. And this, of course, specially concerns the two Republics.

For this, two things are required: (1) to make their own ammunition, and (2) to be well supplied with cannon, and provide a regiment of artillery to work with them. To begin with this last. In this we may praise President Brand. We believe that the Free State is fairly well provided with cannon and with ammunition for cannon. And he has also had for some time past young men drilled in the fort at Bloemfontein to work with the cannon. So that if the English troops were coming over the Drakensberg by Harrismith way, for example, they would not be the only ones to use field-guns, but the Free Staters from the Berg above would have kept them far enough off with their cannon, and if the Transvaal had had just a couple of cannon on Laing's Nek, with a few clever gunners, there would have been still less chance for the English ever to get over that way. Unfortunately, in the betrayal of the country, the cannon that the Transvaal had, also fell into the hands of the robbers, and were used against the Boers at Pretoria. But when once the Transvaal gets its independence back, the Government of the Republic will have learned from the recent war a lesson as to what they must do for the future.

But the other point is of much more importance; the Free State and the Transvaal must make their own ammunition for themselves. This is the matter by which the English have always harassed them. Think how Sir P. Wodehouse was ready to hand over the Boers to the ill-will of the Basutos, by stopping the supply of ammunition to the Free State. And we must freely express our astonishment at President Brand and the Volksraad that they did not have their eyes opened then, and begin at once to manufacture gunpowder. And, again, in the Transvaal war, the one hope of the soldiers was that the Transvaalers might run out of ammunition. And Sprigg * lent himself as a tool to stop the supply of ammunition from the Colony to the Free State, so that the latter might not supply the Transvaal. Now, however, they have their eyes opened, and let them profit by the lesson. The Transvaalers are beginning to make all their own ammunition. At Heidelberg there are already 4000 cartridges made daily. And a few skilful Afrikanders have begun to make shells too. That is right; so must we become a nation. When oppressed, we grow strong. Let us have just a little time, and we will develop our nationality.

And the Free State is also becoming vigilant. At least the *Express* takes the matter up warmly. In its issue of 14th April it says:—

"Lest anyone should think the proposal we made some time since to the Raad about establishing a gunpowder manufactory was merely out of ill-humour caused by the stopping of our supply from abroad, we return to the subject now. Sulphur, as is well known, is found in the country, and the evident proof thereof is the specimen exhibited in the Bloemfontein Museum. All that is needed is to determine the quantity, and Government would do well to instruct its officials to make the necessary inquiries, for we are assured that it is found in more than one place in the State. Saltpetre is found in many parts, and also the best charcoal for gunpowder making, namely that from willow-wood, which is plentiful.

---

* Sir Gordon Sprigg, then and now Prime Minister of Cape Colony.

With an outlay of say £5,000 a factory can be started sufficient to provide for our own needs, which is our special aim at present, though afterwards it could be enlarged as may be desired. We cannot endure to be dependent, as we are now, on the pleasure of ill-mannered and ill-tempered rascals who in a foolish manner enter upon wild, extravagant enterprises from which they have to retreat with shame and then cover it with various lying statements against the Free State, on which they wish to lay the blame of their own folly. Nor can we stand idly looking on while arms and ammunition are sold wholesale to the natives around us, while in the future decisive moment for South Africa we shall find ourselves unarmed. And again, who knows who may be Prime Minister in England then, and what sort of policy will rule the Colony? We wish for peace, and are resolved to have it. We have no glory to win by war. But we may lose that which is precious, namely, sufficient preparation of such means of defence as to make us independent of the favour, friendship, or hostility of the enemy. Thus we hope that one of the fruits of the Transvaal War will be that the Republics shall make their own ammunition, that they no longer suffer England to make a profit by them, and that they will moreover every year set apart £1,000, or rather allow to their Government the amount of charges for powder made on their account."

No Land to be Sold to the British.

And while we are more specially dealing with the Republics we will accordingly give the Boers there one more piece of advice: they must sell no land to Englishmen.

We specially say this to our Transvaal brethren. In any national conflict it is to the advantage of us Afrikanders that we are the landowners. The great majority of the English are only birds of passage (*trekvogels*) that go away as soon as they have eaten carrion enough, or there is no more carrion to be got. Our Boers are really the nobility of South Africa. In England they have a very perverted idea of our Boers. They think they are like the English farmers. Among the English the nobles are the landowners and the "boers" are merely tenants—the slaves, in fact, of the nobility. Here it is just the reverse. The Boers are the landowners and the proud little Englishmen are dependent on the Boers. They themselves are now beginning to see it, and therefore will they try to get our ground into their possession. Watch against that, Free Staters, Transvaalers; sell no land to the Jingoes, even though they offer to pay high prices. Think, if once they get a firm footing (or landed property) then you will never get rid of them again. If you have ground to part with that you do not need for your own children sell it to an Afrikander from the Colony. Here there are too many of us, and there are plenty who will go north if they can get land. Once more, this is a point of great importance—We stand upon our own ground.

WAR AGAINST THE ENGLISH LANGUAGE.

The English and the Anglified schoolmasters and, still more, school-mistresses teach our children from early youth—

(a) That the English language is the finest and best; whereas it is only a miscellaneous gibberish, without proper grammar or dictionary.

(b) That English history is the most interesting and glorious; whereas it is nothing more than a concatenation of lies and mis-representations.

(c) That they must give the chief place to English geography ; whereas all England is nothing more than an island in the North Sea.

(d) That they are educated as soon as they can gabble English; whereas they simply make themselves ridiculous by it, in the eyes of every judicious person.

(e) That English books and periodicals are the finest and best to read ; though really they are the greatest mass of nonsense (with some exceptions) that you can find anywhere ; and finally, in one word:

(f) That it is an honour for everyone to ape the English in every-thing, and, in fact, to become English; whereas it is the greatest shame and disgrace for any people to belie their own God-given nationality.

Among following headings in this remarkable reprint are :—

> Dutch speaking in Parliament.
> Dutch in the Courts.
> Dutch in public offices.
> Dutch in the churches.
> Dutch in the schools.
> Disgrace to speak English.
> The English governess a pest.*

The *Cape Times* of 10th May of this year contains the following comment on the pamphlet just mentioned :—

The pamphlet called the " Birth of the Bond " has drawn from the Chairman of the South African Conciliation Committee (in England) a defence of that organisation in the columns of the *Times*, whose special correspondent in Cape Town had appealed to its evidence of the Afrikander conspiracy to drive the English out of South Africa. Mr. Mackarness must have some personal acquaintance with the operations of the Bond; for if we are not mistaken he was in Cape Town during the period of

---

* In 1882, an Act of the Cape Parliament provided that Dutch in the future was to be treated as an official language, and on an equal footing with English in Parliament and in Courts of Law. Prior to that enact-ment, a British Order in Council of 1828 was in force making English the sole official language.

Sir Hercules Robinson's * experience of Bond machinations concerning Bechuanaland. He may possibly even remember that famous despatch in which the Governor lamented the failure of Responsible Government, in a political condition of Ministerial subjection to an irresponsible power having no constitutional status. We are not quoting the actual words. Sir Hercules Robinson's definition of the situation was neater than any we can give without reference to the text. It was during the same period that Mr. Merriman's † denunciation of the Bond, recently revived as a "Progressive" document, tickled the ears of the groundlings in an Eastern City. Mr. Mackarness, however, the mellowing influence of time having doubtless affected his Colonial memories, now writes : " Since the Bond became a genuine political power in the hands of responsible leaders it has neither in its constitution, its conduct, nor in the speeches of its champions, furnished evidence for the charges of disloyalty so freely launched against it." The champions of the Bond included the late Mr. Borckenhagen ‡ and the present Mr. Reitz.§ The former gentleman was not a British subject ; and, therefore, not amenable to any charge of disloyalty for his consistent hostility to the British influence in South Africa. Mr. Reitz has given ample proof of the sort of loyalty he was likely to foster in the organisation of which the avowed aim was "the formation of a South African nationality." When invited to become President of the Orange Free State in 1888, Mr. Reitz declared that it was his fervent desire to see the day when the United States of South Africa should have become an accomplished fact. It was a perfectly legitimate aspiration for one in his position ; but it was an aspiration excluding the British power from any part or lot in its accomplishment. With Mr. P. Molteno ‖ Mr. Reitz preferred Great Britain as a coast protector to any other European Power. At least, in 1888, he avowed that preference. This, indeed, is hardly the position which loyal British subjects care to contemplate as the future destiny of their country. The Bond, however, must be judged by Mr. Reitz's utterances. The language of Bondmen in the Colony was more cautious. That was all. In aim and aspiration there was no difference.

It is not enough to establish the Bond's innocence of disloyalty. Mr. Mackarness goes on to assert a direct and continuous proof of its active loyalty. " The Bond," he writes, " has actively supported almost every British Ministry of recent years, thus associating itself closely and vigorously with a distinctly British policy." As accurately, might it be

---

* High Commissioner, afterwards created Lord Rosmead.
† A Member of the Bond Ministry at the Cape.
‡ The Editor of the Bloemfontein *Express.*
§ Formerly President of the Orange Free State, now Transvaal State Secretary.
‖ Author of a book entitled *A Federal South Africa.*

said, that an aboriginal cannibal associates himself closely and vigorously with the labours of evangelisation when he has eaten his missionary. Such credulity might be venial in a Courtney or a Massingham, knowing nothing of South African political affairs by personal observation. Mr. Mackarness, however, had his opportunity of acquainting himself with the ways of politicians while the Bond method was being demonstrated with really unblushing candour. From the beginning it was the rule of the Bond to refrain from ministerial office. The rule was, to some extent, forced upon the members by their transparent incapacity to transact departmental business; it was also a convenient rule, inasmuch as it enabled the managers of the party to engage the services of practised debaters, to whom office was precious, both for the personal importance it conferred, and for other considerations that need not be specified. Mr. Mackarness mentions a series of Ministers who enjoyed the Bond support in its close and vigorous association with a distinctly British policy. That is hardly the language Sir Hercules Robinson would have used at the time of Mr. Mackarness's South African sojourn. It certainly was not the language Mr. Merriman used at the same time; nor was it the language with which Mr. J. W. Leonard * electrified the meeting of Cape Town citizens assembled to support the distinctly British policy in defiance of the Bond and its auxiliaries. The curse of South African politics, indeed, was the diabolical ingenuity of the Bond in getting its purposes effected by the instrumentality of politicians who had no natural sympathy with it. The advance was made cautiously, step by step, but with assured progress towards the determined goal. First the native vote had to be dealt with. One set of Ministers began this work; another set of Ministers completed it. Thus seat after seat was lost to the Party now calling itself Progressive, and the balance of power in the House of Assembly transferred to the Party aiming at Afrikander, which, in truth, is nothing else but Republican, domination. "As a matter of fact," Mr. Mackarness says, "neither Mr. Rhodes nor any other sensible person had any doubt as to the Bond's loyalty." What Mr. Rhodes thought about the ultimate aim of the Bond, while he was relying on the Bond vote, we do not know; he is not one who always lets out the full contents of his mind. It sufficed for him that the Bond vote was necessary to keep him in power; nor did he grudge the immediate price. Whether he was satisfied within himself that the union of South Africa within the Empire, and in harmony with British ideals, was the desire and aim of the Bond, is another matter. We doubt, however, whether any "sensible person," who had even a superficial knowledge of South African politics, gave the Bond credit for such an aspiration.

The distinct instances of Bond loyalty quoted by Mr. Mackarness

---

* Late Attorney-General of Cape Colony.

are plausible but not convincing. "In 1894," he says, "the Bond members voted a large addition to the salary of the High Commissioner, and in 1895 supported the Imperial Government in forcing President Kruger to reopen the Vaal Drifts.* In 1896 certain Bond members supported Mr. Merriman in petitioning for the establishment of the British Government in Rhodesia. The enthusiastic devotion of the Dutch towards Her Majesty in 1897 has been placed on record in eloquent terms by Sir Alfred Milner. In 1898 the Bond Members unanimously voted £30,000 a year to the Imperial Navy and gave the British Admiralty a free hand in Simon's Bay." The vote to the Navy was creditable to the Bond; it would have been even more so if the Members of the Party had given a courteous hearing to the arguments by which it was recommended. In the matter of the Vaal Drifts the Bond offered no opinion. What was done was done in Cabinet Council; and we believe that the leakage whereby the decision of the Cabinet came to be generally known seriously disturbed the equanimity of Ministers. They did good by stealth, and blushed to find it fame. The demonstration of loyalty in 1897 goes far to prove that the Bond policy, written large in Mr. Reitz's declaration, is not the policy of all the Dutch-speaking people of South Africa; and upon this foundation is the hope built of a happier condition after the present troubles have passed away. Mr. Mackarness, however, holds his brief for the defence of the Bond, not of the Dutch-speaking population of Cape Colony, and, so far as the Bond is concerned, he has absolutely no case.

The London *Daily News* of the 20th April of the present year contains the following article on the origin of the Bond :—

Mr. Cronwright-Schreiner is not exactly the man to whom one would look at present for a criticism of the Bond, and for evidence in support of the case that the British policy of equal rights and progressive legislation was in danger in South Africa. Neither would anybody think from Mr. Schreiner's and other speeches on the same side that British success means greater protection for the natives. The fact is, however, that no stronger assertion of the mischief that was going on in South Africa, as the result of the Bond's principles and organisation, could be desired than that which is to be found in a paper of Mr. Cronwright-Schreiner's on "Political Ethics and Political Organisation," read to the Cradock Farmers' Association on October 7th, 1893, and reprinted in a pamphlet which we now have in our hands. It will be noted that the date is long

---

* The late Cape Premier, Mr. Schreiner, agreed to the Cape Ministry's active assistance in using armed force to compel the Transvaal to open the Drifts.

anterior to the Jameson Raid; it is even before the commandeering dispute
and Sir Henry Loch's significant questions to the Transvaal Uitlanders
concerning their armament; it is a date when Mr. Rhodes was in favour
with the Dutch.   What at that date was the policy of the Bond in regard
to the British power in Africa?   What were the character and political
aims of the Bond?   What were its ideas with regard to the treatment of
the natives?   Mr. Cronwright-Schreiner (Mr. C. S. Cronwright as he was)
shall say.

" What is the Afrikander Bond ? " said Mr. Cronwright, in his address
to the Cradock Farmers' Association.

" It is," said he, in answer to his own question—" it is anti-English in
its aims; its officers and its language are Dutch; and it is striving to
gain such power as absolutely to control the Cape Parliament."

" What sort of men were they ? "

"The vast majority of Bondmen," we read, " are nearly illiterate,
ignorant, and governed almost entirely by emotion instead of by reason ;
the wisdom of the Bond represents to a very great extent the ignorance of
the farming population of the Colony.   Reason and argument are of no
avail with such men; they are bad, non-progressive farmers, and their
actions, prompted by ignorance, are governed by unthinking prejudice."

The Bond, said Mr. Cronwright, was composed chiefly of a type of
farmer which he had described in an early part of his paper.   Looking
for this description, we find it is part of a general description of the social
conditions of the Colony, most of which we transcribe :—

"The social conditions of this Colony present a most interesting
problem; indeed they are almost unique.   There are three main elements
of the population in juxtaposition such as are not found similarly placed
in any part of the world.   There is first a class fairly representative of
the present-day, nineteenth-century moral, religious, social, and mental
development.   This class is composed partly of people born in other
countries, principally in Great Britain and Germany, and of their
educated Colonial-born descendants, and of the educated Afrikanders,
descendants of the old Hollanders and Huguenots.   The great bulk of
this class is, of course, of English descent, and all speak and write
English.   Next is a class, a peculiar people, such as I believe are found
nowhere else in the world.   It is composed almost entirely of Afrikanders
engaged in farming, speaking a *patois* of very limited vocabulary, called
by them 'the Taal,' the great majority being unable to speak English.
They are descendants of the old Dutch pioneers, and through having
been for a long time almost entirely cut off from communication with
civilisation, as many of them are yet, they have not advanced; their isolation and illiteracy have prevented any intellectual progress; rather they
have deteriorated.   The narrow Calvinism of their ancestors has developed
into a gross fatalism.   They are almost illiterate, very ignorant, and superstitious ; they are out of touch with the world, and out of sympathy with

and behind the spirit of the times; their notions are crude and primitive in the extreme, and their conduct is governed by a standard of morality which had little in common with that which regulates the remainder of the white population. Their reading is practically confined to the Bible, and they are the victims of an effete theology. A most capable writer in 'The Cape Illustrated Magazine' for August remarks: 'No one with eyes to see, and ears to hear, can avoid remarking that we have in our midst a numerous section of the population, mostly rural, content to stand upon the old motto, *Quieta non movere*. This is the section that believe that what sufficed for their ancestors will suffice for them, and which honestly imagines that a *patois*, like the Taal, is eventually to prevail against the onrush of the Anglo-Saxon tongue, the language of the modern world. This is a class whose antiquated piety would arrest the locomotive in mid-Karoo at 12 o'clock on a Saturday night and allow the locusts to feed undisturbed on their growing crops, because once in the dawn of history the shadowy form of a Hebrew law-giver brought the punishment of *voetgangers* to bear on the equally shadowy form of an Egyptian king.' "

Here comes in a sentence or two of Mr. Cronwright regarding the attitude of the population towards the natives, which we reserve till we come to that subject. Then Mr. Cronwright-Schreiner proceeds :—

It is from the ranks of these people that the " Poor Whites," the most depraved section of the population, are being daily augmented. They are lazy, slovenly farmers, with a rooted antipathy to honest, continuous hard work, and they object to be interfered with by law, wishing to be absolute on their farms. They resent any law which tends to protect their more progressive neighbours from their own dangerous methods of farming, and they would selfishly and foolishly subserviate the interests of the whole Colony to their own benighted wishes. Thus we have no Compulsory Scab Act, no Compulsory Destruction of Locusts Act, no compulsory eradication of prickly pear, or *Xanthium Spinosum*, no Compulsory Brands Registration Act.

"These men," said Mr. Cronwright, summing up, "constitute the strength of the Bond; this is the section of the Dutch to whom our pitiable invertebrate politicians are bowing the knee and selling the country for a mess of pottage, to the utter degradation of political morality and to the great detriment of the best interests of the Colony." The third section referred to by Mr. Cronwright-Schreiner were the natives, about whose treatment something will presently be quoted.

Mr. Cronwright found that the Bond's influence on the politics of Cape Colony was "decidedly pernicious," that it dominated the Parliament, was "absolutely powerful" in up-country districts, and that the fear of offending it had (even then in 1893) "too long paralysed our political life."

It is said to-day that the war has raised the race feeling. But in 1893 Mr. Cronwright said, in criticism of Mr. Hofmeyer's reputation as a great statesman:

"We have had our Legislature dominated by a race clique, that clique being composed of men who, beyond all others, know least of politics and are least able to judge of what the real needs of this country are. And the leader of this party, he who, by his clever management, perhaps because he is the only able man among them, has given them this baneful power, he is called great!"

In further criticism of the Bond, Mr. Cronwright-Schreiner objected to the rule of "that section of our people least capable of legislating on sound and progressive principles." Again, we read: "Where the Bond rules there is no political freedom, for its members consider a different opinion from their own as a gross insult, and resent it accordingly." Again: "It" (the Bond) "simply exercises terrorism where it is powerful enough to do so." On the race issue, which Sir Alfred Milner is accused of raising in 1899, see again what Mr. Cronwright said six years before:—

"It is the Bond which, while voting by ballot in its own deliberations, has prevented our voting by ballot for Parliamentary representation, and yet prevents that system being adopted at the coming General Election. With all its power what have we got to thank it for? Comparatively nothing. Weighed in the balance, it is found wanting. It has directed all its energies to resisting the measures the country needs, to introducing the "Taal" into Parliament and the Law Courts, and to raising the franchise so as to give the Dutch Boer element more voting power. In fact, the Bond has sacrificed the welfare of the country for years to the selfish attainment of one object, namely, the supremacy of the Dutch-speaking inhabitants of the Colony, regardlesss of the rights of others; the imagined good of an ignorant clique of the Dutch has been preferred to the good of the country. These men must not have power; they are unwholly unfit to have it. Because it is such a body, and striving solely for its own benighted ends, and is founded and conducted on race lines, and because it cannot grapple with our problems, and not only does not and canno introduce wise and progressive legislation, but also blocks the way whereby we might advance, I say it should not have the power it has, and that we should oppose it instead of temporising with it."

So much for the character of the Bond, its political capacity and its political aims, long before the Raid. Now, as to its treatment of the natives. The triumph of the Bond is, of course, the alternative to the British establishment of the policy of equal rights, and recently there has been an attempt to prejudice the British case by representations (to which the signatures of many labour leaders have been obtained) that the war is a deep design of the capitalist class to obtain cheap native labour for the mines.   On this question Mr. Cronwright gave this opinion in 1893:—

"I am sure the Bond policy would spoil our labour supply."

He also said :—

"The Bond is utterly unfit to deal with the native problem.   It is benighted and dominated by violent and unthinking prejudice.   Such a body cannot be trusted to guide the destinies of our weaker fellow-mortals. Its native policy is fraught with the gravest danger to the Colony.   As I have said, the native question is our one big problem ; it will never be settled on Bond lines.   In the native we have an almost unique supply of labour, a perennial fount of wealth to the Colony.   Treat him justly, wisely and humanely, and we shall always have a supply of good and cheap labour; pursue the Bond policy, and the country will be flooded with a set of roving thieves, who will become utterly demoralised by adding to their own vices those of the lower whites, and be a curse to the country; and endless trouble will be stored up for the future."

Here we recur to the omitted passage from Mr. Cronwright's description of the farmers dominating the Bond.   It is said :—

They still retain the inhuman and primitive ideas with regard to the native—bred of ignorance, and the days when "Zwart Schepsel" was their slave.   They are utterly unable to discuss the native question on its merits ; they do not consider that we have any moral duty towards the black from whom we took the land, and who now contributes largely to the revenue, and fights for the British Empire as loyally as they themselves do.

Towards the end of his paper Mr. Cronwright, recurring to this topic, said the class of Dutch which constituted the majority of the Bond had an utterly degraded view of the native, looking upon him more as a higher type of animal than as a human being, and their behaviour towards him was regulated accordingly.   If they had their way, they would never have "fair play."   These are the views of Mr. Cronwright-Schreiner before the Raid, and before his marriage.

It is set against this explanation of the establishing of the Bond that the leaders of the party under whose auspices the present Cape Ministry have been put in power have persistently, and till to-day, denied that there ever was any such design to oust the British influence.   British colonists, however, meet one's inquiry as to the degree of acceptance which these professions deserve by reminding one that, in a country of diplomatists, the ways of diplomacy are considered permissible in the furtherance of a movement regarded as patriotic; and by telling one that, precisely as every Boer in the field is a general, fully cognisant of the plan of campaign, so is every Boer in political life an ambassador, considering himself entitled to exercise quite as much reticence as any Minister Plenipotentiary from St. Petersburg, or Washington, or Berlin, or Paris, or Rome—or even from the Court of St. James.

The connection between the hopes revivified by Majuba Hill and the immediately started Dutch press propaganda has been sufficiently indicated by the extract already given from the pamphlet on "The Birth of the Bond," which, it is to be noted, is a reprint from *De Patriot*, the leading Dutch newspaper of Cape Colony in 1882.

The nature of that propaganda has been clearly described in the despatches of the present High Commissioner. There is nothing in which the pages of *De Patriot* surpassed those of *De Express*, the Afrikander organ in Bloemfontein in the Orange Free State. The *mot d'ordre* for the whole press in the Cape—where *Ons Land* is now the principal Bond paper printed in Dutch, and the *South African News* the principal Bond paper appearing in English—is clearly to eliminate British influence in every respect all over South Africa. The very title of the journal published in a British colony, an integral portion of the Empire—*Ons Land*—asserting that the land is *ours* in the Dutch tongue, shows plainly the keynote. The British born or descended citizen of the Empire is merely, in the view of the press propagandist, a commorant foreigner, who may remain, and even may be naturalised, if he behaves himself.

De Express of Bloemfontein was conducted by a man of great ability and of striking personality, the late Mr. Carl Borckenhagen. German by birth, he had adopted his new Afrikander nationality with thoroughness, and showed clearly that the dream of his life was the establishing of a new non-British nationality. Whether it was that he loved

the Afrikander more or the Briton less is not quite so clear.
Many of our German cousins seem to dislike us.   But
of the wonderful ability with which he conducted his
journal, there can be no doubt at all, and none, too, of his
astonishing command of the English idiom in its most telling
vigour.

In Pretoria the *Volksstem*, the "People's Voice," was
conducted on practically the same lines as the Bloemfontein
Express.   In Johannesburg the *Rand Post*, published in
Dutch, and the *Standard and Diggers' News*, published in
English, practically adopted—with some waverings on the
part of the latter journal—the same programme.

It would be impossible, within any reasonable compass,
to give extracts illustrating the carrying out by these
journals of the original policy—"Eliminate all that is
British."   It must suffice to say that the very latest, as
well as the earliest of their issues, will convince the most
incredulous.

As far as the journalists of the Republics are concerned, it
is to be remembered that they were foreigners, and not
citizens of the Empire; and, however we may regret their
narrower conception of patriotism, we cannot say that they
acted outside their rights, incumbent though it may be on
every citizen of the Empire to aid in dispelling for ever
their particularist dreams.

Similarly, as regards the anti-British propaganda carried
on by Ministers of the Dutch Reformed Church, it does not
seem expedient to argue over much on what is palpable to
all in South Africa, and what is indeed plainly avowed, if
not boasted of.   Churchmen of other Churches may safely be
left to frame indictments against these preachers of the
Prince of Peace.*   Reading these indictments of the Dutch
Reformed Church by Anglican and Roman Catholic, Scottish
Presbyterian and Wesleyan in South Africa, one historical
parallel forced itself on my memory.   The heaviest article in
the indictment of the Venerable Bede, the Saxon monk and

* See Appendix.

chronicler, against the British native Christian Church—the inheritors of the institutions of Constantine, finally driven to Wales—was that they pushed their hatred of the Saxon invader so far as to refuse to evangelise him, desiring his punishment in the next world to avenge his crimes of the present. The Grond Wet of the Boer Republic of the Vaal River declares that no equality of black and white, in Church or State, will be endured by the people. The missionary enterprise of the Dutch Reformed Church among the Kaffirs is largely conspicuous by its absence.

As to their war spirit, yet another historical parallel. The Dutch Reformed Church is, like its people, of the 16th century—a church militant indeed. The utterances of many predikants recall the King's unanswerable query to the Pope's remonstance against the capture of a mail-clad bishop: " Is this your son's coat ? "

Let me pass to aspects of the propaganda on which I may speak more freely. On a May day of 1891 I was in the garden of the Middle Temple when I first heard of—but did not realise its terrible meaning—the Young Afrikander ideal. A friend of mine was with me, and we were speaking on one aspect of the Law of Nations, on which I have always been interested—the race limits of International Law—the extent to which our rules of international conduct are applicable to savages and savage warfare, or to the peoples of Eastern civilisations—Indian or Chinese or Japanese. I hold that they are quite inapplicable, being the reflex of the consciousness of the white race of Europe. I referred to the manner in which the great groups of peoples were becoming greater—the consolidation of France, from the warring provinces of Brittany and Burgundy and Gascony and the Isle de France ; of the almost completed consolidation of the German-speaking peoples ; of the vast sweep of the Russian autocracy ; of the wondrous stretch of the United States of America ; and last, and not least, of our world-wide Empire, and of how closely we are approximating to the political fusion of the dominant race of Europe, almost realised in the Roman Empire ; and how with each step towards that fusion the inapplicability of our laws of conduct, national and international, outside our own race, tends to become plainer, until at last it would become so plain that no one would conceive these laws as even remotely to relate to European dealings with Kaffir or non-European. The pressure of the non-European must inevitably tend in the direction of consolidation, and therefore of the elimination of particularist national or rather tribal ideas, among the European race the world over. My friend, who is of an old Huguenot name, and a lawyer of the Temple, said: " You are speaking of the Millennium; in South Africa we shall drive the British into the sea."

As, among other reasons, I had immediately before been instructed in the library by a mild Aryan brother of Bengal how the British rulers of India were to be induced to surrender their powers of Government to the educated graduate of Calcutta University—their command of Sikh and Gurkha and Rajput to the men from the plain—by the simple device of holding up a grey-coated bogey of a Russian soldier on the borders of Baluchistan, I confess I did not dream that tragedy was jostling comedy so near. The shadow on the old sundial, the slope of the lawn, and the trees under which I was sitting, seemed more deserving of attention.

In the fierce glare of a Bloemfontein day of March 1897 I met my friend again, holding high office in the Orange Free State. We talked of many things, but one of his first questions was, " Do you still think of the Millennium, as in the gardens of the Temple ? We shall drive the British into the sea." I said, " They shall be as dead and gone as the red and white roses plucked in the Temple Gardens five hundred years ago, and as forgotten as the wars of York and Lancaster." " No, not quite so forgotten. They can keep Simonstown and the Bay." This was the Confederation Week of March 1897, which linked the Orange Free State to the fortunes of the Vaal River Republic. I had returned from attending the " Kwaije Vrouw " banquet, and a perfectly harmless phrase of the President Kruger was being wildly telegraphed over the world.

The latest, although, I hope, not the last, time I met my

friend was in a Johannesburg club in September 1899, in
the dark and gloomy days during the exodus of the Uitlanders.
He said, " Good-bye : we should have preferred this war
twenty years later ; we may fail, but we shall do our best.
You did not believe my prophecies years ago ; you believe
them now." I said, " Of war, I did not believe them ; but
of success, you will be led to believe mine."

Now my friend of these three interviews, and of many
others, was not one of the Afrikanders in power ; he is one of
the most favourable specimens of the results of South African
educational training, and is a marked exception to the
rank and file of the average young Afrikander trained in
African schools, obtaining degrees in English or Scottish
universities, or becoming qualified as professional men—
lawyers, physicians, or engineers—in England. To the
intellectually inferior members of the Young Afrikander
party I shall refer again, when I come to consider the
immediate cause of the war.

What, however, any European who settles in South
Africa cannot fail to see, from palpable evidence, is that
South African educational institutions, judged by the fruits
of their training the minds of their alumni, can only be
described as an anti-British forcing-house. The shibboleth,
" Drive the British into the sea," has clearly been impressed
on their minds at the most susceptible period.

Nothing is further from my design than to institute a
polemic against individuals or individual institutions. So I
do not propose to re-echo the naming of particular colleges
or institutions incessantly reaching one's ears in South
Africa from British residents, although details, if they were
wanted, are easily available. For present purposes it is
sufficient to judge the schools by their fruits—the minds of
those who have passed through their training. " Drive the
British into the sea."*

* See Appendix.

·CHAPTER XI.

GERMAN COLONIAL EXPANSION.—THE ALLEGED "ENTENTE CORDIALE."

ONE of the most impressive speeches I ever heard was one delivered by Mr. Gladstone, then Prime Minister, in the early part of 1885, defending his policy towards German expansion in South Africa—addressing the House of Commons and the foreign ambassadors.   The Prime Minister welcomed Germany to the field of colonisation, and as a helper in the great task of spreading European civilisation over Africa and the world, wished her " God speed."

That Prince Bismarck, then German Chancellor, reciprocated such fraternal feelings one may be permitted to doubt. German interests, and German interests alone, quite legitimately from his nationalist standpoint absorbed his thoughts. Consolidated Germany had become industrial.   Industries require markets all over the world, and trade follows the flag —more especially when other nations' traders are excluded by hostile tariffs.   The Scramble for Africa came rather late or Germany; but Germany took possession of anything that was left.   Among these annexations was that of German South West Africa, surrounding the British possession, administered by Cape Colony, of Walfisch Bay.

A generation or two from this will be better able to judge— as then documents, now in the archives of Continental Foreign Offices, may be published—as to the reality of the anti-British policy freely ascribed to the German Chancellor by British Imperialists in Johannesburg and in Cape Town.   I shall endeavour to show what their theory was and is.   Let us console ourselves by thinking that in a hundred years the incredible may become commonplace. Few people in London at the end of the 18th century would believe that the Empress Catherine of Russia could stoop to send written directions to her ambassador in London to have English journalists who opposed her policy in their articles in the London press waylaid and bludgeoned. Yet the curious may read these directions in the collection of despatches published a few years ago by order of the Tsar, edited by Professor de Martens of St. Petersburg. If these journalists had been warned, and had published their news, they would probably not have got a soul in England to believe them.

British Imperialists in South Africa ascribe to Prince Bismarck, and to a less extent to his successors, a definite anti-British policy, so as to secure for Germany territory where possible, and, when territory was not attainable, trade. They allege that the following ascertained facts are proofs of that policy.

In the first place, the annexation of German South West Africa, always regarded as within the British sphere of influence since 1836, being within latitude 25°; and more than that, actually constituting the Hinterland of the British possession of the town and harbour of Walfisch Bay. There is, in fact, even now, no other harbour of the slightest importance in the territory. Much bitterness is still felt by Cape colonists on what they regard as an unwarrantable intrusion on their ground, and it is another of their grievances against a vacillating Colonial Office in London. They point out to you that a narrow strip of German territory has been prolonged to touch the Zambesi River. They suggest it was meant to facilitate a junction with Transvaal territory, the trek to the North being still expressly permitted to the Republics by the London Convention of 1884; permitted, indeed, until Mr. Cecil Rhodes, by occupying Mashonaland and Matabeleland, headed off the trekking Boer.

In the next place, the subsidising of the German East African line of steamers, running from Hamburg to Delagoa Bay, and preferential trade advantages in the way of Pretoria

Government orders to German traders. Connected with this, the institution of the Government National Bank in Pretoria with German, instead of Hollander or Boer, directors in 1889.

Again, the closing of the Drifts in 1895, an order of President Kruger, to prevent traffic being taken by road instead of rail from Cape Colony to the Transvaal, a measure intended for the benefit of the Hollander railway company primarily, but secondly to divert trade to Delagoa Bay, where the railway ended and the German steamers plied.

Yet again, the introduction of German officers, artillerist and engineers, to Pretoria and Bloemfontein; and the construction, ordered in 1895, before the Jameson Raid, of forts in Johannesburg and Pretoria under the direction of German officers.

The famous telegram of January 1896 of the German Kaiser figures very largely indeed among their proofs of an anti-British Boer-German *entente cordiale*. British South Africans will not accept assurances, such as even a Socialist member of the German Reichstag gave me, that no political significance attached to that telegram; that it was merely the military spirit of the Kaiser leading him to recognise Boer valour. They ask you, why then did the Germans ask permission from Portugal to land marines at Delagoa Bay to proceed to Pretoria to guard German interests, on the outbreak of the Jameson Raid?

As regards President Kruger's desire to obtain German support, or that of any other of the great Powers, there of course can be no doubt. His declaration of January 1896 to that effect is explicit; but we are speaking here of German policy.

Now, in subsequent chapters, I purpose to present both the Uitlander and the Boer version of the Transvaal situation, in the language of their own leaders, directly communicated to me, and my own conclusion on their merits. In this will appear plainly the Boer attitude towards the German Government and German influence, and their desire to utilise both of those forces as buttresses of their independence—as they conceived it.

Here I only record the general sentiment of British South African Imperialists, on German policy, prior to the present war. If I can form no definite conclusion as to German Imperial policy from 1884 to 1892, and from 1892 to 1899, no doubt the fact that the public of foreign countries have no access to the records of the Foreign Office at Berlin will prove a sufficient excuse. Of one thing one can feel perfectly convinced: that if the German Chancellor had conceived designs of ousting British influence in the Transvaal and the Cape and South Africa generally, it would not be for love of the *beaux yeux* of Pretoria.

As to an alleged "Conspiracy" between the two Republican Governments, the German Chancellor, and the Bond party in Cape Town, to oust the British Empire one hears very much; but, except by inference and induction, one is shown no proofs; on the contrary, as I shall make clear later on, we have emphatic denials on the South African side—both in the Republics and the Cape.

Even as to such a design, embodied in an alliance as formal as may be, it must in fairness be remembered that there is no absolute wickedness in a German Chancellor desiring the predominance of Germany, in extent of territory or in trade, in South Africa, or anywhere else; and in availing himself of the absolute independence thrust on one former British dependency—the Orange Free State—and the modified independence surrendered after defeat to another British dependency. And similarly, that the object of creating a Dutch-speaking and Dutch-ruled South African Dominion through the Governments of Pretoria and Bloemfontein is a perfectly intelligible ideal for Dutch-speaking folk, who have had so many reasons not to admire the British Colonial Office, to entertain.

The case of the Bond party in Cape Colony is quite different. Such an alliance would constitute the crime of rebellion in a particularly aggravated form. It would indeed be monstrous, as the present High Commissioner put it, if the Dutch-descended British colonists were not loyal. Absolute liberty, absolute equality, political power to the extent of nominating the Ministers of the Crown, is their lot in the Cape Colony—and in all British possessions no disability rests on any European of non-British descent.

I venture to submit to British South African Imperialists a view of the policy of some of the Bond leaders—for the rank and file have sent thousands of armed rebels to the field, and indeed Bond Members of the Cape Parliament have taken up arms as well—which I have tentatively held, which, if correct, would harmonise their professions, public and private, of loyalty to the Empire with their sympathy with their kindred over the Orange River, and their desire to see them maintain their separate state existence. Living statesmen who have sat in the Imperial Cabinet, even at one time Lord Beaconsfield, looked forward to the future of the Colonies as one of absolute severance from the Empire. "Perish India," is a well-known phrase. The Colonial Minister of Majuba Hill, his successor of the London Convention of 1884, and Prime Minister Gladstone cannot have been inspired with that passionate devotion to the great mission of the Empire and the maintenance of its integrity which now thrills through its citizens. These statesmen certainly considered themselves loyal; and, no doubt, even their opponents would not dispute their loyalty in intention, however they may denounce what they regard as their unwisdom. I have recalled how, at the Queen's Jubilee banquet in Johannesburg of June 1897, I heard a Dutch loyalist—who has sacrificed home and friends for his loyalty —refer to what he assumed to be the inevitable dissolution of the Empire. May it not be that the independent Afrikander nation, contemplated by some of the Bond leaders, was one to be evolved by this peaceful process?

None the less it is incumbent on citizens of the Empire to demonstrate the utter failure of that ideal to rise to the true conception of the destinies of the race. That they will resist it to the death on the field of battle they have shown. But the task remains of convincing the minds of our Boer fellow-citizens, and of some among our allies of the United States. The work before those suited for it in South Africa to-day is to convince all who have, for good or ill, thrown in their lot with the future of South Africa, that the growth of a local patriotism and the cherishing of proud memories of a bygone ancestry are no more incompatible with the wider patriotism of the Empire than the upholding of the ancient nationality of Wales or of the newer nationalities of Canada and Australia.

CHAPTER XII.

THE HEMMING IN OF THE REPUBLICS—THE ACTION OF MR. CECIL RHODES.

OF the policy of Mr. Cecil Rhodes, late Prime Minister of Cape Colony, I have no first-hand information ; as, to my regret, he is almost the only one of the leading men, living in South Africa of recent years, whom I have never had an opportunity of meeting.   My conclusions as to his policy, therefore, have to do rather with its results in action than its intention.

The annexation, by Mr. Rhodes's expedition in 1889, of Mashonaland, on the north of the Transvaal, followed by that of Matabeleland, completely cut off the expansion of the Boer Republics to the north.   For the first time in the two hundred and fifty years of Boer life in South Africa the trek was at an end.   This was a serious social factor in the life of the Boer, whose sons hitherto had always looked to the beaconing off of new farms for newly established home- steads.   This aspect of the end of the trek was seen clearly enough by the Transvaal Boers, and the so-called Ferreira Trek across the Limpopo was attempted in 1890; but the expedition was met and turned back by the then Adminis- trator of the newly-named province of Rhodesia, Dr. Jameson, afterwards to be the leader of the Raid.

The funds for this latest of British annexations were, as Mr. Rhodes has explained, furnished by the famous diamond mines of the De Beers' Company ; and a charter was procured from the Imperial Government, vesting the administration of the new province in a company, framed on the seventeenth-

century English model of the old East India Company.
Mr. Rhodes's party in the Cape Parliament was, until 1896,
the date of the Jameson Raid, supported by the organisation
of the Bond.

The social effects in the life of the Boer of the Transvaal
of the cutting off of the trek were great; the political effects
were greater. As I have pointed out already, the Conventions
of Pretoria of 1881 and of London of 1884 expressly permitted to the Transvaal Boers the right of expansion to the
north of the Limpopo, if they should choose to exercise it,
merely stipulating that agreements with Kaffir chiefs to the
east or the west of the Republic should be subject to
Imperial revision. The Imperial policy was to retain the
trade route to the north, and to control any access to the
sea which the Boer Republics might seek to establish.
Now, the Boers had neglected to exercise the right of expansion; and the Rhodes annexation definitely closed the
door.

As I have explained in what I have said as to the policy
of President Kruger, a substitute, or, at least, some slight
solatium was offered to President Kruger in the shape of a
seaport on the Indian Ocean at Kosi Bay. This in return for
the promise of the Republic to assist the Chartered Company
in the maintenance of order in Rhodesia. But this right,
too, under circumstances already described, was allowed to
lapse, and was not renewed in the Convention of 1894,
annexing Swaziland to the Transvaal.

The extreme importance to the Empire of the annexation
of Rhodesia has only lately been realised in the United
Kingdom. It is not a question of whether Chartered Company Government is good or not, or whether direct Imperial
rule would be preferable. It is that some form of British
annexation was urgently required to maintain the trade route
to the interior of Africa. British Parliaments, unfortunately,
until quite recently, have not taken wide views of foreign
relations, or of the necessity of safeguarding British trade.
Much more than that, a Treasury, with a truly superstitious
reverence for keeping down expense—an economy that in

Delagoa Bay and the Transvaal has cost untold millions
and thousands of lives—would never have consented to
move.

The result, therefore, would have been the expansion of
the Boer Republic to the Zambesi River, and the junction of
its territory with German South-West Africa, where it touches
the Zambesi, and the complete shutting off of British trade
to the vast undeveloped interior.

The policy attributed to Prince Bismarck of ousting
British influence in South Africa, and joining hands with
the Transvaal in holding a steel rope from sea to sea,
became, therefore, incapable of realisation without war with
the British Government, and a general European war, which
the holders of Alsace-Lorraine could not contemplate with a
light heart.

As I have already said, I have no materials, except those
open to the whole world, on which to judge as to Mr. Cecil
Rhodes's intention or methods. As to this service of his to
the Empire there can, however, be no doubt or hesitation.
Without his control of the millions of De Beers and his
promptitude of action, not waiting for the consent of a de-
bating Parliament or an unteachable Treasury at Westminster,
the British annexation of that vast territory would, in human
probability, not have been accomplished. In which case, the
problem now before the Imperial Government would have
been different indeed.

The prevention of Boer expansion to the west effected by
the Bechuanaland Expedition of 1884, under Sir Charles
Warren, showed a similar regard for Imperial interests in
the maintenance of the trade route to the interior. But in
the Bechuanaland Expedition the action was taken by the
Imperial Government. In the annexation of the territory
north of the Limpopo the action was taken by an individual
citizen of the Empire on his own initiative, and at the
expense of resources of which he held the control.

Of the political methods of the late Premier of Cape
Colony, various estimates have been made.

His opponents—and there are some among staunch

Imperialists—tell you that his alliance with the Bond strengthened its power for anti-British purposes.

But the parallel of Prince Bismarck persisted in presenting itself to my mind. One would like to hear what any survivor of forty years ago of the old National Liberal Party of Prussia could tell one of their earlier relations with the Man of Blood and Iron. Even in later days he is said to have kept in his cigar-case a veritable olive leaf, to be tendered by the victorious leader of the Junkers to the National Liberals.

Parendo vinces. As are the powers of nature, so are princes and democracies. Lord Chancellor Bacon's demeanour towards the contemptible Prince, into whose hands the inscrutable designs of Providence had committed the lordship of Scotland and England and Ireland, would too hastilty be deemed mere opportunism.

The stories of Mr. Cecil Rhodes's reputed comment on General Gordon's views of life and action—" Your ideas are admirable, but they lack a gold basis"; of Mr. Rhodes's— again reputed—indignation at General Gordon's refusal to accept the contents in gold of the treasure chamber of the Chinese Emperor, grateful for the repression of Taeping rebels, if, as is to be hoped, they are true, would explain many adaptations of means to an end.

In a speech delivered to the shareholders of De Beers after the relief of Kimberley, Mr. Rhodes referred to a conversation of his with the late Mr. Carl Borckenhagen, editor of the Young Afrikander Bloemfontein *Express.* In this colloquy the late premier of the Cape Colony was, as he says, invited to throw in his lot with the party which designed to oust British influence from South Africa, and to form an independent Afrikander nation; a proposition declined, as being incompatible either with the respect of the Dutch people, which, towards a deserter, would be inconsiderable, or with the duty of a citizen of the Empire.

Singularly enough, I have Mr. Carl Borckenhagen's version of that colloquy. The able journalist described the attitude of the late premier as one of crass materialism. " Money, not the sword of the spirit."

I ventured to tell him that, in all ages, one who aspires to act, and not merely to teach, must use the weapons of the time and generation. In one time muscle; in another tactical skill in arms; in another speech; in another gold. And this is not, of necessity, materialism.

CHAPTER XIII.

THE REFORM MOVEMENT IN JOHANNESBURG.

DEALING with the policy of President Kruger, I have referred to the various restrictions on the attainment of the franchise, imposed after the London Convention of 1884, with the object of retaining power in Boer hands, and excluding any possible participation in power of those who did not entertain the dream of an anti-British Dutch dominion in South Africa, and even of those who were in any respect "Engelsch gezind."

Now, many writers and speakers have blamed the President — while, strangely enough, congratulating the Empire—for not seizing on the undoubted opportunity, presented to him by the influx of the new European population and his control of a revenue of millions, to build up a great Republic on the model of the United States of America, consisting of all Europern nationalities. There is not the faintest doubt that the President had this prospect; had it especially after the Jameson Raid in 1896; and had it even up to a short time before the war of October 1899.

Many, even of British descent in South Africa, perplexed and despairing of ever seeing any sane and consistent policy adopted by the Imperial Government, would most decidedly have thrown in their lot with the formation of such a Republic, destined to ultimate independence, if they were treated by the Boers on terms of equality. Some critics even ascribe to the baleful influence of State Secretary Leyds the President's not having adopted this line of policy. I shall show later on that it was not the policy of State

Secretary Leyds that had the last word in precipitating war ;
but there is a much deeper objection to all those irrelevant
criticisms. They remind me of the ingenious speculations
as to what would happen if an impossible Tsar were a
Socialist, or an inconceivable Pope a revolutionist. The
mind of President Kruger, and of all the dominant caste
among the Boers, would revolt against such a conception of
a Republic. By independence they meant Dutch independence, of a Dutch-speaking, Dutch-thinking, Dutch-ruling,
Dutch-praying and Dutch-fighting folk, and not nineteenth-
century new-fangled Republicanism of a cosmopolitan herd
of unwarlike European Outsiders, of a different religion and
language, whose participation in political power would bring
the Republic into harmony with, instead of opposition to, the
Empire. *Aut Caesar, aut nullus.*

As might, however, have been anticipated, the Outsiders,
more especially the British majority, did not take kindly to
this archaic conception of their position—whether paralleled
by that of Hebrews in Egypt, or of Helots in Sparta ; and
refused to be comforted by any amount of plausible explanations as to the President's necessity of consulting the
prejudices of the veldt Boer. Within five years of the discovery of the Witwatersrand, they started against the
exclusionist legislation of the Volksraad, an agitation ever
increasing in volume and determination.

For the first few years, in fact until 1894, the Uitlanders
addressed their petitions and remonstrances to the Government and Volksraad of the Transvaal. They formed a National
Union to agitate for the removal of their grievances. When,
however, after years of agitation, they found their petitions
rejected with scorn, and a speaker in the Volksraad telling
them that if they wanted rights they could take up rifles and
fight for them, and the President declaring that he would
never yield and that the storm might burst, they turned their
eyes to the Imperial Power. Their appeal to Lord Loch,
the High Commissioner in 1894, primarily induced by the
refusal of the British Helots to take up military service
against the Kaffir tribes, as long as they were refused the

franchise, is one step in this alteration of their appeal. The agitation in press and platform meanwhile continued.

Into the various counts of the indictment brought by the Uitlanders against the Government of Pretoria, I do not purpose to enter here, but shall go into them fully later on. Here I shall deal only with the accusation that the agitation was not a genuine one, but was the outcome of a "Capitalist Plot" to get the gold reefs more completely into capitalist hands; and secondly, with the disastrous Jameson Raid of December 1895.

I came to South Africa fully prepared to give credence to the theory of a "Capitalist Plot," should I find evidence to sustain it. President Lincoln's warning to his people of the danger of capitalist domination—a warning given now nearly forty years ago—has always seemed to me to mark his prescience, and to point to a real danger; to which, fortunately, many American citizens are at last awakening. The exemption of Kimberley diamonds from taxation seemed to prove a similar danger in South Africa. The patient investigation of some years has convinced me that there was no such inception to the Uitlander agitation.

In real fact, the great capitalists, if they looked merely to dividends, were in a much better position with the Government of President Kruger. I do not here refer to possibilities of corruption being greater than under any probable British regime. The gold law itself of the Transvaal played most enormously into the hands of the great houses. In the first place, the amount of taxation levied on the gold product directly was not considered by the resident Uitlanders—whatever the great capitalists might say—as really excessive. What the Reformers objected to was not the actual amount of taxation on gold, but improper expenditure of the sums accruing, and improper of levying of customs tariffs on necessaries of life, which affected the rank and file, and affected the millionaires not at all. If taxation pressing on the Uitlander residents were removed, and if the taxes on the Gold Mines were expended on legitimate objects of public expenditure—roads, bridges, law courts, schools, and other such purposes—and not expended on armaments and secret service funds, the rank and file of the Reformers would never have objected to the taxation on the gold output as excessive ; and, indeed, would not improbably have advocated its being increased.

In the second place, one absurdity of the Transvaal Gold Law played directly into the hands of the great capitalists, and acted detrimentally to the ordinary resident of moderate means.   Gold claims, whether worked or not, had to pay the same amount of monthly licences.   The result was, that in times of depression, for which wealthy speculators carefully waited, poorer men, perforce, were obliged to allow their claims to lapse to the Government, whereupon, of course, the wealthy speculator could afford to buy at the public auction of the lapsed claims, prescribed by law.   In this way all unexploited claims of known value were for a long time, and are to the present day, falling steadily into the hands of a few great capitalist groups.

The great owners, who may be trusted to see to their pecuniary interest, were quite aware of these two cardinal results of the Transvaal Gold Law ; and for them the rule of Pretoria, from a merely pecuniary point of view, was simply ideal.

They appear to have looked askance at the Reform movement.   No conceivable British-ruled community could suit them as well ; witness the terrible example of the British law of Klondyke, giving about 50 per cent. of the gold to the British Crown, otherwise the Canadian Treasury.

To be set against this, of course, is the fact that the high tariffs and the high charge for dynamite exacted by the Dynamite Monopoly, interfered with exploitation of mines of lower grade ore.   But a millionaire need not worry about apples which he was sure of gathering when they became ripe.

Now, a consideration of these facts is alleged by the rank and file of the Uitlanders—such as the men who are now riding in the Imperial Light Horse—to have induced the great capitalists to hold very severely aloof from the Reform movement at first.

Later, when it gained volume and there seemed a possibility of Pretoria giving way and a British as well as Dutch-ruled Republic being created, they decided to cast in their lot with the side which apparently—although only apparently—was going to win and to control, if not "capture," the movement.

Now, I am not to be taken as saying that the capitalists of the Witwatersrand had no public motive in their later action in joining the Reform movement; I was not in the Transvaal at the time, and I have not sufficient *data* on which to judge. Indeed, we must all hope that, in view of the pending settlement, some at least have been and will be actuated by views of higher statesmanship. But it is an historical fact that, for whatever reason, they held aloof from the Reform movement, and that, therefore, its origin cannot have been a "Capitalist Plot."

The Jameson Raid of December 1895 altered the whole political arena. All the winning cards fell to President Kruger.

It is needless here to dwell on either the conception or the execution of the Raid for the supposed aid of the Uitlanders, carried out by Dr. Jameson, the Administrator of Rhodesia, with about 500 of the Mounted Police under his command. Its violation of all the rules of international law is, of course, obvious.

But its result on the position of the Imperial Government and of the Uitlanders of Johannesburg was simply to cause paralysis. To the hands of President Kruger and his Government it committed a magical lever. Enormous armaments might in the future be proceeded with openly, as well as secretly, since proof there was that armed invasion of the territory of the Republic, without challenge or warning, had happened, and might happen again.

Viewed in the light of the subsequent war, the failure of the ill-omened Raid can only be described as Providential. If that body of five hundred men had reached the practically unarmed city of Johannesburg, one shudders to think of what would have been the fate of the hapless citizens. The mighty and unknown power of the two Republics—for both had sprung to arms—the most formidable military force in South Africa, which has defied in war one of the greatest of the world Empires, would have crushed into gore and ashes the whole European population of the gold reef.*

"Dit is de eerste geboortsdag van der Afrikander natie," "This is the first birthday of the Afrikander nation"—is said to have been the exclamation, on hearing that Rhodesian troops had crossed the border, of the veteran judge who was negotiator of the Convention of Majuba Hill. As a blow turns into ice water below freezing-point, so did the shock of the Raid unite all the Boers in the land. The more progressive Boers of the Transvaal, the Boers of the Orange Free State, who always maintained a Liberal franchise, the Dutch colonists of the Cape and Natal, many of whom, unwitting of the old President's deeper designs, had sympathised with the Uitlanders in their grievances, became crystallised into a solid mass, henceforth never to be moved but by the cannon of the Empire.

On the steps immediately following during the year 1896 I need not dwell. The Imperial Government's hands were cruelly hampered by being made to appear in the wrong in the eyes of the world by the action of a few troopers over whom they really had no control. The Uitlanders were reflected on for their apparent lack of courage for not coming to the help of their rescuers; never to have opportunity to show their quality until Elandslaagte. The President was enabled to display his magnanimity in not shooting "the marauders," merely handing them over to the British Government for trial; and as to the "rebels," by restraining himself from the infliction of the death sentence,

---

* It has been objected to by some that the large cannon had not at that time been procured by Pretoria; and that therefore the Raid might have succeeded. But not cannon, by any means. Rifles were and are the strength of the burghers; and Mr. J. P. Fitzpatrick's book shows that at the end of 1895 there were two rifles for every burgher in the land.

contenting himself with enormous fines amounting to a quarter of a million sterling. His Government also was enabled to openly increase with feverish haste that pile of armaments which later on astonished the world.

The trial of the Reform prisoners in Pretoria I have had described to me from the lips of Reform prisoners and their advocates, as well as by their chief prosecutor. The trial of the late Administrator of Rhodesia and his companions of the Raid I have personally witnessed in the High Court of Justice in England, where they were duly sentenced and sent to prison.

The only immediate matter to be borne in mind is that the Imperial Government, for its part, vindicated its non-participation in, and strong disapproval of, the ill-omened expedition.

It is true that the deeper cause of the Raid was the existence of the helotry of the Uitlander, and that public attention was riveted on their position as one result of the Raid. This, however, is one of the compensations incident to many actions whose justice cannot be defended. The peaceful progress of the Reform movement would probably have succeeded in obtaining Imperial intervention without three years' delay, three years' preparation of armaments on the Boer side, and the cost and loss of lives of a devastating war.*

During the following year of 1896 the three most striking aspects of the political situation were the colossal armaments being prepared for the Pretorian Government in all the war factories of the world, the diplomatic intervention of the Imperial Government through the Colonial Secretary, and the growth of an Imperial political organisation through South Africa, called the South African League.

This last carried on the agitation of the Reform movement, though under different leadership, the leaders of the late Reform movement having been sentenced by the Courts of

---

* The present High Commissioner describes the Raid as "a conspiracy of which the great body of Uitlanders was innocent, and which perverted and ruined their cause."

Pretoria either to banishment, or, as a condition of the reduction of their imprisonment to fines, by the imposition of the penalty of abstention from political agitation.

Before taking up the thread of events in the order of time, let me state in their own language the case of the Uitlander against the ruling Boer, as presented to me by leaders on both sides in the end of 1896 and the beginning of 1897.

CHAPTER XIV.

THE UITLANDER INDICTMENT AGAINST PRETORIA.

THE method of investigation of the public problems of South Africa which I had decided on before my arrival, I carried out, with particular care in regard to the Uitlander movement in the Transvaal. I shall give, usually in their own words, the charges of the Uitlanders against the Transvaal Government, which I obtained in 1896 and 1897 from leaders among them ; and the defence, again usually in their own words, as stated to me by leaders in the two Republics.

Let me first say that I have never regarded the real issue as one of the treatment of the Uitlanders, simply regarded as oppressed individuals. The real issue for the Empire and the world was, and is, the maintenance of the integrity and prestige of the Empire, struck at primarily by the relegation of certain of its citizens to an inferior status in the Transvaal : secondarily, by the fostering of an ideal of a hostile Dutch Afrikander Dominion.

The Uitlander might want the franchise in order to use it as a lever to redress his personal grievances. The Imperial Government's demand on his behalf was moved by a sense of self-preservation.

What follows in this chapter was written in 1897.

The grievances of the Transvaal Uitlanders are now a thrice-told tale : one, too, on which public opinion in England is largely made up. As evidencing the existence of the anti-British policy ascribed to the Government, reference has already been made to this long catalogue.

Here I purpose to enumerate the grievances as stated by the Uitlander leaders, taking first those endorsed by Lord Ripon and Mr. Chamberlain.

The Uitlander's exclusion from the franchise, and the reasons why the Uitlanders object to being placed in a position of political inferiority, furnish ground for a sense of resentment which has largely been influenced by what may be generically described as sentimental considerations. The practical results of their exclusion from the franchise are not less entitled to consideration. The present conditions under which the franchise may be obtained are practically prohibitive. If the Uitlander desires to be naturalised, he must first reside two years, and have been during those two years registered in the list of the Field-Cornet of his district. This registration subjects him to compulsory military service. At the end of the two years he may request to be naturalised. His request may be granted—if the State Attorney considers there is no legal objection, and if the Executive considers there is no political objection. The Uitlander who has been permitted to become naturalised must take an oath of allegiance, expressly renouncing his allegiance to his former State. What privileges does he secure by this naturalisation? He can vote in the election of the Field-Cornet for his district, and of the district member for the Second Volksraad. What is the Second Volksraad? An advisory body without legislative power. Membership of the Second Volksraad is open to Uitlanders who have been naturalised for two years, are over thirty years of age, are Protestants by religion, have immovable property, and are actually domiciled in the Transvaal. If the newly naturalised citizen has remained in possession of these qualifications for ten years, he becomes eligible to be appointed a full burgher; that is, if the First Volksraad, the body with legislative power, thinks fit to create him a full burgher by resolution. Seeing that the First Volksraad has absolute legislative power, the Franchise Law would seem to be unnecessary in this latter provision; as the First Volksraad can appoint anyone to be a burgher, whether he has fulfilled the terms or not. The contrast between the provisions regarding the Uitlander and those applying to the Boer is evident from consideration of the fact that every Boer youth of sixteen years of age obtains the full political franchise, with right of voting in the Presidential election and to the First Volksraad, the supreme power in the land.

The consequences of this exclusion from the franchise are alleged by the Uitlanders to be those which may be expected to spring from the absence of control by the tax-payer over those who have the spending of the money. Every item in the impeachment of the Government put forward by the Uitlanders they trace to the monopoly of political power enjoyed by the earlier immigrants. Over-taxation, peculation, mismanagement, favouritism towards Hollanders, defects of municipal government, inefficient police, defective water supply, inefficient educational institutions, imperfect organisation of the Law Courts, and retrogressive legislation affecting the liberty of the citizen—all are ascribed to the exclusion of the Uitlander population from the exercise of political rights.

The educational grievance is next to be considered.

"The Government of the Transvaal," writes a leading Uitlander, "in the exercise of its prerogative subordinates the education of children growing up in the country to the patriotic impulse of compelling them to accept it through the medium of the Dutch language. The consequence is, that last year, whilst £63,000 was nominally spent on State-aided schools, only 1s. 10d. per head was devoted to the education of Uitlander children, i.e., English schools; whilst over £8 per head was spent upon the school-going children of Dutch-speaking parents. Notwithstanding the lavish expenditure upon the "Staats Gymnasium" and Dutch country schools, the scale of education amongst Dutch inhabitants is of the lowest order. In Johannesburg, I have no hesitation in saying, there are thousands of children, both Dutch and English, growing up in ignorance and vice, and their existence in the State must ultimately prove a danger and disgrace."

"The prejudice against English," writes a leading advocate, "is sure to injure the rising generation in the struggle for existence here, for without English it could never aspire to any position either in the learned professions or in commercial life."

Mr. Chamberlain's remark that "Up to the present, it seems to have been practically impossible for the children of Uitlanders to obtain effectual education in the State-aided schools," is as true as when it was made in February 1896. There is no adequate provision for the 7,000 children in the Johannesburg district. As English-speaking parents refuse to allow their children to be taught in schools where the instruction is carried on in the Dutch language, their only alternative is to send them to private schools. As these English-speaking private schools receive no assistance from the State, the expense falls on the parents of the children. In the case of well-to-do parents, this means they have to pay twice over for the education of their children; but in the case of the miners and the poorer population, it means that their children are without instruction, as they cannot afford to pay the fees required by competent teachers in private schools. The newer generation of the poorer classes are growing up without education, to the material detriment of their own prospects, as compared with those of the educated immigrants from Europe, and to the ultimate danger of the population of the Transvaal; ignorance being the seed-plot of crime. Recently the Volksraad passed an Education Bill, to which Mr. Chamberlain looked forward in his despatch of February 1896. What are the provisions of that Bill? The medium of instruction under the new Bill will be the home language of the children (this being usually English) only until they have reached the fifth standard, when the medium is to be Dutch alone.

Financial grievances are next to be considered.

"It is maintained," says Mr. Chamberlain, "that the finances are mismanaged, and that the expenditure escapes proper control and audit; that taxation is maintained beyond the needs of the administration; that unfair discrimination is shown in the collection of personal taxes; that the import duties on the necessaries of life are not only a hardship on the working classes, but so raise the cost of the working of the mines as actually to be prohibitive of the working of the poorer ones, which, if the taxation were better apportioned to the ability to bear it, might be opened up to the general advantage."

As the Manifesto of the Transvaal National Union puts it :—

" We find that taxation is imposed upon us without any representation whatever. That taxation is wholly inequitable:

(*a*) Because a much greater amount is levied from the people than is required for the needs of the Government;

(*b*) Because it is either class taxation, pure and simple; or, by the selection of subjects, though nominally universal, it is made to fall upon our shoulders; and

(*c*) Because the necessaries of life are unduly burdened.

Expenditure is not controlled by any public official independent of the Government; vast sums are squandered; while the Secret Service Fund is a dark mystery to everybody."

As a result of want of control of the tax-payer over those spending the taxes, taxation is excessive; it presses with special weight on the working classes. It discriminates between the Boer and the Uitlander.

The finances are mismanaged in expenditure as well as in the levying. Enormous sums are wasted on war material, unnecessary for any legitimate purpose of self-defence. Vast appropriations are made on account of secret service. The excess of taxation may be measured by the consideration of the fact that a State with the insignificant population of the Transvaal raises £4,462,193 in taxes.

In effect, the whole of this taxation rests upon the gold industry, which produces about £7,000,000 worth of gold during the year, as there are practically no manufactures, and no taxation levied on agricultural produce grown in the country. The annual estimates issued last year show the income and expenditure as follows :—

INCOME.

Customs	£1,200,000
Gold Prospecting Licences	482,000
Hut Tax and Native Poll Tax	162,925
Fines, Special	212,000
Postal	110,000
Telegraph	86,000
Railway	322,327
Stamp Dues	200,000

Transfer Dues	£275,000
Diggers' Licences	58,872
Stand Licences	54,200
State portion of Profit on Dynamite . .	35,000

EXPENDITURE.

War.	£943,510
Total Salaries	898,041
Police	242,421
Telegraph Department	80,909
Postal Department	44,374
Works	730,000
Special Expenditure	585,350
Judicial Department	19,241
Administration of Justice	38,850

The war item of expenditure last year was under
£200,000 ; this year it is £943,510, of which £375,000 is
for the " purchase of fire-arms."

The estimated expenditure, which in 1894 was only
£1,595,000, has now risen to more than three times that
amount, while there is a public debt of nearly £10,000,000
sterling.

The taxes are levied so as to tax the Uitlander and leave
the Boer free from taxation.

"The policy of the Government," says the Manifesto, "in regard to
taxation may be practically described as protection without production.
The most disastrous hardships result to consumers, and merchants can
scarcely say from day to day where they are.

" Is it not a grievance that the townsman has to pay a heavy tax on
almost everything he uses, while the countryman pays hardly anything
on those articles which he himself indulges in ?

The policy of taxing food imports to favour the Boer
farmer—the exact reverse of the policy of the Free Breakfast
Table—renders the cost of living to the working classes
enormously high, and makes their nominally high wages
entirely illusory.

The effect of this policy of taxation on the mining
industry will be considered later.

An Uitlander writing at the time of the Jameson Raid
described the situation as follows :—

" The system of taxation is so organised as to throw nearly the whole of the revenue charges of the country on that portion of the population which is powerless to control expenditure. The revenue a few years ago, before the Uitlander population had risen to its present numbers or developed the mining industry to its present value, averaged about £75,000 a year. In 1894 the revenue was £1,750,000; in 1895 there has been a very great further increase, and, notwithstanding this augmentation in the total receipts, it has been estimated, according to carefully compiled returns, that the share paid by the Boer population is only £5000 more than it was ten years ago. To speak, as is sometimes done, of the share which they contribute to the Exchequer as a tenth is only a form of words. In reality it is much nearer to a twentieth. The system is protective where there is nothing to protect. The Boer consumes no imported produce, and the State does not supply more than a quarter of the produce consumed on the Rand. The customs tax, therefore, falls as a revenue tax upon the Uitlander. The Boer, unfortunately, is cultivating less than before, and the natives, who were good producers, are being dispersed and harried under the Plakkers Wet, or Squatters' Law, which, as will be shown, is enforced also chiefly against the Uitlander landholders. A few other examples will serve to illustrate the direction of the incidence of taxation. The receipt stamp law is made more and more vexatious and burdensome, and the penalties are excessive. But only trade receipts are stamped. The farmer who sells produce does not stamp receipts, and the Boer never engages in trade.

" This tax falls, therefore, exclusively on the alien. The newly imposed 1 per cent. tax on coal falls also exclusively on the alien, who alone makes use of this kind of fuel. These are relatively small matters. The transfer duty, which, of course, falls wholly upon the industrial community, has lately been subjected by the Raad to an increase, which is of the most disastrous importance to the development of the mining industry. Hitherto this duty has been 4 per cent., paid either on the cash consideration passed in respect of claims, or ground acquired by companies, or on a valuation made by the local authorities of the vendors' shares. The Raad have now decided that the 4 per cent. shall be payable on the nominal value of the shares and cash. The tax under the old conditions has given a very large revenue to the State. The proposed change converts it into an absolutely colossal charge upon the mining industry, and will swell the already considerable surplus at the disposal of the Transvaal Government with sums that would otherwise have gone a long way to open up and equip new mines. The duty has to be paid on reconstructions as well as on *bonâ fide* sales, and the fact that the ownership really remains in the same hands is not taken into account."

Mr. Chamberlain's despatch next refers to the exceptional restrictions imposed by law on the right of public meeting.

Mr. Chamberlain adds, however, that he feels bound to admit that, as far as the recent history of Johannesburg is concerned, these restrictions do not seem to have been very strictly interpreted. The Uitlander resident of Johannesburg does not consider the restriction to be merely nominal. Exactly as the effect of an immigration law is not to be measured by the number of immigrants turned back at the border, similarly the effect of a law repressing the right of public meeting cannot be gauged by simply considering the number of meetings which have been formally suppressed. People are deterred from holding meetings when they know they are exposed to hostile Government action. It is also pointed out that the new Acts, the Alien Expulsion Act and the Press Act, render—

" The expression of public opinion liable to be visited by severe punishment. It is right also to point out that under the Press Law letters or articles of a personal or political nature must bear the signature of the author; it may have the effect of deterring the exposure of abuses in any case where the writer has perfectly good reason to feel disinclined to disclose his name."

The grievances of the Mining Industry next come under review. The agitation for the removal of burdens on the industry has been represented in England as a grotesque complaint on the part of the cosmopolitan Jew capitalist that he is not allowed to add to his already superfluous millions. But, it is said, there is more in the complaint than the disaj pointment of the millionaire. The whole prosperity of the country depends on the mines. If by taxation mines of inferior grade are made incapable of being worked at a profit, not merely the cosmopolitan millionaire but all the inhabitants of the Rand, and more particularly the working class, must suffer. Furthermore, the European investor must suffer. £150,000,000 of European capital have been sunk in the Transvaal mines; the return in dividends to the European shareholders has been slight. If the Government do not wish to repress the growth of the industry then they must labour under the economic fallacy ascribed by Edmund Burke to the Government of George III.

They seem not to know that " Taxation is not Revenue," and not to realise the elementary economic proposition that by lowering an impost the Government may obtain an increased return to the treasury. The chief burdens on the Mining Industry fall under the head of the Protective Tariff adopted by the Government to favour the agricultural products of the Transvaal farmers, the policy of granting monopolies, such as the dynamite concession and the railway concession, the policy of obstruction as regards railway facilities with the Cape Colony, the want of facilities for the employment of native labour, and minor obstructions to the carrying out of the business of the mines—such as the official ostracism of the English language. Generally, also, it is alleged that the excessive taxation, direct and indirect, prevents the higher-grade mines giving adequate return for the capital invested in them, and prevents the lower-grade mines being worked at any profit at all. As to the first point, it is clear that taxing food imports raises the cost of subsistence of the labourer, and necessarily the rate of remuneration which he must be paid by the mining companies, although that increased rate is of no advantage to the labourer but passes to the Government in the form of taxation. As regards State monopolies Mr. Chamberlain observes—

" The policy of granting State monopolies as regards mining requisites and other important articles of commerce has given rise to much resentment, and as regards some of them, it is difficult to see how even a plausible justification can be put forward for them from the point of view of the interests of the general community."

It is pointed out that the policy of granting monopolies is one which is condemned by all economies, and is contrary to the practice of the civilised world. On the one hand, it may be looked upon, at the best, as a means of exacting excessive taxation; and at the worst, as a scandalous misuse of the public revenue to enrich a few monopolists. To take the dynamite monopoly. At the lowest estimate this is calculated to be equivalent to a tax of £400,000 per annum on the industry. The Manifesto of the Reform Union put it at £600,000 per annum. The monopolists purchase in Europe a 50-lb. case of dynamite at a cost of 29s., paying carriage from Europe to Johannesburg, amounting to 10s. at the utmost. Their charge is 88s. per case to the mining companies. Even these figures do not represent the whole of the possible loss to the industry. The companies cannot use other explosives which cost less and are more suitable for some descriptions of mining; they are deprived of the benefit of any new chemical inventions, as they are compelled to buy from monopolists whatever the monopolists choose to sell; and as to the dynamite which they purchase, they have no guarantee that it is of good quality, as the monopolists have no competition to fear.

Mr. Chamberlain observes—

"I cannot suppose that, looking to the large interests which the Government of the Republic has in the financial success of its railways, there can be any hesitation in redressing proved grievances, or in adopting measures for the improvement of the personnel or the traffic and other arrangements of the lines."

Opinion in Johannesburg does not justify that confident expectation of Mr. Chamberlain. It is represented that the railway management is not merely incompetent in its personnel, and inefficient in its supply of railway material and rolling stock, but is directed by political motives which have no regard whatever to the commercial success of the mining industry. It is alleged that the policy of the railway administration controlled by the Government is, in the first place, to repress the growth of the industry, the opening up of new mines or the profitable working of mines of lower grade ; and in the next place, to drive such traffic as there is over the Portuguese railway to Delagoa Bay instead of the British' railway to Cape Town. It is pointed out, for instance, that the railway refuses to supply sufficient trucks for conveying coal to the mines; that companies have suffered large losses on account of insufficient supply of coal for their engines. On one occasion the traffic from the Cape was practically stopped at Vereeniging on the Vaal River by the refusal of the railway to forward loaded trucks from the

Cape, on the pretext that the Transvaal Railway could not give more trucks for the Cape service than for Natal or Delagoa Bay. The coal supply is similarly obstructed by the refusal of the railway company to facilitate the construction of sidings, and by their insisting on coal being loaded into sacks, instead of into trucks with movable sides. Their refusal to run sufficient trains to the terminus of the Cape Government Railway is ascribed to a distinct anti-Cape policy to drive traffic from the Cape route. Political motives, however, are said to be not the sole ones, inasmuch as goods coming by the Delagoa Bay route pass for a greater distance over the Transvaal line, and a larger share of the cost of carriage goes to the Transvaal Railway. The railway, in whose stock the Government is largely interested, arranges its tariff so as to be a huge tax on the Mining Industry. The Rand train, a coal and passenger train running from Krugersdorp to Springs (about forty-two miles), is understood to earn enough to pay interest on the whole mining capital of the whole line. The railway has its head office in Amsterdam, where its books are kept, and its accounts are published in Dutch. Refusal to insure undelivered goods, refusal to take precautions against fire, the appointment of Hollander clerks who can understand neither the Taal nor English, a bewildering red-tape system imported from Holland, arbitrary regulations of tariff and traffic, and systematic insolence on the part of the officials, are said to be counted among the facilities afforded by the railway.

In connection with the labour supply Mr. Chamberlain was similarly hopeful.

" As regards the grievances which have been put forward in connection with the labour question by the mining industry, I content myself at this time by expressing the hope that, if, by the abatement of formalities and needless restrictions, by promoting the well-being of the natives when going to, remaining at, and returning from the mines, and by forcing on them wise restrictions as . regards drink and such matters, the labour supply can be enlarged, and the condition of the labourers improved, the President and his Executive Council will not fail to give the question their most earnest attention."

The Uitlanders do not consider that Mr. Chamberlain's hope has been realised to any appreciable extent. A Liquor Law has been passed restricting the supply of alcohol to the natives ; but the working of the native pass law, the arbitrary exactions inflicted on the natives working in the mines, the police arrest of any native appearing even accidentally without a badge in public, their prohibition to walk on the footway, the practical denial of redress if they are ill-used by white men—all these official practices, it is alleged, act as a deterrent on the supply of native labour to the mines. Many minor obstacles are enumerated to the development of the mines of the Rand which fall under the head of charges of general maladministration, to be considered later on. One, however, may be noted here. The ostracism of the English language (the recent law requiring all documents to be written in Dutch) is said to constitute a serious obstruction. Summing up generally the charges against the policy of the Government as regards the mines, it is averred that the action of the Executive, direct and indirect, prevents the higher-grade mines from giving adequate return for the capital invested in them, and prevents lower-grade mines from being worked at a profit. The Government Commission recently appointed to consider the condition of the mining industry is expected to elicit facts bearing out the foregoing contentions.

Mr. Chamberlain's remarks as to the police service are said to be as applicable to present conditions as they were to those of last year :—

" The only other matter of grievance on which I propose to touch now is the condition of the police force; as to which, I may remark, that the difficulties of the reforming party in the Volksraad and the Executive appear to arise from the strong prejudice of the more conservative of the burghers against employing Uitlanders, which would not be unworthy of sympathy were it not for the patent fact that a population like that of the burghers cannot possibly be expected to furnish adequate material from which to select candidates for this department of public service ; and to make difficulties about appointing foreigners amounts, under the circumstances, to a denial to the Uitlander community of what are among the primary rights which the governed may demand of those who undertake to govern them."

The municipal government of the Rand is the last subject referred to in Mr. Chamberlain's despatch. It is complained that residents have no control over the management of municipal affairs; that the streets are ill-kept and ill-lighted; that there is no efficient police—the police being mainly Hollanders appointed and paid by the Government, and under no obligation to consult the wishes of the residents of the town; that the water supply in the hands of concessionaires is very imperfect, and the quality of the water supplied is dangerous to health; that fever has become endemic, and that crime, owing to the want of efficient police and absence of lighting, is rapidly increasing, and that it has become dangerous to go out of doors in the suburbs after sunset. The municipality created by the law recently passed by the Raad is said to be but a slight improvement on the previous system under which such control as Johannesburg had over its municipal affairs was exercised by the Sanitary Board. The Burgomaster of the new municipality is a nominee of the Government, and acts of the municipality are subject to the veto of the Government.

"The municipal affairs of the town," writes a resident, "are controlled by a Sanitary Board, whose powers are limited, and subject in nearly all detail to the veto of the Government.

"The water-supply, which should be controlled by the municipal body, is in the hands of concessionaires. It was the same with the lighting of the town until recently, when the Sanitary Board was empowered to acquire it. The sanitation of the town is extremely defective, greatly owing to the limited powers of the Sanitary Board.

"A municipal law is under the consideration of the Volksraad, but it is understood that the chief officer, namely, the Burgomaster or Mayor, will be appointed by the Government from among the burghers of the country. All these matters occasion inconvenience and discomfort to the inhabitants."

Many other grievances, however, not touched upon by Mr. Chamberlain are enumerated by the Uitlander. The ostracism of the English language is not confined to the

State schools. The language of commerce is English all through South Africa; yet policemen in the streets are unable or unwilling to reply in English, and railway officials profess a similar inability. The discussions at the municipal Board must be conducted in Dutch. It is proposed that all way-bills and other commercial documents should be written in Dutch under a penalty of a fine for neglect. "There has been a deliberate attempt," says the Manifesto of the National Union, "to Hollanderise the Republic, and to kill the English language."

"The use of Dutch," writes a Johannesburger, "as the official language in Courts and public departments naturally causes expense and inconvenience to the trading, manufacturing, and mining classes, whose only tongue is usually English, and in which all business transactions are conducted."

A leading advocate writes :—

"The prohibition of English in the Courts makes litigation twice as expensive and not nearly so effective as it would be if both languages are used; for in cross-examining an English witness who understands, but does not speak, Dutch, the witness has many points in his favour, and cross-examination through an interpreter is often a farce. About 75 per cent. of the High Court cases are between English-speaking people; about 15 to 20 per cent. are between an English litigant and some other party, and from 5 to 10 per cent. are between non-English litigants."

Religious disabilities, unknown in any civilised country, flourish in the Transvaal.

"The Statute books," says the National Union Manifesto, "are disfigured with enactments imposing religious disabilities."

"So far as I know," writes a resident, "these disabilities are felt in this way. No grant in aid of Jewish schools is made on the ground that if such grant were given, Roman Catholics would equally have a claim, and as the State will only support the Protestant religion, Roman Catholics are rigidly excluded."

This retrograde principle is embodied in a clause of the Grond Wet.

Another branch of the action of the Government consists in restricting the right of the Uitlander to carry arms, considered in all countries to be the essential privilege of a free man. Arms are heavily taxed on the frontier. Besides the tax a special permit is required for the importation, a permit which may be refused at the discretion of a Government official. The purchase of ammunition, even by persons who are already in possession of arms, is hedged round with burdensome restrictions. In every single instance of purchasing ammunition, no matter how small the quantity, the Government permit must be obtained. The new law now before the Volksraad may be described as the Uitlander Disarmament Act, as it provides that not merely is importation or purchase of arms, but the possession of arms, to be subject to Government licence, refusable at discretion. Assisting this policy of disarmament is instituted what is described as a system of military terrorism. Powerful forts are built at Pretoria and Johannesburg; vast quantities of Maxims and military supplies are being daily imported, and an elaborate force of artillery is drilled and equipped; military parade is incessant, and everything is done to impress the Uitlanders with a sense of subjection to the armed forces of the Executive, and of being governed by a power which is independent of their opinion. Threats, it is said, are freely made to commandeer obnoxious Uitlanders in the event of disturbances; everywhere the Transvaal eagle, adopted as the symbol of military authority, is paraded in the face of the Johannesburger. German officials assist in this organisation of military forces, and so far from conditions in this respect being better, they are worse than at the time of the publication of the Manifesto.

"We have now openly the policy of force revealed to us: £250,000 is to be spent upon the completing of a fort at Pretoria, £100,000 is to be spent upon a fort to terrorise the inhabitants of Johannesburg; large orders are sent to Krupp's for big guns, Maxims have been ordered, and we are even told that German officers are coming out to drill the burghers."

This anticipation of the Manifesto has been more than verified.

The exclusion of the Uitlander from office in the Republic, quite apart from the resultant misgovernment attributed to it, is considered a serious grievance. Public office has always been regarded among English-speaking people as a reward for public service, and as a stimulus to public spirit. The position under which the permanent resident is excluded from any hope of rendering any service to the commonwealth is regarded as not merely implying a stigma of inferiority, but as depriving the English-speaking population of a valued element in their social life, and an invaluable stimulus to interest in public affairs. This is particularly a grievance felt by British residents on the Rand, accustomed to traditions of self-government and equal citizenship. The special grievance of the Afrikander Uitlanders consists in the preference shown to Hollanders as opposed to Afrikanders in appointments in the public service.

" When we remember," declares the Manifesto, " that those who hold power belong to a different race, speak a different language, and have different pursuits from ourselves, that they regard us with suspicion and even with hostility, that as a rule they are not educated men, and that their passions are played upon by unscrupulous adventurers, it must be admitted that we are in very great danger. . . . In the most important departments of State we are being controlled by the gentlemen from the Low Country, while the innocent Boer hugs to himself the delusion that he is preserving his independence. They control us politically through Dr. Leyds, financially through the Netherlands Railway, educationally through Dr. Mansvelt, and in the department of justice through Dr. Coster."

A Johannesburger writes to me :—

" The railway departments as well as the educational department are manned almost exclusively by Hollanders, and many of the most responsible posts are likewise occupied by Hollanders. It is understood that a good many Germans have within the last few years been imported into the State, and occupy positions in the military and volunteer corps. Few Englishmen are employed in any office of trust by the Government, and the Netherlands Railway is, of course, in German and Hollander hands, as also is the dynamite industry, the mint, and the National Bank."

As a proof that legal oppression of the Uitlanders has

increased since Mr. Chamberlain's remonstrance of February 1896, attention is called to the recent legislation, such as the Press Law, the Alien Expulsion Act, the Judiciary Law, and the proposed Disarmament Act. The anticipation of the Manifesto has again been confirmed.

"The Volksraad has by resolution affirmed the principle of administrative expulsion, and has instructed the Government to bring in the Bill accordingly next session. To-day this power rests justly with the Courts of Law, and I can only say that if this Bill becomes law, the power of the Executive Government of this country would be as absolute as the power of the Czar of Russia. We shall have said good-bye finally to the last principle of liberty."

A year later than the Manifesto the Bill passed the Volksraad.

A lawyer writes to me :—

"The Alien Expulsion Act is scandalous and so repulsive to South African ways of thinking that I doubt whether it will ever be enforced. The Press Act is in direct opposition to the Grond Wet, is most oppressive, and so stringent that it will produce a vast amount of harm."

There is none of that security for liberty which springs from the existence of a fixed constitution, whether written or unwritten. The First Volksraad is legally supreme, and blindly adopts the suggestions of the Executive.

"The Legislature in this country," says the Manifesto, "is the supreme power, apparently uncontrolled by any fixed constitution. The chance will of the majority in the Legislature, elected by one-third of the people, is capable of dominating us in every relation of life.

"Coming to the Executive Government, we find that there is no true responsibility to the people. None of the great departments of State are controlled by ministerial officers in the proper sense ; the President's will is virtually supreme, and he, with his unique influence over the legislators of this State, aided by an able, if hostile, State Secretary, has been the author of every act directed against the liberties of the people."

The recent dispute between the judges on the one hand, and the Legislature and the Executive on the other, is fresh in the public mind. The judges endeavoured to assert the overriding force of the constitution, the Grond Wet of 1858, as against the temporary will of a transitory majority in the

Volksraad.   The Volksraad asserted its supreme power, and, by a resolution, placed in the hands of the Executive the power of dismissing the judges unless the judges agreed to renounce their claim to the right of "testing" Volksraad *besluits* by the Grond Wet.   Now, as a judge remarked, the Volksraad, being legally supreme, may declare the President a king by a majority of one, or may cede the territory to Germany by a like majority.

The administration of justice next comes under consideration.   It is complained that the judges have no stability of tenure, that they are not sufficiently paid, that the Executive and the Legislature constantly interfere in their decisions in specific cases, and have ousted their jurisdiction in many important particulars.   How insecure their tenure of office is may be seen from consideration of the rule for future practice established by the recent Volksraad *besluit* on the constitutional question.   A mere resolution of the Volksraad empowers the President to dismiss the judges, one or all, unless they promise to abandon an obnoxious constitutional theory.   Their insufficient pay has many undesirable results. No complaint is made as to any want of uprightness on the part of the individual judges now on the bench, but it is asserted that their modest salary of a few thousands a year is not a sufficient attraction to secure the best lawyers in the Republic, who would be compelled to sacrifice a large portion of their incomes by accepting judicial office.   It is felt, also, to be anomalous and undesirable that causes involving the ownership of many millions should be committed to the decision of officials so inadequately remunerated.   It is not sufficient that the judges should in fact be upright; they should be placed in such a position of dignity and emolument as to render the complaint of dissatisfied litigants in great causes unworthy of attention or credence.   The interference with the discretion of the judges in specific cases adopted by the Volksraad on more than one occasion has been the subject of comment, instances of which are to be found in the Manifesto.   Even pending cases are said to have been interfered with by Volksraad *besluit*.

The Manifesto declares :—

" The High Court of this country has, in the absence of representation, been the sole guardian of our liberties. Although it has on the whole done its work ably, affairs are in a very unsatisfactory position. The Judges have been underpaid, their salaries have never been secure, the most undignified treatment has been meted out to them, and the status and independence of the Bench have on more than one occasion been attacked. A deliberate attempt was made two years ago by President Kruger and the Government to reduce the Bench to a position subordinate to the Executive Government, and only recently we had in the Witfontein matter the last of the cases in which the Legislature interfered with vested rights of action."

The limiting of the jurisdiction of the Courts is pointed out as another ominous tendency.

" In a law, introduced by the present Government, the Government, instead of the Courts, are constituted the final judges in cases of disputed elections. No election committees are allowed. This operates against candidates opposed to the Government, because the Government has virtually a vast standing army of committeemen and henchmen, officials being allowed openly to take part in swaying elections; and the Government is in a position by the distribution of contracts, appointments, purchase of concessions, the expenditure of secret service money, and otherwise to bring into existence and maintain a large number of supporters who act as canvassers—always on the right side in times of election."

Not merely is the cognisance of election disputes removed from the jurisdiction of the Courts, but the recent Alien Expulsion Act similarly deprives the Uitlander of this protection of his liberty. The organisation of the tribunals in other respects is not favourable to the Uitlander.

" The great bulwark of liberty, the right to trial by jurymen, who are our peers, is denied to us. Only the burgher or naturalised burgher is entitled to be a juryman, or, in other words, anyone of us is liable to be tried upon the gravest charge possible by jurymen who are in no sense our peers, who belong to a different race, who regard us with a greater or less degree of hostility, and whose passions, if inflamed, might prompt them, as weak human creatures, to inflict the gravest injustices, even to deprive men of their lives. Supposing, in the present tense condition of political feeling, anyone of us were tried before a Boer jury on any charge having a political flavour about it, should we be tried by our peers, and should we have a chance of receiving even-handed justice?

"The High Court hardly comes under this censure, although, in a general sense, there is maladministration, first, in the under-payment of the judges; second, in the occasional pressure put upon the High Court by the Government; third, in the absence of any Court of Appeal, which latter defect is viewed as a great hardship in a country in which interests of large magnitude are constantly the subject of litigation."

The treatment of natives is not usually supposed to be an Uitlander grievance, and has not figured largely in their indictment against the Government, nevertheless, it is to be found in the Manifesto of the National Union.

"The administration of Native Affairs is a gross scandal and a source of immense loss and danger to the community. Native commissioners have been permitted to practise extortion, injustice and cruelty upon the natives under their jurisdiction. The Government has allowed petty tribes to be goaded into rebellion. We have had to pay the costs of the 'wars' while the wretched victims of their policy have had their tribes broken up. Sources of native labour have been destroyed, and large numbers of prisoners have been kept in gaol for something like eighteen months without trial. It was stated in the newspapers that, out of sixty-three men imprisoned, thirty-one had died in that period, while the rest were languishing to death for want of vegetable foods. We have had revelations of repulsive cruelty on the part of Field-Cornets."

On the question of the treatment of natives as the main cause of the division between the Dutch and the British, a leading Johannesburger writes to me:—

"The question of the treatment of the natives in the form of the admission or not of the coloured people to political and civil rights still constitutes the main cause which tends to maintain the separation of the Dutch and British. In the Republics, the coloured people are entirely excluded from political and partially excluded from civil rights. In the British Colonies, the principle of political equality, irrespective of colour, is established."

The programme of the Imperialist organisation, the South African League, even in the "Transvaal Province," includes a profession of faith in the political equality of black and white.

The last item in the long indictment against the Boer

administration refers to the general conduct and policy of
the Government as distinguished from inherent vice of
origin.

"In the administration," declares the Manifesto of the National
Union, "we find that there is the grossest extravagance; that secret
service moneys are squandered, that votes are exceeded, that the public
credit is pledged in a manner that is wholly inconsistent with the
interests of the public. Money is said to have been sent out of the
country for secret service purposes, and the public audit seems a farce.

"The administration of the public service is in a scandalous condition;
bribery and corruption are rampant; we have had members of the Raad
accepting presents. . . . A class of men has sprung up who are in constant
attendance upon the members of the Volksraad, and whose special business
seems to be the influencing these members one way or the other. I think
thousands of you are satisfied of the venality of many of our public servants. I wish to guard against the assumption that all public servants are
corrupt; thank God there are many who are able and honourable men; and
it must be gall and wormwood to these men to find the whole tone of the
service destroyed, and to have themselves made liable to be included in
the general denunciation."

"The general administration," writes a leading advocate, "is rotten to
the core; where there is no corruption there is gross ignorance; and in no
department are the bulk of the men up to their work."

A resident in Johannesburg writes to me :—

"Maladministration may come under two heads, first, official corruption, second, official incompetency. Both forms of maladministration exist
very largely in the Transvaal. It is unnecessary to particularise, as the
facts are notorious."

The indictment of Transvaal methods of administration
put forward on behalf of the Uitlanders may therefore be
summarised as follows :—

The Government of the Republic is an arbitrary Government, and is elected by a minority of the population. It is
retrograde and narrow-minded, and opposed to liberal
principles of Government. It is oppressive in taxation and
insulting in demeanour. It affects the methods of a military
autocracy under cover of the forms of Republican administra
tion. It is incompetent through ignorance in the head and
ignorance in the hands. The administration is extravagant
and it is corrupt.

I have endeavoured in the foregoing to set forth in their own language the claims of the Uitlanders of the Transvaal, and their interpretation of the policy of the Government of the Republic.

It will be my task to set out the other side of the question as it has been represented to me by leaders of both political sections of the Boer population. This reply will deal first with the great allegation of an active anti-British and anti-Uitlander policy on the part of the Government of the Republic, and next with the special items of individual grievance as formulated by the Uitlander leaders.

CHAPTER XV.

THE BOER REPLY TO THE UITLANDER.

(Written in 1897.)

I HAVE already set forth in their own language the claims of the Uitlanders of the Transvaal and their interpretation of the policy of the Government of the Republic. It is now my task to set out the other side of the question, as it has been represented to me by the leaders of both political sections of the Boer population.

This reply will deal with the general allegation of an anti-British and anti-Uitlander policy of the Boer Government of the Republic, and also with the special items of individual grievances as formulated by the Uitlander leaders.

The Boer denies that the action of the Government, or of either political section of the Boers, is guided by a sentiment of active hostility towards British interests or British-born inhabitants. A regard for their independence is the impelling motive which dictates their policy; they deny that there is any such design as that ascribed to them by the Uitlander leaders, of desiring to supersede British influence in South Africa. They point out that it is difficult, from their standpoint, to see any identity of interest between the Uitlander in the Transvaal and the Imperial Government in England. If the franchise were conceded to British residents, the effect would be to deprive the Imperial Government of so many subjects; and no State has hitherto regarded it as a matter of political advantage to be deprived of its subjects.

The policy of the Transvaal (a leading advocate writes) is simply one of internal independence; the Government and the ruling burghers want merely to be left alone to shape their own action, to make their own laws, to protect their own homes, and specially to maintain undisturbed their policy towards the coloured races, which is constantly threatened by powerful parties in England. . . . Their policy as to external relations is simply one directed to secure more fully their internal independence. Any suggestion that there is a defined policy on the part of the Transvaal to combine with Germany is without foundation.   The Boers would prefer subjection to Imperial rule to that of any other Power; but they have no desire to be subject to any foreign Power whatever.

As to the various points of evidence adduced to prove the existence of an active anti-British policy, they are all capable of different interpretation.

Coming now to the specific grievances set forth as affecting the Uitlander residents, a somewhat different reply is made by the Progressive from that made by the Conservative party among the burghers.

The Progressives are inclined to admit that there are certain grievances, but not such as to justify the violent attempt to overthrow the Government of the Republic which has been made by the Jameson Raid, or the Press propaganda which has been carried on to discredit the policy of the Government abroad.

To take the question of the franchise first. A Progressive writes to me :—

Inasmuch as compulsory military service is consequent on naturalisation, I think the privileges of naturalisation not adequate to what is expected from the new burgher who can only vote for the Second Volksraad.

A Conservative writes :—

I do not see that the Uitlanders have any grievance as regards the franchise. It is merely in self-defence that they are excluded; and they *should* be excluded, as they would upset the Government if they obtained political power. In no country in the world would an overwhelming body of foreigners be allowed to obtain the franchise and sweep the votes of the original dwellers. As regards the contrast between the franchise law in this Republic and the Free State, and the fact that the law was originally identical, it is sufficient to say that circumstances have altered in the South African Republic, and they are no longer the same as those of the Free State. Thousands of immigrants arrive every month in the Transvaal, but the Free State is afflicted with no such additions to its population.

An eminent judicial authority * writes to me :—

As regards the franchise question, I understand it to be meant that it is felt as a hardship by British subjects that they are not allowed, except under certain stringent conditions, to cast off their allegiance and become burghers of the South African Republic (any idea of dual allegiance is, of course, out of the question and need not be discussed), and what I have here said of British subjects of course also refers to persons of other nationalities; but since no exception can be made of one nationality more than another this restriction applies to aliens of all nationalities. A historical retrospect will, I think, tend to show that what is regarded as a grievance is, on the other side, regarded simply as a legitimate means of self-defence against foreign—one may say British—aggression. I believe I am correct in saying that before the Transvaal annexation no country could have been more liberal as regards granting the rights of citizenship to newcomers than the South African Republic. If I am not mistaken, a residence of six months sufficed to entitle them to burgher rights. The Republics have been liberal in this respect—the Free State still, inasmuch as no aggression upon its independence has as yet rendered it necessary to be on its guard against acts of that nature. When the first goldfields of the Transvaal were discovered a considerable number of strangers (chiefly British subjects) settled in the country, particularly at Pilgrim's Rest. I believe, again, that I am correct in saying that two members were allowed to them as their representatives in the Legislature. The conduct of these new residents was on the whole not such as would encourage any Government to allow them to have a say in the affairs of the country. They hampered, insulted, and misrepresented the Government in every possible way, and it seems to have been partly due to the intrigues of these men, as wel as a number of British residents in the towns, that the country subsequently lost its independence for a time. When the South African Republic afterwards regained its independence that occurrence created the bitterest resentment among the English-speaking portion of the Transvaal community. Some of them buried the English flag and placed a gravestone on the site with the motto "Resurgam." Righteousness was with them accounted for nought. Some of their organs expressed the utmost hostility and disloyalty to Republican Government. A similar spirit has subsequently been not infrequently shown by British subjects: witness the manner in which the head of the State has been insulted when he visited Johannesburg, and also on the occasion when Lord Loch visited Pretoria. British newspapers have been constantly reiterating

---

* Chief Justice Melius de Villiers of the Orange Free State.

that it would not be long before, with the continued large influx of English people, the Transvaal would again be English territory, and these were the same newspapers that demanded the franchise for the British Uitlander. The Uitlander of any other nationality, by the way, is hardly ever considered worthy of being taken into account. The professed Uitlander organs at Johannesburg have always exhibited the most virulent hatred of the Boer; no words of abuse have been considered too bad for the latter. One of them had the hardihood to announce that the Boer must be crushed. More than once have I read rhapsodical accounts of the enthusiastic manner in which in the Transvaal "God Save the Queen" has been sung on occasions when it is certainly quite out of place. Can it be wondered at that after the British Government retired from the Transvaal measures were at once taken to maintain and preserve the independence of the country through the restrictions of the franchise? and can it be wondered at that the old-established population of the country, who love and cherish their independence, should be loth to relax existing restrictions so long as the British Imperial Government remains a factor in South African affairs? Why should we, more than any other people, relish the idea of being extinguished as an independent nation? English people would not wish that England should become subject to Germany. Why should subjection to foreign power be thrust upon us? And surely its own right of continued independent existence must by the Transvaal be regarded as a matter that is paramount and that cannot be subordinated to the alleged right of others to control the destinies of the country. Judging from the press organs advocating the cause of the British Uitlander, it is subjection of the race and of the country to British supremacy that is sought. "The Boer must be crushed," one of their organs has said. If such a spirit prevails, one may, with confidence as to the reply, ask an impartially-minded man whether the old-established population is not justified in treating the matter of extension of the franchise with the utmost caution. This matter cannot be settled in accordance with the doctrinaire theories of what are alleged to be the principles of Republican Government, but the safety of the State is the supreme law which must serve as a guide in the matter.

And another Englishman admits that it is unreasonable to expect the Boers to give full political power to Englishmen, who would be numerous enough to hand the country over to the Imperial Government or the Chartered Company.

Another observes—One Englishman has written, "The Boer is as jealous of his political independence as the Yankee or the Swiss."

As regards the educational grievance a Progressive leader writes to me as follows :—

As regards the language question in the schools, I consider the grievance really exists; I would put the two languages on an equal footing; I distinguish between the schools, the Law Courts, and the public departments. Allowing English to be spoken in the latter might facilitate business; but political considerations make it necessary to maintain the language as a mark of the Boer character of the Republic and an assertion of their absolute independence.

A Conservative on this question writes :—

We give more privileges here to foreign languages, such as English, than are given to foreign languages in England or in any other country. In other countries, if foreigners wish their children to learn their language, they have to pay all expenses; but here the Government pays part. I should like to see the reception which the British Parliament would give to a request that the language in schools should be German in the east end of London, and Yiddish in other quarters. We admit that for commerce both languages should be known, but not that it should be made compulsory in the schools. Tens of thousands in Johannesburg are foreign or Russian Jews. Why do they not make the same complaint?

As regards the use of the language in the courts of law and public offices, both sections of burghers are agreed that the official use of the language is a defence of the independence of the country and a standing protest against any infiltration of anti-Republican ideas. A Conservative writes :—

If the immigrants wish to speak English, why have they come here? As regards the statement that the English-speaking are in the majority, we deny it. They are not in the majority, if you except those who speak both languages. If the English-speaking are in the majority, then we dispute the right of a majority of intruders.

As regards the invitation argument (that the Uitlanders have been invited to immigrate*), it is sufficient to say that the conditions of invitation have been carried out. No promise was made to them that the language of the Republic would be altered. Transgressions of the law have been passed over such as would not have been permitted elsewhere. The invitation addressed to the immigrants was, to come, provided they obeyed the laws; one of the laws requiring the use of the Dutch language. There is no policy on the part of the Boer Government or burghers to oust British influence and British language from South Africa, and substitute Dutch. As to their desire to preserve the Dutch language,

---

* Letter of Secretary Ewald Esselen, 13th December, 1883.

their chief reason for doing so is because they consider it part of their inheritance in the past, and a bulwark of their independence in the present.

English policy, it may be said, allows Dutch to be spoken in the Cape Parliament; but the liberties and constitution of the Republic do not rest upon so secure a basis as to admit of a step which would necessarily be the first towards diminishing the influence of the burgher. It is also pointed out that the Dutch-speaking population have always laid great stress on the right to use their native tongue. And one of their grievances, still remembered, is that Sir Owen Lanyon failed to keep the promise of Sir Theophilus Shepstone in his proclamation that both languages should be used. Sir Owen Lanyon appointed officials who refused to speak Dutch.

As regards the language question (writes another correspondent), in a letter to the *Nineteenth Century*, I referred to the treatment of the Dutch-speaking inhabitants of the Cape Colony by the British Government. There an alien Government stepped in and deliberately suppressed the existing official language then in use by the vast bulk of the inhabitants (seven-eighths, at least), imposed various disabilities upon those using that language, disallowed its use in Parliament, Courts of Law, and subsidised schools. This continued for over sixty years, when first the Dutch-speaking community were in a position to command a majority in Parliament, and to obtain some degree of restitution. They bore their disabilities quietly and patiently, without talking of revolution or making the world resound with the sad tale of their woes. Yet merely it is a far greater grievance for a people to be deprived of their own country, of the privileges which they have enjoyed, than for a new population coming into a country not to obtain equal privileges with the old inhabitants, especially when they knew what they were coming to.

I have more than once heard it said in the Cape Colony, " This is a British Colony; it is quite right that the official language and the language of education should be English. If a people do not know it, they must learn it." It would be considered a monstrous thing, I have no doubt, to make a similar remark, *mutatis mutandis*, in the Transvaal. In South Africa it so seldom occurs that " what is sauce for the goose is sauce for the gander." I do not myself see the " right " of any body of men coming into a country, where a foreign language is spoken, to make a grievance of the fact that such a language is not wholly or partially surrendered in favour of their own; I would, as a matter of grace, *not* right, be in favour of giving the English language every privilege that is reasonable and fair, even at the public departments. In answer to my letter to the *Nineteenth Century* it has been said, " At all events, in the Cape Colony the Dutch-speaking people have had the opportunity of making their voices heard on the language question, whereas in the Transvaal the English-speaking population have had none." To my mind there is no analogy between the two cases.

The financial grievances enumerated by Mr. Chamberlain similarly do not receive a single reply from the Boer, opinion being divided as to the existence and extent of the grievances alleged and as to the remedies applicable. The recent Report of the Industrial Commission is sufficient evidence of the difference of opinion in this matter, therefore it does not need to be dwelt on at any length.

" It is maintained," says Mr. Chamberlain, " that the finances are mismanaged; that the expenditure escapes proper control and audit, the taxation is maintained beyond the needs of administration; that unfair discrimination is general in the collection of personal taxes; that the import duties on the necessaries of life are a hardship on the working-classes, and so raise the cost of working the mines as to be effectually prohibitory to the working of the poorer ones. If the taxation was apportioned to the ability to pay a large number might be open to the general advantage."

It is notable, however, that the amount of admission made by the most advanced Progressives is substantially no more than that taxation has been levied on a wrong basis, that the production of the mines and the working of the low-grade mines has been unnecessarily interfered with. Both parties unite in denying that the finances are mismanaged or that the expenditure escapes proper control or audit, or that the taxation is maintained beyond the needs of the administration.

A Progressive writes : " I do not believe the expenditure is dispropor-tionate to the population. Look at the expenditure in Rhodesia; and as to the taxation being excessive, consider that Rhodesia exacts fifty per cent. on profits of mining ventures. It is a purely English idea that gold in the reefs belongs to a private person; the law of most countries gives the mining rights to the State, and it was for the State, as representing the whole community, to dictate terms on which private persons are allowed to benefit by the participation in public property." "There is no unfair discrimination" (writes a Conservative) "in the collection of personal taxes, nor in favour of farmers. The imposts on luxuries are less than those imposed in the American Republic. A tariff for the protection of the produce of the country may, or may not, be a mistaken policy; but Englishmen should recognise that it is at least a policy adopted by most of the world, and which the burghers are entitled to adopt if they think fit. There is no grievance weighing on the Uitlander residents as the result of that tariff. It is impossible to make a ring in such produce; Boer farmers have no such ideas of combining, and the fertility of the country is too great."

As to the objection to expenditure on warlike preparations they are simply necessities, forced on the burgher by the revolutionary plots of discontented immigrants. If there were no Jameson Raid there would be no such expenditure.

As regards the exceptional restrictions imposed by the law on the right of public meeting, referred to by Mr. Chamberlain, the Boer's position is that, as Mr. Chamberlain himself admits, those restrictions have not been strictly interpreted. The power is only held in reserve, and, as a matter of fact, has not been actually enforced. An advocate writes to me: "The law of the Transvaal on the subject is framed on that of England; show me a meeting that has yet been proclaimed." In any case, it is held that as long as there is in existence a discontented party consisting of foreigners desirous of overturning the Government, every Government, having the right of self-defence, is justified in retaining in its hands these extraordinary powers.

As regards the grievances of the mining industry, next referred to by Mr. Chamberlain, the Report of the Mining Commission and the discussion in the Volksraad show that opinion on the Boer side on this matter is largely divided. The recommendations of the Commission represent the views of the Progressive section ; the opposition thereto, that of the other party. As the Report of the Mining Commission is already before the world it is unnecessary that I should here reiterate their recommendations : I will content myself therefore by giving the arguments of the extreme Conservatives on this matter as they have been presented to me.

"As regards the general policy of concessions," writes one of my informants, "if none had been given at the starting of the industry none would be given now, but it would be dishonest to break our contracts with capitalists who have expended enormous sums of money. The State was obliged to adopt this policy of concession at the time at which it was adopted. The country was poor, there were no industries, and when capitalists offered to bring money for investment they expected reasonable security for their return. As regards the dynamite monopoly—in all Europe there are only two dynamite companies. Nobel enjoys a practical monopoly in the North, England, and Germany, and another group of capitalists that of the South. Their joint action has recently been illustrated, and is additional proof of the danger to this country of being obliged to rely on foreign supplies. It is also to be remembered that not merely the gold industry, but, in case of war, the interests of the State would be affected unless the production of explosives was established in the country itself. As a measure of military necessity powder must be manufactured in this country, as in time of war the ports would be closed, and this Republic, being surrounded by British territory, would not be in a position to obtain supplies from abroad.

" As regards the concession to the Netherlands Railway, the same arguments apply; no one else was ready to construct the railway at the time the concession was granted, and, however desirable it might have been to avoid the resulting restrictions on the industry due to the working of the railway, it is impossible to get rid of the consequences of the past.

" As regards the spirit concession, it is enough to say that the policy of taxing luxuries, such as spirits, has been approved of by all countries, and the Government in this country is entitled to adopt similarly such a policy. The same considerations apply to the protective tariff adopted by the Government to favour the agricultural products of the Transvaal farms."

As to the condition of the police service in Johannesburg and the restriction of recruiting to burghers, who, according to Mr. Chamberlain, " cannot be expected to furnish adequate material from which to select candidates for this department of the public service," the reply is that it is not to be expected that a population which showed itself ready to overturn the Government in armed revolt, and invited a foreign force to invade the country, should be armed, drilled, and disciplined at the expense of the Government which they wished to overturn.

As regards the municipal government of the Rand—the last subject referred to in Mr. Chamberlain's despatch—it has been pointed out that, in the first place, there has for many years past been a body which constituted a municipality all but in name, the Sanitary Board having municipal powers with the right to levy rates and taxes, not being elected by the burghers, but by the inhabitants of Johannesburg rated at £20 a year. This Board contained only two members nominated by the Government and fifteen or sixteen chosen by the people themselves. However, the new municipality just instituted, with largely increased powers, is represented as being as much as can be expected to be given to a town so recently established and possessing a population so floating in character. If, in the future, streets are ill-kept and ill-lighted, if the water supply be imperfect, or if disease or crime be prevalent, the people of Johannesburg, and not the Government of the Republic, will be responsible. As to the acts of the new municipality, like that of the former Sanitary Board, being subject to Government veto, it is sufficient to say the veto has never yet been exercised.

Coming to the grievances not touched upon in Mr. Chamberlain's despatch, the first is the official ostracism of English. Policemen, railway officials, officials in the public offices, and in the law courts, are represented as being unwilling or unable to use the language of the majority of the population. The Boer reply to this is practically that referred to on the use of English in the schools. The use of English being permitted in the Courts and public departments might facilitate business, but the necessity, for public reasons, to retain the Dutch languarge as stamping the Boer character of the Republic, apply even here, though a certain amount of inconvenience may be the result.

As regards religious disabilities, I have not found any section of the Boer population prepared to support them in argument. They are universally represented as a historical survival, to be understood only in the light of the traditions of religious persecution, from which the Huguenot ancestors of the Boers suffered.

"The provision that all officials must be 'Protestants,'" writes a leading Conservative, "we acknowledge under present circumstances to be objectionable. Jews and Catholics are excluded from office under the Grond Wet. But I may explain that this is not merely a Uitlander grievance, but it affects all the inhabitants, including burghers. The only reason for such a provision is that the Huguenots who left Europe under persecution by the Catholic King of France established here the foundation stone of the old constitution, and, rightly or wrongly, considered it to be a political danger if Catholics were admitted to power. The exclusion of the Jews appears to be an unforeseen result. At the same time I may point out that certain reforms have already been introduced. At the time of the foundation of the Grond Wet Roman Catholic churches or services were prohibited. Under President Burgers, who was a Freethinker, this restriction was abolished. It is more than likely in the coming revision of the constitution these restrictions will be removed."

"At the same time," writes a Progressive, "it must be rememberd that a grievance of this kind is not one particularly affecting the working-classes, but rather men of considerable wealth."

The restriction on the right of the Uitlander to carry arms, the building of forts, the importation of military supplies, has been the next of the grievances enumerated by the Uitlander. As regards the military preparations, the answer of both sections of the Boers is that the safety of the State is the supreme law. "Defence, and not Defiance," is the policy of the Government, which is entitled to regard its own existence as legitimate; and it has to provide against revolt as an imperative duty towards the burghers of the State. As regards the carrying of arms, a correspondent writes :—

"The statement that Uitlanders are prevented from having arms is a misleading statement. The law here is as to registration, customs duty, and licensing of arms is the same law as that of the Cape Colony, Natal, and the Free State. As regards registration, it is necessary in order to prevent arms from reaching natives. As regards the customs imposed, they are the same as imposed during the English regime. As regards licensing, the regulations are the same as under the British Government of the Transvaal. As a matter of fact, it is not true that the Uitlanders are unarmed; or, if they are, it is their own fault."

The exclusion of the Uitlander from office, felt as a grievance by British residents, is not admitted as being a grievance by the burgher. Under what circumstances they ask, and in what country, has it ever been regarded as a right of foreign immigrants to assume office. If English miners went to dig the gold of the Ural Mountains they would certainly not be inducted into political office by the Tsar.

As regards the alleged monopoly of public offices by Hollanders, " by gentlemen from the Low Country," as the Manifesto of the National Union terms it, the Boer has two replies.

In the first place, they point out that the political independence of the country being threatened on the British side made every appointment to office of a British resident a matter of considerable risk from a political point of view. Again, the Transvaal population did not till some years ago, and to a very limited extent even now, supply a sufficient number of men educated to fill posts in the administration. Educated Hollanders, who could speak the language, and could not possibly be suspected of having any designs against the independence of the country, naturally were chosen, as there were no others to choose.

Their second reply is that there is no such monopoly by Hollanders. With a few exceptions all the high officials are Afrikanders. I have been handed a list with the names and nationalities of all the chief officials, which appeared to bear out this statement.

The Under Secretary of State, the Surveyor-General, the Assistant Surveyor - General, the Treasurer-General, the Auditor-General, the Registrar of Deeds, the Chief Justice, and one of the Judges, the High Sheriff, the Registrar of the High Court, the Taxing Master, the Postmaster-General, the Civil Commissioner, Judicial Commissioners, Magistrates, and all the five members of the Executive Council, the President, the Commandant-General, the Master of Mines, the Commissioner of Railways are all Afrikanders. Of the higher officials only the State Secretary and the Under

Secretary of State for Foreign Affairs, the State Attorney, two of the Judges, and the Master of the High Court, are Hollanders.

Neither are Englishmen absolutely excluded from office : one of the Judges and the Assistant Treasurer-General are Englishmen.

Coming next to the recent legislation which is quoted as proof of the hostile action of the Government towards British residents, the Press Law, the Alien Expulsion Act, and the Alien Immigration Act, the position of the Transvaal Government and of the ruling burghers has been clearly indicated in the despatch of the Government of the 7th May of this year. It is needless to here recapitulate these arguments, but it may be sufficient to quote the remarks of the correspondent I have already quoted, whose idea is that the Transvaal is perfectly justified in passing a law to curb not the liberty, but the unbridled licence of the press. I do not believe that in any country existing, under circumstances similar to that under which the Transvaal existed and exists, would such open advocacy of sedition and revolution be tolerated as was tolerated there for some time past. If there is anything in the law recently passed that would tend to check the legitimate liberty of the press, it ought, so far as it has that tendency, to be amended.

If there is anything unconstitutional in it, it ought also to be amended in that respect. This is a point, however, concerning which no irresponsible journals but the courts of the country would have to decide.

The law for the expulsion of aliens who make themselves dangerous to the safety of the State, I do not think any reasonable person could object to; such aliens, of course, would object. If they did not wish to come under the provisions of the law, they need only be quiet and law-abiding. Without going into details of this law, such measures may be necessary for the security of the State, though it should not go beyond the necessities of the case.

As regards the Alien Immigration Act, it is pointed out that in compliance with remonstrances as to the inconvenience occasioned by its operation it has been repealed ; but that its principle was the same as that adopted by every civilised country, with the exception of England, and its provisions were not nearly so severe as those existing in the United States of America.

A lawyer writes, as regards the Alien Immigration Act, " I agree with it in principle; this is not a No Man's Land." A *res nullius.*

Any order under the Alien Expulsion Act, or under the new Press Act, is subject to an appeal to the Courts, as has been illustrated in practice in the case of the *Star*, when the President's order was set aside by the decree of the Court. That is an amount of power left in the hands of the Court of the Republic such as none of the Courts on the Continent of Europe possesses. The order for the expulsion of an alien in any European country, with the exception of England, is not subject ¡to appeal to the law courts. As regards the alleged absence of security for liberty, which springs from the non-existence of a fixed constitution, or from the legal supremacy of the Volksraad, it is pointed out that Parliament in England is legally supreme, and that no Court of Justice or other authority could question the validity of an Act of Parliament. The Manifesto of the National Union makes it a grievance that the chance will of the majority in the Legislature can alter the law, but the same criticism would apply to English methods of legislation. At the same time, and as a result of the recent dispute between the Bench and the Executive, a Commission is sitting for the purpose of drafting a new Grond Wet, in which provision will be made against the possibility of hasty legislation, and provision made for the security of the independence of the judges.

As regards the treatment of natives, it is denied that there has been any habitual cruelty in their treatment.

The Boer position is, as has been already explained, that it is a political and social blunder of the first magnitude to attempt to put into force the British theory of equality of black and white. In any individual case of ill-treatment the aggrieved have full access to the Courts, and the Courts have no hesitation in giving them justice, but justice in their case does not mean equality.

Finally, the last item in the long indictment against the Boer administration, a challenge of the general conduct and policy of the Government as distinguished from what is alleged to be its inherent vice of origin, the reply on the side of the Boer is an emphatic repudiation of the truth of the charges.

" It is simply false," writes a correspondent; " it is simply false to say that the Government is incompetent and corrupt. Vague charges of that kind are very easily made, and a partisan press is only too ready to exaggerate the slightest irregularity such as may occur under any Government; but to say that the administration as a body can be so described is a falsehood circulated for political purposes."

Another writes—" The general administration is not as corrupt as in England, certainly not as corrupt as in the United States of America. Cases of occasional corruption are inevitable in any country."

Another correspondent writes—" We await Mr. Chamberlain's withdrawal of the extraordinary statements attributed to him on this head."

Another writes—" As to the corruption alleged to exist in the administration, if it does exist, that would be a sad and pitiable fact. It must be remembered, however, that all over the world the experience of the United States, of Canada and other countries show that where opportunities are given to men to make money on a extensive scale by illegitimate means such means will be adopted. Under Great Britain, where opportunities for corruption are afforded, as in the case of army contracts and the like, corruption exists; and curious tales could be told as to what has happened in South Africa outside of the Republics. In a young country such practices are perhaps more difficult to be stopped; but stopped they certainly ought to be as the administration becomes stronger. In course of time such practices no doubt will cease. Also it must not be forgotten that unfortunately it was the Uitlander who introduced such practices, and that in the opinion of some of them (*vide* Lionel Philips's letters, published by the Transvaal Government), the administration was unfortunately not quite corrupt enough. Whether such corruption really exists to the extent as has often been asserted seems to me doubtful, but loose talk of the clubs proves nothing, and half-a-dozen men will strenuously deny what half-a-dozen others will as strenuously assert."

Passing now from the catalogue of the grievances of the Uitlanders regarded merely in the light of hardships to themselves, we have next to consider that portion of their indictment against the policy of the Transvaal Government, which I have already said must present the greatest share of

interest to Englishmen at home. Reference has been made
to the various matters put forward as evidence of an active
anti-British policy on the part of the Government, anti-
British in the sense of trying to depress the condition of
British residents in the Transvaal, and anti-British in the
wider sense of trying to minimise or expel the influence of
the Imperial Government in South Africa. First among
the proofs of such a policy as are enumerated in the alleged
grievances of the Uitlanders, I have given the Boer reply to
this indictment, and have shown that their position in defence
of these matters of legislation and administration complained
of is that they are necessitated by their desire to safeguard
the independence of the country. That where that has not
been the impelling motive of the Government, economic
necessities of the past have induced some of the present
conditions complained of. As to the other matters of which
it is admitted that legitimate complaint may be made, the
answer is that time is required to adjust methods to circumstances. Briefly it may be said that the Boer Government
deny that any of the alleged matters of legislation or
administrative complaint are dictated by a policy in any
respect anti-British.

" The policy of all parties among the burghers," writes a correspondent
" the policy of the President and of the State Secretary are simply to have
the Republic left alone by any outside Power. There is nothing distinctly
anti-British, and never has been in the sense of hostility towards Great
Britain in particular, on the part of the Government or the people of this
Republic. Apparently the action of the Government has been anti-
British, but the reason has simply been because the attack has been from
the British side. Dr. Jameson with Maxims, and the Jingo press with
their pens, have both had a common object. But the burghers would be
as ready to resent attack from German, from Portuguese, or any other
quarter, as from British."

" Neither President," writes another correspondent, " nor the burghers
have any expectation or wish to see the British power eliminated from
South Africa. They are perfectly aware of the defence of the internal
security of the white men in South Africa afforded by the presence of
British power on the sea. No doubt many Transvaalers, like many
Afrikanders generally, believe that *ultimately South Africa will become
an independent nation,* but that is a far-off event towards which things

are slowly shaping themselves, and such an independent South Africa would have no reason for being hostile or for being in any other relation to the British Empire than that of the closest alliance."

" The burghers," writes another correspondent, " have had reason to believe that the English people are religious and desirous of doing justice, but they have also reason to believe that the English people are under the control and direction of persons who are not religious and sometimes have little regard for justice."

As to the other matters adduced as evidence of such a policy, negotiations with foreign Powers, confederation of the Free State, desire to acquire a port, their refusal to comply with Mr. Chamberlain's suggestions of reform, general expressions of hostility towards Englishmen, their reply is distinct.

" There is not the least intention," writes a correspondent, " on the part of the burghers of this country to subject themselves to the power of Germany, or any other foreign Power. What German policy may be is a different thing; but what the policy of the burghers is, is to safeguard their independence. If by cultivating relationship with Germany as well as other foreign Powers, this object can be effected, such a line of action is distinctly the duty of the Government."

" The Government," writes another correspondent, " wishes to use Germany to protect the country, but not to use Germany to injure Great Britain."

" The Transvaal," writes another correspondent, " would prefer subjection to England to subjection to any other Power, but would fight to the last before submitting to any foreign force. If the Transvaal made application to Germany or France at the time of the Raid, a fact not as yet established, such a course would be quite within its rights, as the idea in the Transvaal, and even among the officers of the expedition itself, was that the Administrator was acting on behalf of the British Government, and that his armed Raid had the Imperial sanction.

" German policy towards the South African Republic need hardly, I think, be considered seriously. The people of that State do not want to come under German rule or influence, nor, if they did, would they go so far as to estrange the people of the Orange Free State, who would bitterly resent any assumption of power in South Africa by the German Government."

A leading representative of the Press observes :—*

" I am positive there is no diplomatic purpose behind German action. The only German policy in South Africa is that Germany is anxious to

---

* Mr. Carl Borckenhagen.

cultivate good relations with the Republic, and so preserve the trade which it already possesses with the Republic.

"One may briefly say that Englishmen are distrusted because there is an English policy in South Africa, and Germans are trusted because there is no German policy. The German Emperor's telegram meant no hostility to England ; he telegraphs to everybody, even to the Count of Turin. The Boers, turning out in force against the Jameson Raid when they thought that the whole might of England was arrayed against them, appealed to the military instincts of the Kaiser."

A leader of the Progressive party tells me—

"Even the Conservatives are much more against Germany than against England. All parties are united on this point.

"As regards the adherence to the Geneva Convention, and the other negotiations with foreign Powers, whose conclusion has been made a matter of complaint by Mr. Chamberlain in his recent despatch, the despatch of the Transvaal Government of the 7th May shows that they were acting within their rights. The expressed object of the Convention of 1884, as set out by Lord Derby in his accompanying despatch to the deputation, was to give the Republic full power of conducting negotiations with foreign States, and that power the Republic has done no more than exercise. There is no danger to British interests in such action of the Government, as any treaty with a foreign Power, other than the Orange Free State, is subject to the veto of the British Government, should it prove contrary to British interests.

"As regards the confederation of the Free State, and the recent treaty granting special rights to burghers of the Free State, such step is one not merely of the most natural, of alliance between two kindred peoples, but one distinctly contemplated by the framers of the Convention of London of 1884. Treaties with the Orange Free State are expressly exempted from the requirement of the sanction of the British Government, and are expressly exempted from veto.

"A former British Governor, though, as usual, his policy was reversed by his successor, was strongly in favour of the fusion of the two States ; and that fusion would have taken place forty years ago but for the action of Sir George Grey, the successor in question. The mere suggestion that there is an anti-British design on the part of the two Republics, evidenced by the treaty of alliance, is in itself a sufficient indication of the nature of the criticism to which every action of the Government of the Republic is subject. The two States of common race, history, and language and interests are naturally compelled to draw as close as possible the bonds between them, when their independence is threatened, as it has been by the action of a large section of immigrants within their borders, backed by an aggressive power, the administration of the Chartered Company in the north. As regards the acquisition of the port, it is to be noted that there is a very serious division of opinion among the burghers themselves as to the advisability of such a step."

On one side, we are told, the existence of the Republic is an established fact, and England must be contented to recognise it as an established fact.

" Her wisest course would be to cultivate the friendship of the Republics. Let her renounce entirely all thought of repression. Let her policy be, where she can, to assist in strengthening the power of the Republics. If the Transvaal hungers after a seaport of its own, let the Transvaal have one, if one is to be had. To think that by hampering the Transvaal in that direction a great advantage is gained, is a mistake. Irritation is produced, and no good is evolved. If the South African Republic is anxious to have a fleet of men-of-war of its own, let it have its way. The fleet will not be employed to bombard London; it may assist in the defence of Cape Town."

The President and the State Secretary are known to favour the project, but differences of opinion on this matter do not run on party lines. For instance, a leader of the Progressive party tells me, " We regard the absence of a port as a grievance against England; we think she is trying to surround us." On the other hand, a member of the opposite party tells me—" Many agree with me in preferring to be as we are. I do not think that the Republic requires a port. It would simply give greater facilities for attack; just as the possession of Constantinople might not be such an advantage to Russia as seems to be assumed."

As regards the refusal of the Government to adopt Mr. Chamberlain's suggestions of internal reform, it is pointed out that no independent Government, whose power of internal management of their own affairs is conceded, could adopt any measures of the suggestion, however friendly, of another Power; such adoption would be taken as a precedent, and would constitute only the first of a long long series of intermeddling with the internal affairs of the Republic.

As regards Mr. Chamberlain's declaration of the existence of an anti-British policy, and the official information which, it is assumed, is such as to warrant such a declaration, one is told that there is no necessity for answering such vague declarations until something more tangible than Mr. Chamberlain's expression of opinion is adduced by way of proof. And one is asked to compare Mr. Chamberlain's recent expression of opinion as to the existence of a suzerainty, the abolition of which was one of the objects of the visit of the Transvaal delegation to England—an abolition effected by the Convention of London of 1884.

Lastly, as regards the loud-spoken expressions of intention to drive out Englishmen, attributed to certain irresponsible persons, one is assured that no Government of any people can control the acts of hot-headed and injudicious individuals. If the policy of the British Government and the British people were to be judged by the declaration of certain sections of the British Press, repudiation of treaty obligations and an armed conquest of a friendly State would be assumed to be the object on which the British Government has set its heart.

Summarising, then, the attitude of the Boer Government in regard to the Uitlanders, it may be said that the Progressive party admit the existence of certain grievances, such as the exclusion from the franchise, but do not admit that the existence of these grievances justified an armed insurrection or a political propaganda for the purpose of generally discrediting the Boer Government. The Conservative party's position is practically the same.

On the question of the independence of the Republic and its right to manage its own internal affairs, free from interference on the part of the British Government, both parties are agreed.

The Conservative section—being that in power, and likely to remain in power—one is justified in taking their position as of more practical importance than that of the opposing section of the burghers. The position of the typical Conservative burgher may be summed up as one which upholds the general policy of retaining power in the hands of the burghers, and of excluding, as far as possible, British interference with internal matters of legislation or administration :—

" We have been the first in the country, we have fought for it, and we are the owners of the land, and we own all that it contains. It is for us to dictate terms to the strangers who come here for the purpose of making a fortune.

" They need not have come if they did not wish ; they did not stipulate that they should get the franchise. If they had stipulated we should have replied, ' You come for dividends, and you shall not get political rights.' In no country have strangers ever claimed as a right political privileges."

As to the claim of these strangers that they assisted us in defeating the Zulus, the reply is easy. The Boer has been the pioneer of South Africa, and the burden of nearly all the fighting has fallen on him. If the British Government adopted the policy of Sir Bartle Frere and defeated the Zulus, they did that for Imperial purposes, and not for the purpose of assisting the Boers :—

" The retrocession to the Transvaal, however creditable to an English Government, is, it must be remembered, simply reversing an act of violent and unjust aggression ; and we cannot forget that the English Prime Minister who directed the retrocession, thought the country to be a howling wilderness. Nor can we either forget that the political opposition of the Boers in the Cape played a great part in determining the policy of giving back the land to its owners. We never have yet heard that gratitude is due to a brigand for restoring what is not his, more especially when the restoration is hampered by restriction on the subsequent liberty of the aggrieved party. Nor can we forget that it suited the exigencies of the British party system, which the Government of the Republic perfectly understands, to retrocede the Transvaal and to avoid an unpopular and expensive war."

" Need I do more," said a burgher, " than quote this, what two English writers have said on the subject of the magnanimity of the retrocession of the Transvaal. Mr. Edward Dicey says, ' I for one am not going to endorse the futile theory that Great Britain, having annexed the Transvaal, gave it back to the Boers out of a sentiment of magnanimity. That sort of twaddle may have been good enough to remove the compunction of Mr. Gladstone and his followers in 1881, at having to consent to a discreditable surrender on the morrow of a disgraceful defeat, but it is not good enough to satisfy the demands of historical truth. England, at the instigation of the Government of the day, gave up the Transvaal, because the resistance of the Boers proved more formidable than we had anticipated, because South African wars were unpopular at that period with the British public, and because the game of reconquering the Transvaal after Majuba was not thought to be worth the candle.'

"Lord Randolph Churchill says: 'Had the British Government of that day taken advantage of its strong military position and annihilated, as it could easily have done, the Boer forces, it would no doubt have gained the Transvaal, but it might have lost the Cape Colony. The Dutch sentiment in the Colony had been so exasperated by what it considered to be the unjust, faithless, and arbitrary policy pursued towards the free Dutchmen of the Transvaal, that the final triumph of the British arms mainly by brute force would have permanently and hopelessly alienated it from Great Britain.'

"We cannot see how we owe gratitude to the Imperial Government for giving our kinsmen in the Cape political privileges. The institution of self-governing Colonies is part of the British political system, which experience has taught them conduces to greater efficiency, and let us not forget also greater economy.

"The policy of the President is simply to maintain the independence of the country, and to establish, on a firm basis, the prosperity of the burghers. It is not reasonable for immigrants, who have come to make their fortunes, who have no intention of fighting in defence of the independence of the country, and who have no permanent dwelling-place here, to ask the original inhabitants to step aside, and to give them political domination. Franchise to the Uitlander means foreign rule. If not annexation to Charterland or to the British dominion, at any rate it would mean political domination by cosmopolitan Jew capitalists. The capitalist is welcome to make his money, but he shall not have power over our children or over our country. We do not worship Mammon; we set a higher store on liberty. This may be an old-world prejudice, but it is the spirit which drove our ancestors from France, and drove our fathers from the Cape. To tell us that our policy diminishes the output of the mines may be, in your mind, to use the heaviest words of condemnation, but we refuse to consider our policy simply from the point of view of its effect upon the production of gold.

"Even if newly-enfranchised Uitlanders would not attempt to surrender the territory to the British Government, we distrust their Aborigines' Protection Society policy, which has made Natal, a land wrested by us from the tyrant Chaka, a coolie reserve. We do not wish to see another garden of South Africa made a hot-bed of heathendom, with the British Government of India insisting on the right of the brown men to take possession of the soil, fought for and won by white men. We are keeping one section, at least, of South Africa free from the Kaffirs and the coolie."

CHAPTER XVI.

MY VIEW OF BOER v. UITLANDER.

IT will be seen, from the foregoing, that it was not without hearing what both sides had to say on the issue of Boer against Uitlander that I have been led to form my opinion on the first question, Was there reality in the claims made on behalf of the Uitlander? and on the second, Was there a definite purpose behind the treatment of the Uitlanders and the military preparations of Pretoria and the Afrikander propaganda through South Africa of ousting the British power from the whole sub-continent?

That the indictment of the Uitlanders was, in the main, well founded, subsequent facts have made but too clear. Criticism of people with genuine grievances is easy to those who have not suffered under them; but, nevertheless, it may not be without political use, if I point out the errors, some of them of mere political tactics, but others much deeper, threatening the future peace of South Africa in the conduct of the Reform movement and the Uitlander agitation generally.

As to the deeper mistakes there seems to have been a complete failure to grasp the Imperial importance of the policy of repression of the outsider followed by the Pretoria Government, and a marvellous under-estimate of the fighting power, of the dogged tenacity, of the far-sighted policy, of the next to superhuman secrecy of the leaders of the Boers, and an equally wonderful over-estimate of the Hollander influence—the Uitlanders failing to see that the old President had not the least objection to being supposed

to be led by Hollanders or " my Doppers," when he knew very
well that he was leading in all the main lines of policy.
If continued in, these errors bode ill for future peace and
stability in South Africa.*

"*Huis toe*" was a theory too familiar to all the Uitlander
centres. It meant that, after the most trivial reverse, the
Boer commandoes would disperse to their farms, crying their
call, "Let us home."   Again, the theory that the ruling
caste in the two Republics had no really national, however
perverse, ideal, and were simply intent on the spoils of
office, has been refuted by events.   Their nationalist project
was thought to be non-existent, partly because the British
citizen saw that it would be desperate and dangerous to the
Boers themselves, and partly because a money-making
community, like that of Johannesburg, is apt to ascribe
money-making motives to every action it does not understand.   Nevertheless, it is clear enough now that there was
a national purpose behind the exclusion of the Uitlander
from office and from the spoils of office.

The unfortunate episodes attendant on the Jameson Raid
may be ascribed on the side of the raiders and the Johannesburgers largely to want of judgment.   One section of public
opinion in England was alienated from the raiders for
lawlessness, and another from the Johannesburgers for want
of gratitude to the raiders, displayed in not going to their
assistance.   The persistent putting forward of the grievances
as if personal, and not as *lèse-majesté* against the Empire,
the asking for the franchise, and swearing allegiance to a
flag stated by the petitioners to be foreign, puzzled and
alienated people in England.   "Why do people calling
themselves British ask for the franchise ?   Either they are
coming away and so remain British, and so have no right to
it, or they are staying to swear allegiance to the *Vierkleur*,
and, if so, what claim have they to our sympathy ?"   There

* The old President noted this error of the Uitlanders with grim
amusement.   After the Jameson Raid he observed : " I am supposed by
the Uitlanders to be always guided by some one or other ; it used to be
Nellmapius, and then Dr. Leyds.   Nellmapius is now dead, and Dr.
Leyds is in Europe.   Who is leading now ? "

is much in this illogical, but understandable all the same. Lastly, the violent language and personal diatribes of some journals of the Uitlander press alienated British sympathy. It is true they were paralleled and surpassed by some of the Dutch journals, but Dutch is not read in England. Besides, such is not the tone of English controversy. The public taste is prejudiced against a course upheld by violent language and indulgence in personalities. The English public suspects it is a case of abusing the plaintiff's attorney.

From what has been said, in dealing with the policy of President Kruger, it will be seen to what conclusion I have been led as to the anti-British purpose really underlying his treatment of the Uitlanders, as well as the other portions of his action to which they objected as primarily affecting their own lives.

In the preceding chapter I have given a full statement of the reply of the Boer leaders to the Uitlanders' indictment. It will be admitted that it shows considerable skill in dialectics. But most important, as bearing on the present war, will be noted the repeated repudiation of anti-British purpose or policy. Independence is their aim in excluding the Uitlander from equality of vote or language. Defence is the meaning of their armaments: no aggression on the British power. Such are the protestations of Presidents and State Secretaries, Judges and Advocates, Journalists and Volksraad Members, Commandants and Field-Cornets, and Commanders of Artillery.

There is a sense, of course, in which these assurances may be taken as being meant to represent the truth. Independence means Dutch independence, of a Dutch-ruled State, in which the resident foreigner cannot become a citizen. Defence means defence of the rule of a privileged race. No aggression on the British power means no present aggression; only aggression at a favourable opportunity.

CHAPTER XVII.

LET us now resume the thread of events after the Jameson Raid. Early in 1896, the Reform prisoners—as the Members of the Reform Committee of the National Union of the Uitlanders have come to be known—were placed on their trial in Pretoria charged with high treason, and were sentenced, four of them to death (afterwards commuted to a fine on each of £20,000) and the remainder to imprisonment, commuted to a fine of £2000 on each prisoner applying for release. Two of the latter refused to do so, and were not released until the Queen's Jubilee in June 1897.*

The late Administrator of Rhodesia and the officers of his Expedition were handed over to the British Government, and, after trial in the Queen's Bench in England, under the Foreign Enlistment Act, were sentenced to various terms of imprisonment in May 1896.

The next event of importance was the triumph of the militant Afrikander Party in the Presidential Election of 1896 in the Orange Free State. The former President (afterwards State Secretary Reitz of the Transvaal, referred to in the already quoted letter of Mr. Theophilus Schreiner) had resigned owing to ill-health, and Judge Steyn, a member of the same party, was elected, defeating Mr. J. G. Fraser,

---

* These two were Messrs. Wools Sampson and W. D. Davies, now commanding in the Imperial Light Horse, a force composed almost exclusively of Uitlanders. The State Attorney, Dr. Coster, had consulted me on this matter, and I had recommended their unconditional release as a compliment to the head of the Imperial Government.

for some years Chairman of the Volksraad. Mr. Fraser's policy was that of the President for twenty-five years, the late Sir John Brand, a policy which his opponents described as pro-British, but which was in reality statesmanlike in the highest degree, being a policy of fusing the Dutch and British people, by according equal rights to all new residents and a liberal franchise; and, above all, of working in harmony with the great Imperial Power which kept the seas and secured the safety and autonomy of his pastoral State. It was an evil day for South Africa when Sir John Brand's enlightened policy was defeated in the person of its standard-bearer. If it had not been so, Brand's favourite saying " Alles zal recht komen " would have been realised.*

The increase of armaments in the Transvaal proceeded with feverish haste during 1896 and the following years. Orders already issued before the Raid, as is recited in the National Union Manifesto of 1895, for forts and artillery, were executed.   Military experts, German and Hollander officers, were introduced from Europe to drill the younger Boer in the artillery; a short service system, enabling a large number to pass through this training to constitute a reserve force.

Meanwhile, an Imperial organisation was instituted, called the South African League, to take the place of the disbanded National Union and the Reform Committee. It was not directed by the same leaders—part of the conditions of the release of the latter being three years' abstention from politics—and while advocating the redress of the Uitlander grievances, it was absolutely Imperialist in policy, placing in the forefront of its programme the maintenance of British supremacy in South Africa.   There was no question here of swearing allegiance to the *Vierkleur*.   Furthermore, by

* I have memoranda of discussions of Sir John Brand's policy with the public men to whom I have just referred, with the late Mr. Carl Borckenhagen and with Members of the Free State Volksraad. They are instructive, and in one sense encouraging, by showing that some at least among the Dutch-speaking people could grasp the truth that the unity of the European people is the only way of salvation in South Africa.

advocating the rights of civilised natives, it was even more at variance with Boer sentiment than its predecessor. Later on we shall find, in considering the last agitation in Johannesburg, in connection with the Edgar murder in January 1899, that the action of the League, coupled with the prosecution of its leaders,* finally determined the resolute intervention of the Imperial Government on behalf of the Uitlanders.

The negotiations of the Colonial Secretary, Mr. Chamberlain, during 1896, need not be gone into in detail. They may be summarised as follows : The Imperial Government repudiated all responsibility for the Jameson Raid, and prosecuted the leaders to conviction, and agreed, in principle, to the payment of compensation, to be assessed on the Chartered Company of Rhodesia, for the invasion. A system of Home Rule for Johannesburg and the Witwatersrand was tentatively suggested and declined by the Government of Pretoria ; the grievances of the Uitlanders were championed, as set forth in a preceding chapter, and were dealt with primarily as breaches of the Convention of London.†

Furthermore, various steps taken by the Transvaal Government in concluding agreements with the Netherlands, with Portugal, the signing of the Geneva Convention, and other matters, were dealt with by the Colonial Secretary as being breaches of the Convention of London, which subjected agreements of the Transvaal with foreign Powers to a veto of the Imperial Government.

Lastly, two steps of the highest import were taken by

---

* Mr. Clem Webb, now an officer in the Imperial Light Horse, and Mr. Dodd.

† Article XIV. " All persons other than natives conforming themselves to the laws of the South African Republic (a) will have full liberty, with their families, to enter, travel, or reside in any part of the South African Republic; (b) they will be entitled to hire or possess houses, manufactories, shops, and premises; (c) they may carry on their commerce either in person or by any agents whom they may think fit to employ; (d) they will not be subject, in respect of their persons or property, or in respect of their commerce or industry, to any taxes, whether general or local, other than those which are or may be imposed upon citizens of the said Republic."

the Imperial Government. The first was the dispatch, at the end of 1896, of Mr. Conyngham Greene, an experienced diplomatist in the service of the Foreign Office, to the post of British Agent in Pretoria. His predecessor had been—with an interval during which an acting Agent, Mr. Henry Cloete, had been appointed—Sir Jacobus de Wet, a British colonial of Dutch descent. The next and most important was the sending, in March 1897, of Sir Alfred Milner as High Commissioner for South Africa.

Early in 1897 two other events on the side of the Republics occurred of the most far-reaching consequence. In January 1897 the High Court of the Transvaal delivered a judgment in a case of a claim to mining rights against the State, deciding that a right of declaring a law or a resolution of the Volksraad illegal, if in conflict with the Grond Wet, or Constitution, rested with the judges. A similar right was possessed by the High Court of the Orange Free State, and, as is well known, by the Courts of the United States of America. I do not here propose, as it is not necessary for present purposes, to enter into the merits of the controversy, although I discussed them fully at the time with Chief Justice Kotzé of the Transvaal, who delivered the judgment, and with his colleagues, all of whom supported his action, as well as the President of the Free State, Chief Justice Melius de Villiers of the Free State, and Sir Henry de Villiers, Chief Justice of Cape Colony, and also with the State Attorneys of the two Republics. However interesting to lawyers may be the legal questions involved, it is rather the result of the subsequent action of the Transvaal Government that told on the political world.

The Transvaal Government procured the immediate passing of a law by the Volksraad giving power to the President to summarily dismiss any or all of the judges who did not give him satisfactory assurances that they would not exercise the so-called "testing right," and would hold as law every resolution of the Volksraad, whether in conflict with the Grond Wet or not. The fact that resolutions of the Volksraad might also be retractive and *ex post facto*, and so overturn in a moment vested rights of property, caused this action of the Government to create the greatest alarm and unrest in the whole Uitlander community.

On a promise of a new Grond Wet, providing for the independence of the Courts, the judges gave the required undertaking; but the Grond Wet was not passed two years later.

The next great event occurred in March 1897—the confederation of the two Boer States. This was the crowning stone of the policy of the militant Afrikander in power in Bloemfontein since President Steyn's election in the previous year. It was strongly opposed, but it was passed. Events have proved that it sealed the fate of the Free State.*

The arming of the Orange Free State burghers, at the expense of Pretoria, is generally understood to have proceeded rapidly from this date, and continued for the two following years, in fact, until the ultimatum of the 9th October, 1899.

The only other event of considerable importance in the same year, was the opening of the Rhodesian Railway from Cape Town, inaugurated by the High Commissioner, in Bulawayo, in November 1897. This event, bringing a great concourse of journalists and other visitors from all parts of the world, fixed still more on the South African problem the attention of the home-staying British public.

Not, indeed, that there was much likelihood of relaxing that attention, the grievances of the Uitlanders still being unredressed. The negotiations of the Colonial Secretary with the Transvaal still continued on the same lines as those already indicated; to secure remedy for the Uitlander disabilities, and to assert the claim of the Imperial power to control the relations of the Transvaal with foreign States.

---

* It was during the festivities of what was called "Confederation Week," in March 1897, that the "Kwaije Vrouw" banquet took place, in which President Kruger was supposed by some journalists, owing to their imperfect knowledge of Dutch, to have made some derogatory observations with reference to he Queen. Any one who was there could see that the term was reall meant to be complimentary, meaning "One who insists on her rights."

New legislation, such as the Alien Immigration Act (restricting immigration of aliens, repealed on remonstrance by the Imperial Government, remonstrance emphasised by sending warships to Delagoa Bay), the Alien Expulsion Law, the Press Law, were among the topics dealt with.*

In October 1897, Mr. Chamberlain, the Colonial Secretary, based the right of the Imperial Government to refuse to submit certain claims to arbitration on the ground that suzerainty, created in the preamble of the Convention of 1881, remained, through the survival of that preamble, although the Articles of 1884 were substituted for those of 1881.

The chief political events of 1898 were the dismissal of the Chief Justice of the Transvaal, by order of the President, in February 1898; the Suzerainty Controversy, beginning in April 1898; the accession to office and power in Pretoria, in July 1898, of the militant Afrikander party, led by Mr. State Secretary Reitz and State Attorney Smuts, a party in power in Bloemfontein since President Steyn's election in 1896; the controversy between the Imperial Government and the new power in Pretoria over the Swaziland Convention, from June to October 1898; and the accession to office of a Bond ministry in the Cape Parliament, with Mr. Schreiner as Premier, in October 1898.

Of the accession to power in Cape Town of the Bond Ministry little need be said, except that it certainly was not calculated to damp the ardour or lower the militant tone of the Afrikanders in Pretoria, into whose hands had fallen the conduct of the negotiations with the Imperial Government.

The dismissal of Chief Justice Kotzé had lasting and widespread effects. The Chief Justice, considering that the non-introduction of the new Grond Wet, promised as a condition of his temporarily relinquishing the "testing

---

* At this time I began to take considerable interest in these questions of the legal interpretation of the Conventions, having accepted in May 1897, from Dr. Coster, then State Attorney, a retainer as Advisory Counsel to the Republic, after having consulted the Chief Justice, the leaders of the Bar, and the British Agent, Sir Conyngham Greene, none of whom saw any objection to that course.

right," released him from his agreement to that effect, wrote to the President that he held that the agreement had lapsed. The answer was his instant dismissal by order of the President. Among the British public at home, alarm and distrust of the Pretoria Government was increased tenfold. Among the Uitlanders there was consternation, as the British reliance on the courts of law as the last and surest defence of life, liberty and property is inherited in the blood.

The Suzerainty controversy, brought forward by the reply of State Secretary Leyds, of the 16th April, 1898, excited much interest, but does not seem to have been attended by much political consequence. I have always agreed with the position of State Secretary Leyds, that the Suzerainty—a most elastic term, conveying no specific meaning at the present day—established by the Pretoria Convention of 1881 was abolished by the London Convention of 1884. Lord Derby, the Colonial Secretary, in his speech in the House of Lords of the 17th March, 1885, says, "We have abstained from using the word." But to assert, as proving the existence of the Suzerainty, the persistence of the *preamble* of the 1881 Convention (as the Colonial Secretary had been advised to do in his despatch of the 16th October, 1897), when Lord Derby's printed draft of the 1884 Convention encloses " within a black line " as " proposed to be omitted " this very preamble of 1881, is as extraordinary as it is unintelligible.*

* The matter is really one more of interest to lawyers than to the general public. It is worth noting, however, that every lawyer of eminence, who has published an opinion on the subject, agrees that the Suzerainty and the *preamble* of the 1881 Convention were abolished on the conclusion of the Convention of 1884. Professor Westlake, in the *Revue de Droit International* of 1896, holds this view, and expressly refutes the *preamble* theory. M. Arthur Desjardins and M. Asser, both leading members of the Institute of International Law, have written similar opinions. In England Sir Edward Clarke, and in South Africa several leading lawyers, have expressed the same opinion; and none the contrary. Among these are Mr. W. P. Schreiner, Q.C., the late Prime Minister of Cape Colony, who published his opinion in the press, and Mr. Advocate J. W. Wessels, of the Pretoria Bar, the defender of the Reform prisoners, who gave me in 1896 his opinion in writing that the Suzerainty had been abolished. A foreign Chargé d'Affaires at Pretoria asked me why the Colonial Office had not consulted Professor Westlake.

The most fateful event of the year was, however, one which excited little attention at the time, and any attention that was attracted was rather of a friendly kind. This was the accession of the militant Afrikander party to office in Pretoria in June 1898.

State Secretary Leyds having been appointed Minister of the Republic to Europe, State Attorney van Leeuwen being promoted to the bench, and Foreign Sectretary van Boeschoten being sent to the newly-established Legation in Brussels, their offices were filled by the election of State Secretary Reitz (formerly President of the Orange Free State, and founder of the Afrikander Bond), State Attorney Smuts (a young man of no experience, understood to have been appointed on the recommendation of Mr. J. H. Hofmeyr, of Cape Town, leader of the Afrikander Bond), and Foreign Secretary Grobler, a relative of the President, all three being members of the Afrikander party. Three Hollanders were thus succeeded by three Afrikanders. Changes were also made in their respective offices ; but what really made the alteration of the *personnel* important was that the conduct of the negotiations with the Imperial Government—and necessarily, therefore, the policy to be adopted towards the Uitlander cause in the hands of the Imperial Government— fell to the militant Afrikanders instead of to the trained Europeans who had preceded them.

The mistaken rejoicing of Johannesburg is still recalled by many of the victims of the expulsion of October 1899, at the order of Messrs. Reitz and Smuts. A very prevalent theory for years had been that the Hollander public servants, introduced by the President, were the cause, instead of the effect, of the policy against which the Uitlanders strove in vain.

In Pretoria, therefore, State Secretary Reitz of the militant Afrikanders was, at last, in a position to influence the action of President Kruger—not in policy, for in policy they were in absolute agreement—but in choosing of times and seasons. Educated in England, he was supposed to understand the Imperial strength and purpose. In Bloem-

fontein, Executive Councillor Fischer, in conjunction with
President Steyn—also educated in England—at last could
join hands with Pretoria in a militant pan-Afrikander
policy.*

* Mr. J. P. Fitzpatrick, in his valuable work, 'The Transvaal from
Within,' an accurate record of the facts which fell under his immediate
notice, reproduces the Johannesburger's error as to the real character and
purpose of the Young Afrikander.   Contrast his estimate of Messrs. Reitz
and Smuts with the letter of Mr. Theophilus Schreiner, already quoted,
and with the view of Messrs. Scoble and Abercombie, cited in the note to
Chapter XXIII.   Johannesburg realised its error in October 1899, and
rated plausible professions at their real worth; but the British of Pretoria
had understood long before.   The speech of Mr. J. W. Wessels, given in
the Appendix, shows that it was the Young Afrikander party that were
the immediate cause of the resistance to the Imperial demands on behalf
of the Uitlander, and, consequently, of the war.

CHAPTER XVIII.

IN June 1898, at last in the councils of Pretoria, the Afrikander party kept steadily in view the Pan-Afrikander anti-British goal. To preserve the nucleus round which was to group the Dutch domination from the Zambesi to the Cape, from the Atlantic to the Indian Ocean, a most jealous grasp was to be kept on political power, on the gold in the reef, on the command on rifles, forts and armaments, on the exclusive use of the Dutch tongue. Just as two hundred years before the use of the French language was suppressed by force, so was English to be steadfastly ostracised.

Towards the British Uitlander, vigorous exclusion from political power, while feeding him with fair words, lest he might mould the Republic in other than Dutch models. Towards the Imperial Power, a steady resistance to its interference to protect the Uitlander—such treatment of the Uitlander as he received being a purely internal affair—and equally endeavour to shake off the Imperial control of foreign relations. Evade or openly disregard the Conventions ; weariness and English party spirit, and all other well-known causes of Imperial vacillation in the past century will do the rest. What has often been flouted, becomes obsolete at last.

On the origin and history of Boer distrust and under-estimate of the power of the British people and the Imperial Government I have already written, and of the Afrikander propaganda which has created an Afrikander Separatist party. But in the case of the men in Pretoria and Bloemfontein their education in England has really served to further mislead them. Their brief and fragmentary experience of English life, acquired during a professional education, has given them little or no opportunity of seeing the higher aspect of public life in England. But it has produced an illusion of knowledge, the most dangerous form of want of knowledge. And their education has produced an illusion of intellectual superiority—as regards the rest of the world, the British portion included—a superiority which is real only in contrast to the veldt Boer.

> "Dans le pays des aveugles, le borgne est roi."
> "In het land der blinden, is eenoog koning."*

The reason why this small body of men had such weight with the action of President Kruger—for his policy they did not require to sway as it was identical with their own —both as regards the Uitlander and the Imperial Government, is clear enough to all familiar with the typical Boer's distrust of all but his own people. The President and, with him, the Executives and Volksraads, had complete trust in their support of his anti-British policy. But much more than that, they were credited with special knowledge (which in reality they did not possess) of British politics and parties, and the probabilities of Imperial action. Of Boer blood themselves, educated (at least as to their professions) to some extent in England, they were regarded by the older members of the ruling class as counsellers, whose residence in England had enabled them to master the intricacies of British statesmanship and politics, and whose duties in Holland had inducted them into the mysteries of Continental policy—an assumption which, curiously enough, they would have seen to be absurd if applied to the politics of a Kaffir chief's head kraal, and the casual stay of a European traveller. Lastly, until, at the Bloemfontein Conference of June 1899, the present High Commission raised—what should have been raised long ago—the wider issue of the status of British citizens in the Transvaal, involving the majesty and there-

* See Appendix. The Young Afrikander.

fore the safety of the Empire itself—an issue having no
relation to the terms of Conventions between the Transvaal
and the Imperial Government—until this issue was raised,
all the questions between the Governments turned on the
legal interpretation of stipulations of the Conventions. And
these separatist Afrikanders are all lawyers, and, with few
exceptions, educated in the law schools of England. So,
anti-British, skilled in British and foreign politics, skilled
in law: this was the President's conception of "Le borgne
dans le pays des aveugles"—"Eenoog in het land der
blinden."

The new directors of the negotiations showed their hand
when very early in office, and a long series of new departures,
challenged by the Imperial Government as breaches of the
Conventions, were taken under their direction.*

The first matter of negotiation arose under the Swaziland
Convention of 1894. By that Convention Swaziland had
been placed under the protectorate of the Transvaal; certain
stipulations being made in favour of the Swazis, including
the preservation of their native usages, so far as they were
not in conflict with civilised laws and customs, special
reservation being made as to cases between Swazi and Swazi
to be decided, as previously, by their own custom, and to be
excluded from the jurisdiction of the High Court of Swaziland. The privileges of the principal chief of the Swazis
were specially guarded, and by an express article it was
stipulated that the Imperial Government retained the right
of diplomatic remonstrance, in case the provisions of the
Convention touching the reserved rights of the Swazis were
not observed.

By order of the principal chief, what the Swazis regarded
as a political execution took place early in 1898. In
previous decisions, the High Court of Swaziland had held
that cases of this kind fell within the category of those
excluded from its jurisdiction, by the Convention, inasmuch

* These will be seen enumerated in a memorandum to the two
Governments of the Republics, which I issued during the Bloemfontein
Conference.

as it was matter between Swazi and Swazi, and no European was involved.*

The Government of the Transvaal, on the advice of its new officials was proceeding to arrest the principal chief, who was called Bunu, when the High Commissioner interposed, and pointed out that, under the Convention, the Swazi usages were maintained intact, unless in conflict with civilised laws and customs, that the privileges of the principal chief were specially protected, and that the High Court had already decided that there was no jurisdiction.

At the same time the Imperial Government were quite prepared, by means of a new protocol, to enlarge the jurisdiction of the High Court, and in every way to facilitate the maintenance of order and the gradual introduction of European civilisation.

The Transvaal Government, on militant Afrikander advice, refused to admit that the Imperial Government had any right to a voice in the interpretation of the Convention —a bilateral instrument to which it was one of the parties. No remonstrance from the Imperial Government would be entertained—although the right was expressly reserved— unless there should be a breach of the Convention ; of which, apparently, Pretoria alone was to be the sole judge. They moved Transvaal troops—drilled volunteers as well as burgher commandoes—into Swaziland to seize the Swazi chief, who fled to British territory in August 1898.

The High Commissioner evidently saw that, behind the apparently minor dispute as to the interpretation of a convention there was a spirit and purpose to discredit conventional obligations, and to weaken the whole authority of the Imperial Power. Through the Acting British Agent, Mr. Edmund Fraser, what was practically an ultimatum was presented to Pretoria ; and, as times were not then deemed ripe for war, the Transvaal troops were withdrawn from Swaziland ; an arrangement was made that the Chief Bunu

* The merits of this decision are immaterial; as most lawyers will agree, that another judge might very well have held that such a proceeding was " contrary to civilised laws and customs."

was merely to be fined, and not hanged, as intended, and a new Protocol was signed, in October 1898, extending the jurisdiction of the High Court of Swaziland to cover cases of violent crime, even where only Swazis are concerned.

So within two months of succeeding to office in Pretoria, the Young Afrikanders had brought South Africa and the Empire to the verge of a war, such as has now convulsed the world.

This, of course, was quite undreamt of in England, where the declaration of the Colonial Secretary that five times within recent years war with the Transvaal was imminent, has hardly even yet been realised in its literal correctness.*

As it will explain much that follows, I may say that it was at this point, in October 1898, after many doubts and long enquiry that I realised the real trend—notwithstanding the most pacific professions—of the Afrikander movement. It meant war. The question was one only of time. That the leaders were absolutely assured that actual fighting would be necessary is another matter. If the Empire were at war with another Great Power, possibly the Imperial Government would peaceably cede South Africa to the Dutch-speaking dominion, and even accept a subsidy for policing the sea by its fleet, until the new dominion could spare time to create one of its own.

---

* I entered a strong protest against this method of interpreting Conventions, which is only meant as a political device to evade public obligations, and finally to ensure their destruction by desuetude.

The position taken up by State Secretary Reitz and his colleague, State Attorney Smuts, and their followers, was obviously—apart from their political purpose—that there is no real validity in stipulations pledged on the public faith. In fact, that International Law has no real existence, being "largely a matter of opinion, inasmuch as it has no law courts to enforce it," to quote Secretary Reitz's sagacious phrase. This must be interesting to English lawyers, being an instructive survival of English legal education—the Austinian heresy. It would no doubt surprise that amiable theorist, John Austin, to find his harmless abstractions helping to excuse the evasion of treaties.

The commandeering of British subjects in the Free State to fight against their own people, and the express declaration of Executive Councillor Fischer and President Steyn, " We don't recognise International Law here," will illustrate the same spirit (in the case of Dr. Dalgliesh, referred to in Sir Alfred Milner's despatch, 5th December, 1899.

My absolute conviction that there would be war was induced by the fact that I had learned to know the mind of the young Afrikander, and well knew the mind of the British people. It was as if one were looking through a stereoscope, from two points of view at once. In England no one could believe in the combined ignorance and audacity of two petty States rashly challenging the world-wide Empire; and so, no one dreamt of war. In the Transvaal and among the mass of half-educated Afrikanders, not to mention the veld Boer, although war was conceived as possible, their invincible ignorance of the extent of the resources, of the reserve military power, of the determination of the Imperial people was as great as British incredulity as to the magnitude of an audacity, the result of a hundred years of Imperial mistakes.

CHAPTER XIX.

AFRIKANDER ACTION AGAINST THE UITLANDER AND THE EMPIRE.

LEAVING Pretoria, in November 1898, I made a tour through the Portuguese territory, the town of Lourenço Marques on Delagoa Bay; thence to Durban and other districts of Natal; and, visiting on the way the Eastern Province at East London and Port Elizabeth, arrived in Cape Town in January, 1899. My return to the Transvaal took place in April following.

Impressed as I had been on leaving the Transvaal, with the pending certainty of war, I endeavoured, while pursuing my other inquiries, to ascertain the views of leading men, of all political parties, in all these districts of South Africa on the possibilities of war. Among those who views I sought were the Governor of Natal, Sir Walter Hely Hutchinson, and the Acting High Commissioner, Sir William Butler; the leading members of the past and the present Governments, and of the legislative bodies; as well as of leading lawyers, of leading merchants and landowners in Natal, the Eastern Province and the Cape. With only two exceptions, I was assured that the prospects of war between the two Boer States and the Empire, or between Dutch and British in South Africa, were so remote that no sensible man would think about them. There were only two exceptions who, neither of them South Africans, realised the menace of the situation; one holding a high Imperial post; the other a friend, whose position in the Diplomatic Service, had given him exceptional opportunities of understanding the South African problem.*

The last agitation of the Uitlanders of Johannesburg took place in January 1899, arising out of the outrage known as the Edgar murder.   A British resident, being involved in some street brawl, took refuge in his own house.   The Boer police—British being excluded from the force—broke in the door; and, although several in number, one of them shot the fugitive dead, instead of arresting him.   The policeman was brought to trial, and after a charge from the Boer judge, was unanimously acquitted by the Boer jury.   The Uitlanders determined to protest and to appeal for Imperial protection. Under the auspices of the South African League they drew up a petition to the Queen, and transmitted it in February to the Acting High Commissioner in Cape Town.   It was returned on account of some informality in the presentation, and the Acting High Commissioner expressed himself in terms somewhat unfavourable to the methods of the League. A new petition of the 28th March, 1899, bearing 21,684 signatures was drawn up, and a deputation proceeded to the British Vice-Consul of Johannesburg to request his forwarding it to the Queen.   For this exercise of the elementary rights of a British citizen, the leaders of the demonstration, Messrs. Webb and Dodd, were prosecuted at the order of the Afrikander State Attorney, Smuts, for infringement of the Transvaal law prohibiting public meetings.   Incidentally to this proceeding, an illegal subpœna to attend the trial was served on the Vice-Consul, who refused to obey it.

At this point, the Uitlanders of Johannesburg began to suspect the genuineness of the sympathy felt with their lot by the educated Afrikander.

* A member of the present Cape Ministry reminds me that, in January, 1899, I told a party of friends at his house that war was inevitable during the year, and that a quarter of a million of Imperial troops would be required to cope with the Boer forces.   This, no one present could be brought to believe; the theory of "Huis toe" and under-estimate of the veld Boers, prevailed among Imperialists at the Cape as well as Johannesburg; and, as regards their leaders, the educated Young Afrikanders, no one could realise that they could be so ignorant and so audacious.

The High Commissioner's despatch to the Colonial Office of the 4th May, practically adopts the prayer of the Petition. As I have already pointed out, it takes the question away altogether from the region of legal interpretation of the Conventions. It raises distinctly, and for the first time, the issue, that not the grievances of the Uitlanders, not the woes of the capitalists, but the prestige and therefore the life of the Empire is at stake; if the continued oppression of British citizens is to be endured. The despatch makes clear the existence of a distinct policy of calumny against the Imperial Government, and of claims based on the assumtion on some superior right in Dutch over British, all over South Africa; and shows how the Dutch in British Colonies are becoming disaffected at the spectacle of the British in the Transvaal appealing vainly for protection to the Imperial Power.

The despatch of the Colonial Secretary, dated 14th May, is a confirmation of Sir Alfred Milner's endorsement of the Petition, and states the views of the Imperial Government :—

" It results from this review of the facts and conditions on which the Petition is founded, as well as from information derived from your despatches and other sources, that British subjects and the Uitlanders generally, in the South African Republic, have substantial grounds for their complaint of the treatment to which they are subjected.

" Her Majesty's Government, however, attach much less importance to financial grievances than to those which place them in a condition of political, educational, and social inferiority towards the Boer inhabitants of the Transvaal, and even endanger the security of their lives and property.

" Her Majesty's Government earnestly desire the prosperity of the South African Republic. They have been anxious to avoid any intervention in its internal concerns, and they may point out in this connection, that if they really entertained the design of destroying its independence, which has been attributed to them, no policy could be better calculated to defeat their object than that which, in all friendship and sincerity, they now urge upon the Government of the South African Republic, and which would remove any pretext for interference by relieving British subjects of all just cause of complaint."

During the last Johannesburg agitation, in January 1899,

I had no special sources of information, although I followed the proceedings with attention.; but, inasmuch as, during my then recent tour through the various States, I found that all the leading public men, and the press, without exception, ascribed the action of the Transvaal Government, both as regards the Imperial Government—a series of quite new breaches of the Conventions having begun under the later régime in Pretoria—and as regards the Uitlanders, to my advice as a lawyer, interpreting the Conventions, I wrote a letter of remonstrance to State Secretary Reitz, dated Cape Town, 4th February, 1899, to which reference will be made in the summary of my memorandum to the Executive and Volksraad, dated Pretoria, 1st May. To the Minister to Europe, Dr. Leyds, with whom I had interviews in January and March in Cape Town, I repeated the same remonstrances.

In April I attended—for, as it proved, the last time—the opening of the Volksraad of the Orange Free State. I had several interviews with the President, and with members of the Executive and Members of the Volksraad, of both the Progressive and the Conservative sections. I endeavoured to impress on them the extreme gravity of the situation, the urgent necessity of inducing the Pretoria Government to listen to more moderate counsels, and, if they wished to retain their independence, to redress the grievances of the Uitlanders. The introduction of the Free State Franchise Law into the Transvaal would be the simplest solution. Above all, I endeavoured to convey to them my own conviction of the imminent risk of war; and that the calculation obviously being made by the militant Afrikander that, once again, the Imperial Government would waver and retreat, was due to absolute want of knowledge of the courage and resolution of the British people or Government, when once roused. Although at that time I had not had an opportunity of discussing the situation with the High Commissioner, I had formed a sufficiently accurate estimate, not so much of his policy, as of the result on the mind of the British people at home, of his presentation of the case of the Uitlanders,

and of the gravity of the crisis as affecting the stability of
the Empire. I pointed out, too, the boundless wealth and
the reserve military force of the Empire in case of the war,
towards which militant Afrikander policy in Pretoria was
impelling the two Republics.

I found that, with the exception of certain progressive
members of the Volksraad, including Mr. J. G. Fraser, there
was not the least confidence in the resolution of the Imperial
Government. And as to the chances of war, that they
inclined in favour of the Boer States; more especially in
view of the likelihood of foreign complications.

For much of this I was prepared, but I confess I was
surprised to find the President holding—as he told me—
that the presence of the Bond Ministry in office in the Cape
would interfere with the Imperial troops making use of the
railways. I reminded him that the Molteno Ministry was
dismissed by a word from Sir Bartle Frere, for endeavouring
to control his military operations; and that, at an order
from Sir Alfred Milner, the Bond Ministry would cease to
hold office. And also, that neither an Ollivier Ministry nor
a Gambetta Government prevented the German army from
using the French railways.

I was impressed also to find that, in addition to the
many historic reasons for doubting the resolution and firmness of any Imperial Government, they relied on a new one,
as rendering improbable any British redress by arms of the
Uitlanders' grievances. This was the Queen's well-known
dislike to any war, and her desire that her long reign should
close in peace. In Pretoria I found the same impression.

Now, one of the strange things in this most strange field
of South African politics, is that, almost until their expulsion, the Uitlanders of Johannesburg retained a certain
confidence in the friendly intentions of the Free State
Government in particular, and also in the militant Africanders in Pretoria; thinking that the execution of their
conciliatory designs was prevented by President Kruger
and the Boers of the older school; whereas the very reverse
was the case.

From Bloemfontein I proceeded to Pretoria, arriving there on the 9th April. I there conferred with several members of the Volksraad, including Mr. R. K. Loveday, the only English member of the First Volksraad, and other Progressive members, and, at their suggestion, drew up a "Memorandum on the Present Aspect of the Foreign Affairs of the South African Republic," dated Pretoria, 1st May 1899. This memoradum was translated into Dutch and circulated among the members of the Executive and of the First and Second Volksraad, and was also sent to the Executive of the Orange Free State.

The Memorandum was read at a private meeting of members of the First Volksraad, at which I was present. It is too long to reproduce here; but the following are the chief passages :—

" In view of the grave aspect of the external affairs of the Republic, it has been suggested to me that it would be well if I were to place on record, for the information of the Executive and the Volksraad, my opinion on those features of the situation which seems to call for special attention at their hands.

" The maintenance of the independence and of the free initiative in South Africa of this Republic, and of the sister Republic of the Free State, must necessarily be the first care of those charged with the Government of the State. As I have more than once pointed out during the period in which I acted as advising Counsel on the foreign affairs of the Republics, the maintenance of that independence by the Burghers is not alone now, as it has always been, a high object of their immediate personal concern, but a trust which committed to them by destiny, should be carried out for the benefit of the present and all future people of the European race in South Africa."

Among the causes alleged as threatening the independence of the State, I enumerated the three which appeared to weigh most with them—the hostility of great capitalistic groups, the discontent of the Uitlander population, and a " policy of aggression ascribed to the present British Colonial Secretary " As to the last, I pointed out that

" It would be unwise to assume, without the amplest evidence, that any Statesman in such a position of responsibility to his Empire and to other States would lightly seek cause of war. The wisest course evidently is to avoid, by every means short of the surrender of the independence of a Republic, giving occasion for either pacific or armed intervention."

I then proceeded to point out the circumstances favourable to armed intervention and the rashness of challenging the unfettered power of the Empire. The friendly attitude of Germany, the distractions of France; the Imperialist tendencies of the leaders of the former Gladstone party; the irritation of the ruling class in England at what they regard as ingratitude on the part of the Transvaal burghers; the change of tone among the Liberal press in England, formerly in favour of the burghers.

I then refer to the general opinion, which I had recently ascertained in all the states of South Africa on the gravity of the crisis, to the recent increase of Imperial troops on the border and to the

"Disadvantages and disasters attendant on war, however victorious— the loss of lives, of money, the check to industry, the recrudescence of race divisions among the rapidly amalgamating white people of every descent."

I then combat a fallacy impressed on the Volksraad by the Afrikander party, and which lured the burghers to their destruction. "Forcible intervention is impossible under British Constitutional Government, and so may be dismissed from our consideration." I show how fallacious it was to think that the capitalists, fearing the destruction of their mines could hold the hands of the Imperial Government; who, in the issues of peace and war, have only to commend themselves to the judgment of the ruling class in the United Kingdom, whose characteristic is their "strong sense of justice."

"The ruling class, however unfavourably impressed by the former policy of this State, would never sanction war, unless what in their eyes constitutes a just and sufficient cause should arise. Should, therefore, the Republic, by a strict adherence to its external obligations make certain that it is in the right in its foreign relations, not only would it have the security which springs from a sense of having fulfilled the obligations of justice, but it would bave perceptibly diminished the chances of foreign intervention."

I then proceed to consider the two aspects of the situation into which the Afrikander party has led the Government of the State. The first aspect, that of the negotiations with the Imperial Government, the second, that of the position of the resident Uitlanders.

I first referred to the negotiations with the Imperial Government with reference to actions held by them as breaches of the Conventions, which, "for a considerable time were referred to me for advice; advice usually, though not invariably, acted upon by the Executive," but which had become extraordinarily numerous during the preceding year, since the accession of the Africander party to office.

The enumeration of the pending questions included the Suzerainty Question and the Dynamite Concession and the Convention of 1884; the proclamations with reference to Dynamite in Swaziland, and the Swaziland Convention of 1894; the Extradition with Rhodesia and the same Convention; Indian Immigration and the Convention of London and an arbitral award to which the Imperial Government had assented; and the privileges of the British Vice-Consul. I also enumerated the previous questions already settled on which I had advised.

Desiring the Volksraad to clearly understand my dissent from the method of interpreting conventions adopted by the Afrikander party—with the real object of evading them—and which I was surprised to find even members of the Volksraad had ascribed to my advice, I referred to the fact that my advice had not been followed on the last occasion on which I had been consulted by the Executive—the Swaziland proposed Protocol—until and ultimatum had been received from the High Commissioner.

" As more fully explaining what I consider to be the just and prudent way of considering all questions under the Conventions, I may here quote from my letter addressed to the present State Secretary on the 4th of February, 1899, the substance of which I requested him to communicate to the Executive.

" I am, for my part strongly of opinion that no insistence should in any case be made either as to matters in which there is nothing of real substance in dispute, or where there is room for doubt as to the extent of the legal rights of the Republic; or, above all, where an insistence on a technically valid right would entail disproportionate consequences of public danger."*

Lastly, I referred to the position of the resident Uit-landers as follows :—

" I may be permitted to express my satisfaction that the President has given proof of his proposals of adherence to the policy of securing the stability of the Republic, and removing the prospect of foreign intervention by widening the electoral basis of the State. There can be no doubt that the Volksraad, relying on the advice of the President and the Executive as their trusted Councillors, will duly weigh all the arguments to be adduced in favour of liberal franchise proposals." And, in conclusion, " I trust I may express the hope, that, notwithstanding the present grave outlook, the Volksraad, by the exercise of wisdom and prudence, both in enforcing a scrupulous adherence to the public faith of the State, pledged in its Conventions and Treaties, and in a wise and timely concilliation of those residents from other States, who, for good or ill, have thrown in their lot with the Republics, will so guide the future of the people that the cause of the Republic will be that of justice and right."

This appeal to the Volksraad had an appreciable effect at the time; and several members expressed agreement with its recommendations. But the reactionary forces of the Afrikander party were too strong; with the result which was seen in the Bloemfontein Conference.

It will be seen that the arguments I used were those most useful to convince the burgher members—being an appeal to their desire to preserve their independence and to their sense of justice. It may be convenient here to state my reasons for desiring to see that independence preserved, if such were at all compatible with the higher interests of the race and of civilisation in South Africa. †

---

* I had ascertained that this letter had not been communicated to the Executive in Pretoria, some of whom were—as well as Executive Councillors in Bloemfontein, under an impression that I had advised the legal steps taken in connection with the aggressive policy of Messrs. Reitz and Smuts. In the same letter (4th February), I recorded my dissent from other legal action which I had read of in the newspapers.

† The reasons had already been set forth in a pamphlet stating the arguments in the " Suzerainty Question " in 1898.

The reasons which have evidently influenced the Imperial Government not merely to support, but to offer to guarantee the independence of the Boer Republics, if a policy of equal rights for European inhabitants and justice for the native races were adopted, must influence any one who dispassionately considers the subject.

The promotion of the gradual fusion of the European race in South Africa must be the object of any statesman, Imperial or local, who looks into the future. Dutch as well as British are here in South Africa to stay.

One obvious step in this direction would be gained by conciliating, if it were possible, as some until the present war had hoped, Dutch feeling in favour of Republican forms ; leaving their Republics and local institutions intact.

Again, still bearing in mind the ultimate object, the free initiative of the Republics in regard to the native problem would be more likely to conciliate Dutch feeling, than any hasty super-imposition of home-born British methods, which have caused so much bitterness in the past. But, of course, this initiative to be in the hands of British as well as Dutch residents in the Republics; and the object of retaining it would not be the stereotyping of present Transvaal and Orange River legislation, but to control the application of what is known in South Africa as Exeter Hall methods.

Yet again, for the good of all South Africa, a free initiative in the hands of the Republics in regard to the exploitation of minerals—for the public service and not for the multiplication of millionaires, would undoubtedly present advantages. Here again, however, the control of this initiative to be in the hands of British as well as Dutch residents in the Republics; who would be more likely to take the British law of the Klondyke Gold Fields as a model, or the present Orange Free State law, than the old Free State law, under which titles are held the Kimberley Diamond Mines, in which no rights are reserved to the State.

Immediate harmony with the policy of the Empire, and an ultimate federation of all South Africa under the Imperial protection, would be directly the result of a policy so marked out.

Not least of all, the danger of war and race feud, which we are now experiencing would be dispelled; and a newer generation would have forgotten the particularist dreams of to-day, as a Breton has forgotten that his country was once separate from France.

The young Afrikander idea of independence, we have all now discovered was very different from this; although it is true, pacific protestations of goodwill (in Johannesburg more especially) made the discovery much later in most cases than in mine. The real object of that party in power in Bloemfontein and Pretoria, the meaning which they attached to the " Independence of the Republics " was intolerant and most jealous Dutch domination in South Africa. Their action was impelled by bitter envy and jealousy of the Uitlanders generally, and of the British in particular; and by insane hatred of the Imperial Power, whose sway meant equal rights. They well knew that under any system based on equality of opportunities, they would be compelled to take an inferior position; and they were determined to hold to their factitious superiority arising from the military strength of the veld Boer, and their grasp on the arms and the gold. Their anti-capitalist statements were a mere rhetorical device—*ad captandum vulgus*—in England and elsewhere. Their plausible professions of friendship to the Uitlander, and their ascribing their inability to procure redress of their grievances to the Dopper and Hollander influence—to President Kruger and Minister Leyds—were a mere diplomatic ruse to blind the Philistines, at whose simplicity in believing them they were amused : witness their attempt to bring over the capitalists in March 1897, by concessions of mining facilities if they would abandon the Uitlanders' political claims.*

It is not sufficiently appreciated that their opposition was not merely to the Empire and the British. Anti-British always, it is true; but also anti-Hollander, anti-German, anti-French, anti-foreigner *au fond*. They have always regarded their Hollander public servants as mere instruments,

* Fully described by Mr. Fitzpatrick.

to be dispensed with at the earliest opportunity. No concession of equal rights to any foreigner was dreamt of.

In my sketch of the policy of President Kruger, I have pointed out their misapprehension of this fact as one of the mistakes of the Uitlanders of Johannesburg.*

---

* This mistake was partly realised by Johannesburg on the occurrence of the resignation, in July, 1897, of State Attorney Coster, after an unworthy aspersion on the courage of his fellow Hollanders, offered to him by President Kruger. Dr. Coster has since been killed, as I have already mentioned, fighting gallantly at Elandslaagte; while President Kruger and Messrs. Reitz and Smuts and Fischer, and the rest of the young Afrikanders have kept well outside the range of the British guns.

President Steyn made no secret of his intention to dispense with the service of his Hollander officials, as soon as he could get educated "land's sons" to take their place; and openly averred that, neither in Pretoria nor Bloemfontein could they cause the Afrikander policy to waver by a hair's-breadth.

An Oxford University graduate, appointed to lecture at the Pretoria gymnasium, told me in July of last year, that he had been introduced by the Afrikander State Secretary Reitz to a stranger, as holding his chair only until some " *waare Afrikander* " could be got competent to take it.

The young Afrikanders have been correctly described as the Boer "Boxers!" and, indeed, resemble in more ways than their anti-foreigner policy, the Chinese anti-foreigner party. Among these resemblances, however, must not be included any deducible from a too servile imitation of the Chinese fanatical courage.

One very militant member of the party, a barrister of the Temple, whom I have known for some years, said to me in Pretoria, in April 1899, when I endeavoured to convince him of the necessity of a conciliatory policy:—"The time for discussion has gone by. My horse and my rifle are ready."

During the war, the horse and the rifle may have been ready; but they were not used. At least, the rifle was not; conceivably because its use might involve getting the marksman within range of other rifles. The warrior in question served first on a Red Cross Committee, and then in the Commissariat; the latter an undoubtedly convenient department, with an eye to the strategic difficulty of procuring supplies. He at present reposes under a protection even more secure than that of the Red Cross— that of the shadow of the Imperial flag at Pretoria; as a burgher who has taken the oath of neutrality—while the fighting is going on.

CHAPTER XX.

DURING the month of May, in Pretoria, I had interviews with most of the members of the Transvaal Executive, and with nearly all the members of the First and Second Volksraad, and with many of the official heads of departments. As in Bloemfontein, I found a widespread disbelief in the firmness of purpose of the Imperial Government, and an idea that they were seeking to obtain control by peaceful means which they knew they were unable to get by the use of force, thinking war too dangerous and expensive.

As I have already mentioned, I found in Pretoria, as in Bloemfontein, the same singular reliance on the Queen's dislike to war, as a contributing cause, among all the well-known other causes, towards preventing the Imperial Government from ever, under any circumstances, redressing the Uitlanders' grievances by force of arms. It was useless to endeavour to explain—what the most superficial acquaintance with home politics tells any one—that, however great the influence on foreign negotiations the Queen's unique experience has naturally given her, and however intelligible and laudable her desire for peace, Her Majesty could not conceivably entertain the wish—even if she had the power —to prevent the adoption of measures, military or other, recommended by responsible Ministers as essential to the dignity, and therefore the safety, of the Empire and its citizens. The Afrikander, educated in English law schools knew all about Royal policy, as well as everything else political. A statement by the Afrikander State Secretary and a

letter from General Joubert, published at the beginning of
the war, showed their reliance on the Queen's influence, and
their disappointment at its not having interfered with the
firmness of the Imperial Government.

Nevertheless, there was a small but well-informed section,
who eventually would have influenced the President and the
Executive, but for the Afrikander State Secretary, State
Attorney, and others of the party, who ultimately decided
the fate of the negotiations.   General Joubert was strongly
opposed to a war policy, and advised redress of the Uitlander
grievances and harmonious co-operation with the Imperial
Government; he was alone in the Executive Council.

Before the Conference I had interviews in Pretoria with
members of the Free State Executive, who, however, so far
from being more pacific, as Johannesburgers imagined to the
last, were far more warlike, following implicitly the lead of
Councillor Fischer.

When I went to Bloemfontein, therefore, I felt assured
that the Conference would be abortive.'

It is needless to go at length into the proceedings.   Very
few words will explain them.   The High Commissioner, as
a basis for discussion of all differences between the two
Governments, proposed that immediate and satisfactory
representation in the Legislature should be secured to the
Uitlanders ; and proposed, as the minimum concession which
would secure this end, a five years' retrospective franchise
law for all inhabitants, and one-fourth representation in the
Volksraad.   When the Uitlanders were thus put in a position
to redress their own grievances without calling on the
Imperial Government, the High Commissioner would be
prepared to discuss the settling of questions of the legal
interpretation of the Conventions by an arbitration Commission—from which all foreigners were excluded—and to
settle, by personal negotiation, matters which were neither
Uitlander grievances nor questions of legal interpretation.

President Kruger, relying on the assurances of the
Afrikander party, led by Executive Councillor Fischer in
Bloemfontein (followed by President Steyn), and State Secre-

tary Reitz in Pretoria, miscalculated the Imperial policy. He thought the minimum demand was a maximum ; that a mere bargain was being introduced; that, if he held firm, the Imperial Government would retreat; and never, under any circumstances, would resort to arms to redress the balance of power between Boer and Uitlander.

The President, therefore, in regard to the franchise claim produced a most wonderfully-drafted franchise law—honey-combed with pitfalls—a product of the ingenuity of Executive Councillor Fischer—six months' notices, and proofs of law-abidingness, and of right to franchise in country of origin, and continuous two years' registration, and income of £200 a year; and, after five years, the same proofs all over again. So, at the end of seven years and a half from 1899, if one had spent a large portion of one's life attending to the matter, the franchise would be attained. And then offered this boon, only if Swaziland would first be annexed to the Transvaal, and only if an agreement were made that all future contro-versies with the Imperial Government would be settled by arbitration.

The High Commissioner pointed out that this extraordi-nary scheme did not provide for the immediate, or even the speedy, attainment of the franchise by persons who had been for a long time in the Republic; and on the 5th June declared the Conference altogether at an end.

As will have been seen, I was not surprised at this result. Nevertheless, I did my best to avert it. On the 1st June, the first day of the Conference—after the preliminary meeting to settle hours and procedure, of 31st May—I issued the following memorandum which was printed at the Official Printing Press, and circulated among the members of the Executives and Volksraads of the two States :—

SUPPLEMENTARY MEMORANDUM ON THE FOREIGN AFFAIRS OF THE SOUTH AFRICAN REPUBLIC.

I.—Since the issue of my memorandum of the 1st May, addressed to the Executive and the Volksraad of the South African Republic, I have ascertained several facts, some unknown at the time of writing and some occurring since, which necessitate some further observations.

1. I have ascertained that the majority, if not all, of the members of the Volksraads of the South African Republic and Orange Free State have been under an impression that the action of the former Republic, as regards the negotiations with the British Government during the last six months, as previously, has been taken under my advice.

2. That certain matters enumerated in my memorandum of 1st May, as being in a condition in which the proper course was still open to discissusion, have been advanced a step further (and complicated) by replies sent to the British Government and other action.

3. That further questions under the Conventions with the British Government have been opened by acts of which I was unaware.

II.—I, therefore, find it necessary to inform the Executives and the Volksraads of the two Republics that this impression on the part of the Members to whom I have referred is unfounded.

My advice during no period has been given on all matters relative to the foreign affairs of the South African Republic, but only on matters specifically referred to me. These matters I have already enumerated in my memorandum of 1st May.

For all action taken since October last the present legal advisers of the Government are solely responsible.

III.—I desire to place on record the following facts.

1. I strongly disapprove of the course adopted in connection with the Swaziland protocol negotiation, in which the offer of the High Commissioner to negotiate a new protocol extending the jurisdiction of the High Court to include Bunu was, contrary to my written advice, in the first instance rejected, and then, after strong remonstrance from the High Commissioner, accepted, after unnecessary friction had been created and a loss of dignity had accrued to the Government of the Republic. (The facts are more fully set out in my last memorandum.)

2. I consider the action of issuing a subpœna to the British Vice-Consul of Johannesburg highly inexpedient in view of the strained relations with the Imperial Government, as well as being contrary to International Law, in view of the special practice concerning consuls in Pretoria.

3. I consider it was exceedingly inadvisable, in view of pending negotiations with the British Government, to prosecute Messrs. Webb and Dodd, of Johannesburg, in connection with their presenting a petition to be forwarded to the Queen.

4. I consider the tone (I do not criticise the arguments) of the reply to the Dynamite Concession despatch of the British Government exceedingly ill-advised; and more especially ill-advised the reference to an alleged British opium monopoly, a reference calculated to have no effect but that of arousing ill-feeling in Great Britain and South Africa alike, and consequently of aiding the efforts of those desirous of precipitating a war.

5. I dissent, as I have already stated, from the published opinion of the present State Attorney, unfavourable to the power of the Government of the South African Republic, to cancel the Dynamite Concession; and I agree with the contrary opinions of Mr. Schreiner, Prime Minister of Cape Colony, Mr. Advocate Curlewis, and Chief Justice Gregorowski. As the British Government claim that the monopoly is a breach of the Convention of 1884, unless the Republic has power to cancel the concession, a new cause of controversy, over a question of no material interest to the Republic, arises.

6. I hold illegal, and a breach of the Swaziland Convention of 1894 with the British Government, the proclamations of the Government of the South African Republic of 6th March and 28th April, 1899, relative to the importation of dynamite and fire-arms into Swaziland, rendering practically useless the existing concessions. Here, again, a new controversy with the British Government has been quite recently created. This is more gratuitous, as the Swaziland Convention of 1894 provides for the expropriation of any concession by compensation to be fixed by arbitration.

7. I consider, from what I have learned of its purport, the recent reply of the Government of the South African Republic to the last suzerainty despatch of the British Government has placed the claim of the Republic to be free from suzerainty on a wrong legal basis—a basis unwarranted by the facts. (The original reply of April, 1898, was based on my opinion of 11th February, 1898.)

8. I am of opinion that the legal advice on which the recent war tax on non-burghers was imposed of highly doubtful validity, at the least, but quite apart from that question, of singular inopportuneness. Here again another controversy with the British Government has been needlessly occasioned.

9. I am strongly of opinion that the proposed clause in the new Grondwet (and the legal advice on which it was based) subjecting all foreign residents to military service in time of war, is a flagrant breach of international law; one sure to incur the reprobation of the whole world, and to exclude the Republic from the category of civilised states. I adhere to the conclusions in the learned opinion of advocate J. W. Wessels on this subject, published in the Press.

10. I consider the legal advice on which was based the recent resolution of the Volksraad disfranchising those burghers on whom the franchise had been conferred for defending the Republic during the Jameson Raid, not merely unfounded on legal principle—being *ex post facto* and retroactive legislation—but most inopportune and calculated to hamper the negotiations with the British Government at the Conference of Bloemfontein. Doubt has thus been thrown on the reality and the permanence of any grant of franchise to resident Uitlanders as the result of the Conference.

IV. Finally, I desire to place on record my strong dissent from the whole tone and temper of the negotiations with the British Government, during the last six months and up to the date of the Conference of Bloemfontein—a Conference the result of the mediation of the President of the Orange Free State.

If the object of those on whose advice the Government of the South African Republic acted on the legal questions affecting the British Government and its subjects had been to precipitate a war with the British Government, a more direct course could not have been taken.

As I have explained in my previous memorandum, the very causes which would lead the educated ruling class in England—which alone influences foreign policy—to sanction war are precisely those which touch their sense of justice. Their sense of injured national pride has already been sufficiently awakened by events in South African history. A strong war party exists in every great state—its nucleus in its army and navy. To go out of the way to strengthen the hands of such a party on the part of a small state by committing acts of administration, none of which were of the least immediate urgency as to time, and some of which were either illegal or of doubtful legality or discourteous to a great power, is simply to incur an unjustifiable risk of the lives and fortunes of the burghers of the Republics, and to commit them to a war in an unjust cause.

Want of knowledge of external political conditions, in England or elsewhere, may be an explanation of such a line of action, but it is no valid excuse.

V. It is true that the permanent danger to the independence of the South African Republic, and indeed to that of the Orange Free State, is the discontent of certain of the resident Uitlanders, mostly subjects of the British Government in the former Republic with their position under the constitution. This, however, is a matter to be considered separately in its bearing on the foreign affairs of the two Republics.

The purport of this memorandum is that I wish to make it clear to those Members of the Executives and of the Volksraads of the Republics with whom I have had the honour of conferring, and to their colleagues, that most of the acuteness of the present crisis, threatening the independence and welfare of the Republics, and the evils of war, have been due to measures (with the responsibility for which I have been mistakenly credited), the unwisdom of which I trust I have sufficiently demonstrated to all interested in the fortunes of either State.

M. J. FARRELLY, LL.D.

Bloemfontein, 1st June, 1899.

The only comment I need make on the memorandum— which explains itself—is on the reference to the Suzerainty claim. In a despatch of 9th May, 1899, State Secretary

Reitz makes the following extraordinary proposition. Inasmuch as in the London Convention of 1884 there is no mention of—

"self-government belonging to the Republic, it follows of itself that the now existing right of absolute self-government of this Republic is not derived from either the Convention of 1881 or that of 1884, but simply and solely follows from the inherent right of this Republic as a Sovereign International State."

This is obviously a very different thing from merely saying that the Suzerainty Preamble of 1881 was abolished, and that the Transvaal was a Sovereign State, the rights of which were defined in the 1884 Convention.* However, the legal side of this argument I leave to the appreciation of lawyers. To prove that you have everything, because the instrument which is the historical record of your title grants you nothing, is certainly in keeping with the view that "international law is only a matter of opinion, as it has no law courts to enforce it"; under which circumstances you no doubt can evolve it as you go along.

It is the political side which is truly startling. It is a claim of the Sovereign State of Monaco against France. It is no less than a claim to stand on the same plane with the Empire—which had restored its separate existence to the Republic and still held a veto on its foreign treaties: a claim that the Republic differed from the Empire only in degree of power and not in kind: and stood in the circle of communities as an International State, equal in rights to any in the world. This, of course, was a direct challenge to the Imperial supremacy in South Africa.

The High Commissioner fully appreciated the relative importance of an argument faulty in law, and a claim dangerous in politics. In a despatch of the 14th June, 1899, the State Secretary's proposition is thus commented on :—

"Mr. Reitz's contention is that the Convention of 1881 is completely gone, and that on its disappearance the Transvaal emerged as a Sovereign

---

* The High Court of Justice of England, Chancery Division, declared the Transvaal a Sovereign State. (*Times* Law Reports, 22nd April, 1898.)

International State, not, however, by virtue of the new Convention, which, according to him, absolutely abrogated that of 1881, but by its inherent right to be something which, as a matter of fact, it had ceased to be seven years previously. The way in which the State-Secretary juggles with the Convention of 1884 is rather irritating to a plain man.

"But the importance of the matter does not consist in his arguments. It consists in the assertion that the South African Republic is a Sovereign International State. This appears to be contradicting the position consistently maintained by us, and is, in fact, in the nature of a defiance of Her Majesty's Government."

A defiance it was, and was meant to be. It is easy to defy or to juggle with a giant when you are quite sure he will not hit back; and that mental position of the Afrikander in power is the key to the failure of the Bloemfontein Conference.*

* A brilliant reception was held in the Presidency of Bloemfontein—of late occupied by Lord Roberts—on the evening of 31st May, to meet Sir Alfred Milner and President Kruger. As I looked round the room, I told my friend, Commandant Ferreira, of the Volksraad, afterwards Commandant-General of the Orange Free State, since killed at Ladysmith, that I saw the handwriting on the wall.

CHAPTER XXI.

THE POLICY OF THE HIGH COMMISSIONER.

THE appointment of the present High Commissioner for South Africa (Sir Alfred Milner) was viewed by Boer and Uitlander in the Transvaal, and Bondmen and Imperialists in the Colonies with more than usual attention, largely mingled with apprehension. The general consensus of approval shown by both political parties, within as well as without the Imperial Parliament, while accepted as tolerably reliable evidence of exceptional ability, did not in the least tend to allay this apprehension; nor yet his monumental work on the British regeneration of Egypt. To have an able administrator, Imperialists argued, who fails to grasp the real facts of the situation, will only make matters worse for the Empire. An extreme Liberal in office (the new High Commissioner having been co-worker with Mr. John Morley on the then Radical *Pall Mall Gazette*) was a portent in many eyes, and men spoke of Majuba. On the other hand, the Boers in the Republics were equally apprehensive. The High Commissioner had been appointed by Mr. Chamberlain, whom they loudly charged with complicity in the Jameson Raid, and with designs of annexing their country. Even after the new Commissioner's coming the famous Suzerainty controversy arose.

In Johannesburg the Liberalism — or Radicalism — weighed most; and the long silence of the High Commissioner while conducting his investigations, and the fact that he was accessible to politicians of the Bond as well as Progressives—ending in the alarming report that he was learning to speak Dutch—induced an accusation of his being "Pro-Boer," the Johannesburg analogue of "Engelsche zind."

After nearly two years of inquiry—an eminent writer has been found who thinks six months sufficient—the High Commissioner apparently grasped the situation, that there was a distinct purpose to oust the Imperial Power from rule in South Africa, and to substitute a Dutch-speaking Afrikander dominion, separated from the Empire.

In the Swaziland Convention negotiation in 1898 it was impossible not to see the purpose of the Young Afrikander Party—in power since July 1898 in Pretoria, as well as in Bloemfontein since 1896. They denied the right of the Imperial Government to a voice in the interpretation of a Convention to which it was one of the parties. They held that unless there should be a breach of the Convention —of which Pretoria was to be sole judge—the Imperial Government had no right to remonstrate. Their obvious purpose was gradually to eliminate any effectual Imperial control based on the Conventions in force. On this point, however, the High Commissioner was firm, and the negotiation of a new Protocol, extending a disputed jurisdiction of the High Court, acknowledged the Imperial right.

It was not, however, until the delivery of a speech at Graaff Reinet, in the Cape, when, at the end of 1897, a Bond deputation who had protested their loyalty were told: "Of course you are loyal; it would be monstrous if you were not," that the apprehension of the Uitlanders were relieved as regards the policy of the Imperial representative.

In a series of despatches, ending with the memorable message of 5th May, 1899, shortly before the Bloemfontein Conference, the High Commissioner displayed a vivid picture of the whole political scene. There are pointed out the intolerable assumption—in the press and in the pulpit, in the school and on the platform—of some inherent superior right to the land of South Africa of Dutch-speaking people over those of British descent: the disloyal propaganda of calumny against the purpose and character of the Imperial Power: the anti-British and anti-Imperial purpose of depressing the Uitlander of the Transvaal to the rank of a helot. The destruction of Imperial power in South Africa is clearly shown to be the intended and inevitable end of the Afrikander policy.

The most striking feature of the High Commissioner's policy, however, consisted in his boldly removing the whole controversy between the Imperial Government and the Transvaal from the arid and profitless ground of academical discussion as to the legal interpretation of the Conventions between the two Governments. The basing of Imperial rights on the alleged persistence of the Preamble of the Convention of London of 1881, declaring a suzerainty—a contention held invalid by so many eminent lawyers that it is surprising how the Colonial Office should have adopted it—was succeeded by a much more statesmanlike and indeed an incontestable ground for intervention—the right of self-preservation inherent in the Empire. The Imperial Power, holding the greatest extent of territory, wealth, and population in South Africa, and its continual hold on South Africa being essential to its retention of the sea route to India and Australia and to its retention of all the Colonies, the Imperial Government could not, as a matter of right of self-preservation, endure the maintenance of its borders of a hostile military State, keeping in political subjection a majority of inhabitants of British descent. To endure this injustice was to destroy its prestige in the eyes of the world, with British subjects of both white races in South Africa, with the subject native races.

The spectacle of British subjects in the Transvaal appealing vainly for protection to the Imperial Power was leading into disaffection the Dutch-descended inhabitants in the Cape and Natal, and, in conjunction with the incessant Afrikander propaganda, was bringing them to turn their eyes to Pretoria as a Mecca—and indeed as a Golconda and a Woolwich as well.

Not Conventions, but rights apart from contract altogether, formed the base of the High Commissioner's policy. *Proximus ardet Ucalegon.* In fact, his action rested on the

principle of President Burger's address to the Pretoria
Volksraad in 1877, in speaking of the Boer ill-treatment of
the natives :—

> "If you ask me what the English have to do with it, I tell you that as
> little as we can allow barbarities among the Kaffirs on our borders, as
> little can they allow that in a State on their borders anarchy should
> prevail."

Nor did the High Commissioner allow the Jameson Raid
to be successfully used as a reason for putting the Uitlanders
on terms of inequality, referring in one of his despatches to
the Raid as a " conspiracy of which the great body of
Uitlanders was innocent, and which perverted and ruined
their cause."

The key to the solution, without war, of the situation,
the only peaceful way of ending the menace to South Africa
and to the Imperial Power was to adopt some means by
which the power, guided by the anti-British bias dominating
the wealthy military State of the Transvaal, could be paci-
fically brought to work in harmony with instead of against
the Empire.   The franchise for the Uitlander was the only
conceivable means, if the majesty, and therefore the integrity,
of the Empire, as well as the autonomy of the Republics
were to be preserved.   At the negotiations of Majuba,
President Kruger had promised the continuation of equal
treatment of new-comers with burghers, and that this
explicitly referred to the political franchise was explained
by Dr. Jorissen, one of the Transvaal negotiators.   In the
Convention of Pretoria of 1881 the grant of self-government
was to "all the inhabitants," not merely the Boer inhabitants
of the Transvaal.   The letter of invitation of December 13th,
1883, by the Secretary of the Transvaal deputation to
London, addressed to European investors and immigrants,
expressed indignation at being asked to furnish assurances
of fair treatment ; but the High Commissioner took his
stand on none of these contractual rights over which lawyers
might argue.   The majesty—the integrity—of the Empire,
the loyalty of its South African citizens were at stake, and this
gave rights to the Imperial Government apart from contract.

Therefore, at the Conference at Bloemfontein, the demand of a real and not illusory franchise, and substantial representation in the legislation of the Transvaal was put first. As it was not conceded, a thing of gins and pitfalls being proffered instead, it was also the last. Nothing but this minimum demand could remove the menace to the Empire by establishing race equality and bringing the Republic into friendly co-operation with the Imperial Government.

Now, many Imperialists, including several Reform prisoners, expressed to me after the Conference, and even quite recently, their satisfaction that this minimum demand of Sir Alfred Milner at Bloemfontein was not acceded to, and that the Conference failed.*

These objections were put to me in this way : Either the Franchise Law would be evaded in administration, or an omnipotent Volksraad, three-fourths Boer, would alter the law when Sir Alfred Milner, in the course of time, was promoted to some other sphere of public service, and a more pliable High Commissioner took his place, or British subjects in the Transvaal, unwilling to forfeit their citizenship of the Empire, would decline to take the franchise, no matter how liberal or genuine, and so no Uitlander majority could be obtained in the election of President or Commandant-General; and, therefore, the last state of the Uitlander would be wore than the first, as they would have exhausted the fore of their appeal to the Imperial Government and the British public, who would say to them : " Now you can work out you own salvation."

A little consideration will show that these objections are not well founded. In the first place, guarantees, embodied in a new Convention, providing that the franchise was genuine, and not subject to variation or repeal without the express consent of the Imperial Government, would necessarily be insisted upon. In the next place, an Imperial Act

* Some of my Imperialist friends of the Imperial Light Horse, and of the Guides, were also good enough to add that they were glad that the Republican Governments would not listen to my advice ; as, if adopted, it would have averted war.

of Parliament could easily be framed, providing that British subjects, naturalised in the Transvaal, could regain their British nationality by going to British territory; and also, of course, that a reciprocal franchise in British territory would be granted to Transvaal burghers who applied. A rather close precedent for such a law is provided by the Swaziland Conventions of 1890 and 1894, by which British residents in Swaziland were granted political franchise in the Transvaal.

The result of these combined provisions would obviously be that every British resident in the Transvaal would accept the franchise. And what would instantly follow, under the law of the Transvaal?

In the first place, rifles; rifles supplied by the State at the public expense to all the new citizens. In the next, the power of electing the Commandant-General, which carried necessarily with it the control of the forts and of the artillery in Johannesburg and Pretoria. Again, the power of electing the President, which also involved the control, and if necessary dismissal, of all officials in the permanent public service. And last, and not least, the complete control of the municipalities of Johannesburg and Barberton, and other mining centres.

Of these rights, clearly, the rifles—the immediate arming of the British inhabitants, would be the greatest. To ensure the control of the forts and artillery it would not be necessary for the new voters to elect a new Commandant-General, or, to control the officials, even a new President. General Joubert was a very enlightened man; President Kruger would be a changed man in the presence of 80,000 British rifles. In a word, all officials would have to play to the pit instead of the gallery. A Plantagenet might safely be trusted with privileges by an England in arms, privileges destructive of English rights when exercised by James I.*

* In the recent occupation of Johannesburg, Lord Roberts re-appointed the Boer Commandant of the Town, and his subordinate officials. It is obvious that though the person remained, the *mot d'ordre* was changed; British bayonets being prevalent.

The change in the position of the British inhabitants would be immediate; the change in the *personnel* of the officials need not be other than gradual.

To my mind, one of the clearest proofs of the complete efficacy of the High Commissioner's proposed franchise was that the Young Afrikander advisers of the two Executives of Pretoria and Bloemfontein advised its prompt rejection. They saw that a real, and not an illusory, franchise would destroy the purely Boer domination in the Republic, and with it their nucleus in Pretoria, their control of arms and gold, wherewith to build up a Boer dominion over all South Africa.

It remains for me to give here, as fairly as I can, an appreciation of the High Commissioner's policy and method of carrying it out, as derived from a careful consideration, among other things, of his published despatches, and from personal interviews in Bloemfontein and Cape Town. I may say that I came to the consideration of the subject with no predisposition whatever in its favour, rather the reverse, as the past history of Colonial Office appointments in South Africa has not been very encouraging; and even the policy of the Colonial Office with reference to the Transvaal as, for instance, in the Suzerainty controversy, before the present High Commissioner took a stand of his own, left something to be desired.

The High Commissioner deserves credit for being the first to see and to proclaim the great Imperial issues involved in the dispute with the Transvaal, both as to the Imperial control of its foreign relations, and to its treatment of the Uitlanders. Even the Uitlanders themselves had not insisted on this, the all-important aspect of the situation.

As to his methods, of slow and patient investigation, of accessibility to all parties in the State, and taking every pains to ascertain Dutch as well as British Colonial views, I have shown that they even excited suspicion among Imperialists. They were methods the very reverse of those of the purely imaginary "prancing pro-consul" of Mr. Gladstone's burning periods.

The objects aimed at by that policy, on which it has chiefly been challenged, relate to war, and the independence of the two Dutch States.   As regards the prospects of war, mere quietism and inaction would never have averted it. On the first international trouble in which the Empire was involved, the dominant Young Afrikander Governments of the Republics would have moved.   Unless, indeed, that was anticipated by the disgusted British Colonials taking the law into their own hands and marching to the relief of their kinsmen in the Transvaal, in which civil war the Imperial Government would of course be immediately involved.   For the threats of British Colonials throwing off the Imperial connection and making terms with the Boer, though no doubt meant when uttered, I do not think more than the petulance of just indignation at Imperial betrayal, though as to this I am not certain.   But if this were the third one of three courses, one of which was inevitable, this again meant war for the Empire, and one ten times more terrible than the present.   The High Commissioner's policy was the sole one that made for peace.

The independence of the Republic in the legitimate sense of that term, its freedom from external interference and its perfect autonomy, provided a régime of liberty and political equality for all civilised men were established, has never been threatened by that policy.   Of this I am convinced, not alone by the High Commissioner's personal assurance to myself, but from a dispassionate consideration both of his methods and of what would be, if it were attainable, the most advantageous course to the Empire, to Europeans in South Africa, and to their mission of civilisation.   As I have already stated, as my reason for supporting the independence of the Republics—constituted on a basis of equal rights for civilised men—I had hoped that their maintenance would conciliate the Dutch historic preference for Republican forms, and so promote the gradual fusion of Europeans in South Africa, which must be the aim of European statesmen of wider views.   In this way, the self-ruling people of the two Republics would no longer have cause for race division, and would gradually fall into line with the world-wide Empire—a fusion towards which the first step would be the Confederation of all South African States under Imperial protection. It would not be the first time that the Empire sheltered a Republic within its bounds. The Seven Isled Republic rested once under the *Pax Britannica*, until that Minister, afterwards to live to be the Premier of Majuba Hill, ceded, as High Commissioner, the Ionian Islands to Greece.

But, above all things, the conservation of that glorious heritage of the past, the Imperial power, so lightly regarded even now by some of our fellow-citizens, has been shown, by the desperate war being waged, to have been jeopardised by the policy against which was set the action challenged of the present Imperial representative. As I have shown, war was sought to be averted by that action; but, if that action had not been taken, war would soon have come in a worse form.*

* This book deals with policies and actions of persons rather than with appreciation of persons. Nevertheless, as it conveys a public moral, may I ask my countrymen to reflect what reason had they to expect that any Imperial representative, in full sight of a century's examples of Imperial vacillation and ingratitude, would be found at a crisis of the Empire's fate to reject a safe quietism for a path of duty almost certainly involving loss of fortune and fame and career?

The pathetic figure of a Frere going to his grave in obloquy, denounced by a wizard of eloquence—obloquy now, indeed, to be remedied by the slow wisdom of a tardy bust—might well have served to deter.

CHAPTER XXII.

MY LAST REMONSTRANCE.

ALMOST immediately after the Conference of Bloemfontein, I returned to Pretoria. The failure of the Conference to end as the Afrikander Party had hoped it would—in the High Commissioner's accepting an illusory scheme of franchise— had somewhat disconcerted their leaders. The High Commissioner—unlike some of his predecessors, as the old President ruefully recalled—had shown most unexpected firmness and penetration in dealing with the negotiators of the simple pastoral State. Still, the Afrikanders persuaded the Volksraad that it was merely a splendid chess move in the detested British game of diplomacy. They proceeded to try a long series of tedious and fatuous jugglings with issues soon to become so terrible. I made one last effort to awaken their misled people to the realities so soon to be upon them. I conversed with many members of the Volksraad, who were very courteous and willing to hear, and evidently doubtful whether, after all, as I had rightly foretold the Imperial policy before the Conference—and predicted the failure of the Conference, on the ground on which it failed—I might not now also be in the right as to the necessity of redressing without delay the Uitlander grievances, of unreservedly accepting the Bloemfontein minimum, and of working on the policy of Sir John Brand, in thorough accord with the Imperial power.

My views on the critical nature of the situation having become known—partly owing to an imperfect version of my memorandum of the 1st June having been published in a

Johannesburg journal—I was requested by a representative
of the Pretoria *Press*,* a Government organ, to explain my
views to the general public, already explained to the
Executives and Volksraads in memoranda.

The *Press* of Pretoria of 13th June, 1899, accordingly
published a report of an interview between its representative and myself, from which the following extracts are
appended :—

The situation is one of extreme gravity. There is a distinct danger
of war, a danger not fully realised by many in both Republics. As far
as I can see I do not think there is any party in the Republics desirous
of precipitating actual (and immediate) war. But I am certain that a
want of knowledge of the actual conditions of English politics and of the
character and power of English statesmen, and of the present state of
English public opinion with reference to the Republics and the status of
the Uitlander, has led many men of influence in public affairs here to
believe that war is impossible, and that therefore extreme steps may be
taken, either in the direction of a denial of the rights claimed on behalf
of the Uitlander, or of a demeanour towards the Imperial Government
which, in my opinion, is unwise, without incurring any risk of actual
warfare. Many here apparently think, even yet, that the Imperial
Government is not in earnest in championing the claims of the Uitlanders
to political rights. Possibly they will continue their disbelief until an
actual concentration of troops on the border convinces them too late, when
a spark may cause an explosion. I do not think that any true friend of
the Republics or of the burghers should keep silence under such
circumstances.

The High Commissioner gave me his views fully at Bloemfontein. I
have seen nearly all the public men in all States and Colonies of South
Africa, and all appear to me to be much more impressed than here in
Pretoria with the gravity of the crisis and the necessity of the redress of
the grievances of the Uitlanders. It will be readily agreed, I think, tha
the attitude of other countries endorses this view. The attitude of
Germany, evidenced through the fact of the Anglo-German Agreement
with reference to the Rhodesian railways and telegraphs—the position of
France with reference to the Dreyfus agitation precluding its taking part
in outside matters—and the recent *rapprochement* of the United States
and Great Britain, seem to me to indicate a strengthening of the position
of Great Britain. It must also be remembered that only a small section

---

* The assistant editor, Mr. Williams, now serving with General
Buller's force in Natal.

of the British public exercise an influence on foreign affairs, viz., the educated upper and middle class, from which the officers of the Army and Navy are drawn. While there is, of course, a warlike feeling among the greater part of this section, they have a strong sense of justice, and they will sanction no war except for what seems to them a just cause. But it is not merely on the ground of the possibility of armed intervention, but of the necessity of doing justice, that steps should be taken to meet the just demands of the resident Uitlanders for equality of treatment as to political rights; and the burghers of the Republics have always wished to have justice and right on their side.

The present claim put forward on behalf of the Uitlanders by the Imperial Government is a purely political question, and avowedly is not based on any rights secured to the British Government or its subjects under Conventions with the Republics. Therefore, no question of the legal interpretation of the stipulations of those Conventions can arise at all. The Imperial Government claims political rights for its subjects resident in the Republic, not under the Conventions, but on account of its predominant interest in the peace of the whole of South Africa, and its concern for the welfare of its subjects resident in the territory of the Republic. There is, evidently, no room here for lawyers' arguments.

I am in favour of the widest possible extension of the franchise consistent with the retention of a considerable majority in the Volksraad for the present burghers.*

The resident Uitlanders should have a strong minority representation. A qualifying term of residence of five years, dating from the actual commencement of the residence, seems reasonable. With a settled scheme of redistribution there can be no prospect of overwhelming the power of the old burghers.†

I have no hesitation in saying that I have always maintained that to apply a wide and liberal interpretation to the provisions of the Conventions with the British Government is the right course to follow; and that controversies on trivial matters, and on any matters as far as possible, should be avoided. I hold that it is unsound to interpret international agreements of this kind in any merely technical way, such as might be defended in reference to a commercial contract drawn up by a solicitor. Critics may consider this as applying ethics or politics to the interpretation of Conventions. I consider it merely the application of common sense. And I also hold that a courteous and friendly reception should invariably be accorded to any proposition as to the interpretation of the Conventions put forward on behalf of the Imperial Government. It is undignified on the part of a small State; it is dangerous, inasmuch

---

* The Bloemfontein Minimum.
† This was pointed out by the High Commissioner at the Conference.

as it plays into the hands of the war party which exists in every great State, and it is unjust to the great Power which guards the seas and preserves the peace of South Africa to adopt any line of controversy capable of being regarded as discourteous.

With regard to the claim for equal political rights, advanced by the British Government on behalf the Uitlanders, this claim by the Imperial Government marks a perfectly new point of departure. In view of the predominant interest of the British Empire in the peace and order of South Africa and the welfare of the immediate subjects of the Empire, this measure might easily have been foreseen as natural and inevitable. It is evident from the proceedings of the Bloemfontein Conference that the Imperial Government, as represented by the High Commissioner, have no desire to set aside the independence of the Republics. Their claim is, substantially, to secure for British residents in the Republic treatment somewhat analagous to the treatment accorded to citizens of the Republics in British territories. The law of the Orange Free State is more liberal than the claim now made on behalf of the British residents in the South African Republic.

The maintenance of the independence of the Republic must necessarily be the first care of the Volksraad. All Europeans, even those who are not African by birth, can sympathise with this desire. Apart from being a matter of the immediate personal concern of the burghers, all who consider the future of South Africa must regard it in the higher light of a trust which is committed to the Republics, to be carried out for the benefit of the present and future people of the European race in South Africa.

What the Republics now should realise is that to preserve that independence, which is a heritage for the benefit of all South Africa, the stranger within the gate must be considered. And, again, quite apart from any consideration of the desirability of maintaining the independence of the Republics, the claim of the Uitlander to participate in political privileges is one founded on considerations of justice, equity, and international usage.

These were my last words to the Governments and the burghers of the Boer Republics.

CHAPTER XXIII.

AFRIKANDER NEGOTIATION: FROM THE CONFERENCE OF BLOEMFONTEIN TO THE ULTIMATUM.

THE Afrikander party, still believing that force would never be resorted to by the Imperial Government, and knowing British unpreparedness for war, and still resolute on refusing any franchise that was other than a pretence, tried, as regards the Imperial Government, a policy of illusory offers and wearying delay; towards the Uitlanders one of " *Divide et impera.*"

Negotiations had been opened with the capitalists in the preceding March to endeavour to detach them from the Uitlander cause by the offer to grant them greater facilities for working the mines, by reducing the price of dynamite, and other such concessions. When it was found that it was impossible to separate them from the rest of the Uitlanders in their demand for political reform, the proposed concessions were promptly withdrawn by the State Secretary, after an acrimonious correspondence. Similar attempts were now made to detach the Jews by promising to relieve them of their political disabilities under the Grond Wet—a promise, it is needless to say, never kept.

The negotiations with the Imperial Government extend from the 9th June, the date of a despatch of State Secretary Reitz, to the 22nd September, the date of the reply of the Colonial Secretary—that he deemed it useless to continue the discussion, and that the Imperial Government would proceed to formulate its own proposals.

It may be divided into two sections as to time, one very

long, from the 9th of June to 10th September; the other from the 10th September until the 22nd.

In the first stage of three months, the Afrikander party's idea was that the Imperial Government were not really in earnest. They would never fight, however they might bluster. They were known to be unprepared.

Finding, after three months, the Imperial Government unexpectedly firm, and a body of about 5000 British troops from India having been sent to Natal, the Afrikander State Secretary at Pretoria and the Executive Councillor at Bloemfontein decided that a still bolder front would surely cause the Imperial Government to withdraw from the position for which they were not really going to fight. So, without knowing, the young Afrikander party made a fatal move. It meant irrevocably war. About the 10th September the burgher commandoes were ordered to the Natal border.

In three weeks, precisely as I had predicted in the interview in the Pretoria *Press* of the 13th June, a spark on the border caused the explosion. It was not from a concentration of Imperial troops but of burgher levies that the occasion arose. The veldt Boer on the border was intended to frighten the Imperial Government out of its supposed policy of pretence and bluster. The Imperial Government, never having been pretending or blustering in its demand for equality for the Uitlander, was not deterred in the least by the apparition of commandoes on the border.

On the receipt of the Colonial Secretary's reply of the 22nd September, closing the discussion, the Afrikander party, at long last, saw that they had fatally miscalculated the spirit and purpose of the Imperial Government, and that the clock had struck for war. Even then they might have tried more delay, waiting for foreign complications, if delay were open to them.

But the monster evoked by the Pretoria Frankenstein was not to be laid. The veldt Boer, absolutely certain as to his superiority in arms to the despised red-coat, got out of hand, and insisted on seizing the formidable strategical positions on the borders of Natal.

The insolent ultimatum of the 9th October was not intended in the least as a diplomatic document; the deciding on war had already passed out of the hands of State Secretary Reitz and Executive Councillor Fischer. It was the parting insult of a player at a desperate game, who sees he has under-estimated his adversary's intelligence and courage and skill, and knows that nothing has been left him by the chances of fate and fortune but a mad appeal to force.

Understanding, so well as I do, the series of evasions and devices the kaleidoscopic succession of supposed offers of franchise really were, I could not find patience to attempt to summarise them, but that it is alleged even by some people in England that the faulty diplomacy of the Imperial Government caused the war. There was no faulty diplomacy on the British side after the Conference at Bloemfontein; at least, in the direction of being peremptory. If anything, it was too patient.

As I have shown, war was forced on the Afrikander leaders by the veldt Boer. But it was they who sent the veldt Boer to the border; and there would have been no war if they had agreed to treat the Uitlander as a political equal.

But even if, with their eyes wide open, they had believed what I had told them—that the Imperial Government was in earnest, and would fight to the death sooner than see the Empire shattered as a result of the degradation of its citizens in the Transvaal—even if they had believed that assurance, I am convinced that, sooner than give up the political power, which all their lives they have dreamt of as the lever with which to build up a Dutch Afrikander Dominion, they would have deliberately gone to war; hoping for chances of foreign complications, of British party see-saw, of all the forces that for a hundred years have sprung up to unnerve the Imperial arm. They knew not how the spirit of the Empire, within one short generation, expanding with its ever-widening dominion, has entered into the souls of its citizens.*

It is a tedious task, but let me endeavour to state briefly the course of the correspondence.

On the 9th of June State Secretary Reitz addresses a note to the British Agent in Pretoria, containing a proposal for arbitration " on differences arising out of the varying interpretations, approved by the parties, of the terms of the London Convention of 1884."

In his despatch of the 14th June the High Commissioner observes :—

" The whole point and gist of my contention " (at Bloemfontein) " was that redress of Uitlander grievances must come first. . . . My proposals for a settlement of the Uitlander grievances on the basis of a moderate measure of enfranchisement having been rejected by the President, and a totally inadequate scheme put forward in their place, he now comes forward with an arbitration proposal. . . . I cannot see the smallest reason why Her Majesty's Government should not at once reject this particular proposal."

In a telegram of the 19th July the High Commissioner intimates that the Volksraad have passed a seven years, retrospective franchise, with multitudinous conditions.

In a despatch of the 27th July the Colonial Secretary suggests a Joint Inquiry by nominees of both Governments to ascertain and report on the practical reality and permanence of the franchise recently enacted. If such Joint Inquiry should result in a favourable report, then a new conference should be held to discuss the proposed Tribunal of Arbitration.

The Afrikander party know very well that their recent seven years' retrospective franchise law is quite illusory ; they do not like any Joint Inquiry. So, in the first place,

---

* I find that Sir William Dunn, M.P., for several years Consul-General of the Orange Free State in London, has come to a like conclusion. In a speech delivered in Scotland on the 6th June, he states : " While the Raid undoubtedly hastened the outbreak of hostilities, the Dutch had, long before that date, been doing all that they could to undermine British supremacy in South Africa, and were simply biding their time until they saw their way clear to striking an effective blow."

their State Attorney offers a simplified seven years' franchise,
on condition that there should be no inquiry.*

The British Agent was unwilling to accept less than the
Bloemfontein Minimum of five years' retrospective franchise.†

* High Commissioner's despatch, 15th August.

† Immediately preceding the illusory offer of a five years' retrospective franchise, the negotiations at Pretoria were being conducted
through the medium of interviews between the British Agent, Sir
Conyngham Greene, and Mr. Smuts, the Transvaal State Attorney.

Mr. Smuts subsequently had the hardihood to accuse Her Majesty's
Agent of "tricking" and "decoying" him, by misleading promises of
accepting his conditions, into making an offer of a five years' retrospective
franchise. This accusation startled and shocked the British public at
home, and helped to give them some slight inkling of the calibre and
character of the young Afrikander negotiators.

As I told the British Agent at the time, if he had known Young
Afrikander methods and persons as well as I did, he would probably have
preferred to conduct his negotiations through the medium of writing,
instead of personal interview. Sir Conyngham Greene's diplomatic
experience in civilised lands, such as Holland and Greece—and Persia—
had misled him as to what he was reasonably justified in expecting. A-
veneer of European civilisation is at times disconcerting.

The deceit of the typical Young Afrikander is scathingly dealt with by
Advocate J. W. Wessels in his speech which appears in the Appendix. I
have no comment to make on that speech, except that I think my friend
Mr. Wessels under-estimates—or at least does not insist upon—one of the
greatest causes of Young Afrikander depreciation of British character and
power. It is the illusion of half knowledge and deficient insight. The
saying "No man is a hero to his valet" is often quoted as if it were
depreciation of the man, instead of criticism of the valet. To appreciate
a great painting one need not be a painter, but one must have some slight
degree of artistic feeling. To appreciate a high character or a high
intellect, one must have some insight springing from the presence,
although it may be, in a lower degree, of the qualities to be appreciated;
whereas the valet can only see the exterior, and—this is the irony of it—
he thinks he knows everything about his master. A man who can see
nothing but the foibles of some of the officers of our Imperial army is
really worse off towards correctly estimating British military efficiency
than if he had never met a British soldier in his life.

In an interesting work by Messrs. John Scoble (an old resident of
Pretoria) and H. R. Abercrombie, 'The Rise and Fall of Krugerism,' the
following instructive passage, illustrative of educated Young Afrikander
diplomacy, occurs:—

"Towards the middle of last year, and just after the termination of
the Bloemfontein Conférence, a bold attempt was made to inculpate
certain persons alleged to be officers holding Her Majesty's commission
in the army as conspirators against the State. Some half-dozen persons
were arrested during one night and taken to Pretoria, where they were
incarcerated in the common gaol upon a charge of high treason. For
some time these persons were kept in prison, and strenuous efforts were
made by officials and one or two of the persons arrested to induce the

Next, we have State Secretary Reitz's despatch of the
22nd of August offering a five years' retrospective franchise,

---

principals to make a confession of guilt or guilty knowledge of a plotting
to overthrow the Government of the Republic. With great difficulty the
principals managed to communicate with Mr. Conyngham Greene, Her
Majesty's agent at Pretoria, and he took the necessary steps to bring the
matter to an issue. The State Attorney, Mr. Smuts, approached Mr.
Greene, and offered to withdraw from the prosecution upon the ground
that he felt reluctant to proceed against men holding commissions in the
British army. Mr. Greene, however, knew what this cunning suggestion
meant, and after consulting the Colonial Secretary, Mr. Chamberlain,
informed the State Attorney that the British Government insisted upon
the matter being sifted to the bottom, and that an advocate was to be
appointed to defend the accused. For this purpose Mr. Greene procured
the services of Messrs. Tancred & Lunnon as attorneys for the defence,
and they appointed Mr. Advocate Duxbury as counsel. The Government
was in consequence forced to proceed with the investigation, and preliminary examinations extending over several days took place. It then
appeared that some of the secret agents of the Government had been
imprisoned intentionally, with the object of enabling them to gain
incriminating evidence, and of becoming State witnesses at the trial.
Mr. Duxbury subjected these gentry to such a severe cross-examination
as to fully expose the intention of the plot, which was to identify the
Imperial Government, through the agency of British military officers,
with a revolutionary propaganda in the Transvaal, and thereby justify
the hostile attitude which the Transvaal intended to adopt. Through
the able efforts of the counsel engaged for the defence the charge broke
down completely, and eventually, the Government deciding not to
proceed with the case, the accused were released from custody. At this
time the authorities of the Republic shrank from no means to further
their end, and the case in question seems to us one very nearly
approaching to the crime of subornation of perjury. The secret agents,
having their instructions from the head of the department, were ordered
to make the necessary affidavits against these British subjects so as to
set the criminal law in motion; and these same wretches were set on the
watch to entrap persons who allowed themselves to audibly condemn the
actions of the Government.

"The suggestion made by the State Attorney, that he would abandon
proceedings if desired by the British Government, is essentially Krugerian.
If Mr. Greene or Mr. Chamberlain had fallen into the trap, the Transvaal
Government would have claimed that the charge was so absolutely true
that the British Government was afraid of the circumstances being dragged
into the light of day, and it would have been used as a reason for the
earlier declaration of war. As it is, there can be little doubt that the mass
of the people believed that it was only by the vigilance of the Government
that a serious conspiracy against the independence of the Republic was
brought to light, and the fact of the State Attorney declining to prosecute
was solely in deference to the wish of the British Government, and, therefore, a magnanimous forbearance on the part of the Transvaal. The report
on the proceedings at the preliminary examination has been published in

providing the Imperial Government comply with the following singularly reasonable conditions :—

First,—The Joint Inquiry to be waived.

a recent Blue Book, and it shows clearly the quality of the means used by the Government in order to gain the desired end.

"The circumstances relative to the illicit purchases of gold under the authority of the Government have often been dwelt on, but the charge of purchasing gold amalgam brought against a certain Count de Sarigny, and the State Attorney's interference, is perhaps less generally known. The accused was discharged before evidence could be adduced, simply because it would have involved the Government in the scandalous affair. Sufficient, however, leaked out to show that a system of permits was instituted by which certain persons were held free of damage in case of being detected in purchasing gold. The ostensible reason for the institution of special permits was to ascertain how and by whom the thefts of gold were made from the batteries of the mining companies. That was a sufficient reason for the adoption of extraordinary means in order to ensure the destruction of a system of pilfering which had grown up on the Rand gold fields. But it is a remarkable fact that not a single amalgam thief has been discovered through this agency, while there is reason to believe that the gold bought under special permit has not been less than £750,000 in value. It is difficult to trace gold obtained by theft or by the authorised robbery countenanced by the Government; but it is pretty certain that a considerable amount of the stolen gold found its way to agents stationed at Delagoa Bay, where the price of amalgamated and cyanide gold is openly quoted."

The methods and the civilised regrets of the Young Afrikander are well expressed in the following extract from a despatch appearing in the London *Times*, dated, Pretoria, May 22 :—

"To-day I have had conversations on the present situation with President Kruger and Mr. Smuts, the State Attorney. In discussing the prospects of speedy peace Mr. Kruger said, with great emphasis, 'Unconditional surrender on our part is absolutely out of the question. The Transvaal will fight on until the greater part of her burghers are dead; but plenty of life remains to her yet.'

"Mr. Smuts declared that the Transvaal had no choice but to fight to the bitter end. The Republics were now well aware of their ultimate fate, but, for all that, the war would not be concluded for a long time yet. Speaking of the proposed destruction of the Johannesburg mines, Mr. Smuts said that he greatly regretted that Johannesburg should suffer, but that the Government had no choice in the matter, as the popular pressure upon them was too great to be resisted."

Mr. Smuts' regrets were spared, and the fiendish project of wrecking the mines and plunging into hopeless misery for years tens of thousands of innocent men, women and children—to which he was compelled by popular pressure to assent—was prevented from being accomplished by the action of Dr. Krause, the Boer Acting-Commandant of Johannesburg, who arrested the leader of the wreckers, sent by Mr. Smuts, the day before the surrender to Lord Roberts.

Second,—A definite promise of no more interference on behalf of the Uitlander.

Third,—An abandonment of the Suzerainty Claim.

Fourth,—An agreement to refer all future questions to Arbitration.

The object of these singular stipulations—if they were really expected to be accepted—is of course clear. If the Imperial Government promised never to interfere again, an omnipotent Volksraad could soon dispose of the five years'—or a five months'—retrospective franchise—if, indeed, it were not illusory from the first, in the stipulated absence of inquiry. So the Uitlander would still be repressed. If an agreement were made to submit all future disputes to arbitration, the Imperial Government's power of interfering in the foreign relations of the Republic would be reduced to a very small compass.

The stipulation that the Imperial Government is to agree not to " further insist on the assertion of the Suzerainty " is even more subtle and dangerous, taking the circumstances of the time into consideration. Let us, therefore, consider this at more length.

In his despatch of the 9th of May, the Afrikander State Secretary had quite shifted from its original position the discussion on the relationship between the Governments. The original contention of State Secretary Leyds in the despatch of the 16th of April, 1898, was that the Suzerainty preamble of the 1881 Convention was abolished, and that the 1884 Convention was the instrument defining the relationship. But State Secretary Reitz, on the 9th of May, 1899, took the strikingly original ground, that the Transvaal was a " Sovereign International State," whose rights did not spring from any Convention.

Now, seeing that the Imperial Government, in their despatch of the 13th July, 1899, had declared that " they had no intention of continuing to discuss this question," that was, for all practical purposes, all that a reasonable Transvaal Government could want. They would have heard no more of the Suzerainty.

What, then, was the political meaning of State Secretary Reitz's introducing the subject again, instead of letting it drop ? *

In the first place, we extort from the Imperial Government a formal promise not to reassert the Suzerainty. Now, the assertion of the Suzerainty, as most lawyers hold, was simply an error made in good faith, and was due solely to the fact that the Colonial Office relied on incorrect legal advice. (Why they did not procure competent advice, and why our War Office also made not very dissimilar mistakes, is another matter, not undeserving of the attention of the British people.) But a formal renunciation would be represented as an admission that the Imperial Government had been wilfully, instead of mistakenly, in the wrong, and had attempted an unjustifiable aggression. This sort of easily misrepresentable step no Great Power can afford to take.

In the next place, such a renunciation would instantly be represented to the Foreign Powers and to the veldt Boer as an admission of State Secretary Reitz's theory that the Transvaal was a Sovereign International State, whose right of self-government did not spring from the abandoned Suzerainty preamble or from any Convention.

It seems hardly likely, however, that the Afrikander party thought that these terms would be accepted.

The Colonial Secretary's despatch of the 28th of August intimates that the Imperial Government are willing to agree to a Unilateral Inquiry instituted by the British Agent, but cannot renounce the Imperial Government's right to interfere; can make no normal renunciation of the Suzerainty Claim; are willing to discuss Arbitration; and suggest a further Conference.

State Secretary Reitz in a despatch of the 2nd of September withdraws his offer of a five years' franchise as his remarkable conditions will not be accepted, and falls back on the already enacted seven years' franchise—pitfalls included.

* There were other than political meanings, but they are unimportant.

The Colonial Secretary's despatch of the 8th September refuses to go back to the seven years' franchise proposal, as the Imperial Government are satisfied it is insufficient; but is willing still to accept the lately proposed five years' franchise; assumes that the English language is to be used by the new Volksraad members; and suggests a new Conference to discuss the Arbitration and other outstanding questions.

Now we reach the fatal despatch of State Secretary Reitz of the 16th September, after the commandoes had been ordered out and sent to the Natal border. Pretoria will not agree to a five years' franchise unless on the conditions already imposed, and refuses the use of the English language in the Volksraad, but will now agree to a Joint Inquiry.

The reading of this remarkable diplomatic correspondence at this point should be accompanied by a war map. The explanation has already been given. It was the effect on the Imperial Government of the presence of commandoes on the Natal border that was awaited, more than the tenor of this despatch.

The reply of the Colonial Secretary of the 22nd September closes the discussion, and announces the intention of the Imperial Government to " formulate its own proposals for a final settlement of the issues which have been created in South Africa by the policy constantly followed for many years by the Government of the South African Republic."

Last comes that most insolent document, flushed with insane arrogance—the Ultimatum. It is, as has already been stated, not a diplomatic document at all. The Afrikander leaders saw that war had come upon them through the impatience of the veldt Boer; and now was their last chance of a parting greeting to the foe they had so fatuously contemned. Its modest demands deserve enumeration :—

First.—All matters of difference to be settled by Arbitration.

Second.—British troops on the borders to " be instantly withdrawn."

Third. —" All reinforcements of troops which have arrived in South

Africa since the 1st of June, 1899, shall be removed from South Africa."

Fourth.—"Her Majesty's troops which are now on the High Seas shall not be landed in any part of South Africa."

"An immediate and affirmative answer" is requested "before or upon Wednesday, 11th October, 1899, not later than 5 o'clock P.M."

Failure to accept these terms before 5 o'clock P.M. is to be regarded as a declaration of war.

Any further movement of British troops is also to be regarded as a declaration of war.

These terms would have been rejected with scorn by Montenegro. The Imperial Government is calmly requested to evacuate British territory and to recall British troops on the high seas.

Still, with all this insolence, even to the last is to be perceived the note of non-European subtleness. This arrogant Ultimatum attempts to lay the responsibility for a declaration of war on the Imperial Government, because, indeed, they will not evacuate British territory and will not prevent British troops from landing at British ports.

But, as has been seen, it was intended as nothing but a parting insult to the Imperial people and Government, whom the separatist Afrikander had foolishly despised since Majuba Hill. And so, once again, is the Chancellor Oxenstierna justified of his saying—" *Vides, mi fili, quantilla sapientia homines regantur.*"

CHAPTER XXIV.

ON WHICH SIDE WAS THE AGGRESSION?

FROM what has been seen of the methods and objects of the Afrikander in power in Pretoria and Bloemfontoin, it will be clear that the aggression and the making war was not on the side of the Imperial Government.

There was no aggression or undue or unwarrantable interference in the Imperial interposition to put an end, as a measure of self-defence, to an intolerable menace to the peace of South Africa and to the very existence of the Empire, involved in the presence of a formidable and hostile military Power on the border, ever ready to attack at a moment when the Empire should become involved in foreign complications. It was no aggression to intervene for the protection of the oppressed Uitlanders; it was an Imperial duty to citizens of the Empire and of friendly Powers; it was self-defence to prevent the growing disaffection of the Colonial Dutch.

This is the real justification of the Imperial position; the situation was so menacing and intolerable that it would have justified armed intervention and occupation of the Boer states.

I prefer to call attention to this—the real inwardness of the situation—rather than to the platform question, " Who struck the first blow?"

As a matter of fact, the militant Afrikander led his misguided people into striking the first blow, by seizing, annexing, and renaming British towns and territory in Natal and Cape Colony; and by looting and destroying houses and property of British citizens; and by cruelly expelling and maltreating the majority of the European inhabitants of the Transvaal.*

But, we are told, although it is admitted that the Boers struck the first blow, seized British territory and expelled and maltreated British citizens, still their action was only technically aggressive. Believing they were going to be attacked, they, in their simple way, took up defensive positions on alien soil. As Mr. Leonard Courtney put it, they, in entire innocence, took the Colonial Secretary's intimation that discussion was useless, and that the Imperial Govern-

* As it is not my intention to write in this book a history of the unprecedented scenes of the Exodus from the Transvaal, or of the progress of the war, I, therefore, deal with that unparalleled outrage on civilisation, by order of the Afrikanders in power in Pretoria, in connection with the question of the responsibility for the war. I resided near Johannesburg during most of the period, and had abundant proof of the misery wrought at the instance of the Afrikander office-holders, Secretary Reitz and State Attorney Smuts, who, as lawyers, advised the Pretoria Government to take this step. Johannesburg at last appreciated the educated Young Afrikander.

It is, of course, true that, under International Law, a State at war is entitled to order the withdrawal of subjects of the other belligerent. But here, if ever, must be applied the exception, " Summum jus, summa injuria." The general rule, taken from the custom of States in Europe, applied to far different circumstances. Nowhere in the history of the civilised world has the majority of the inhabitants of a territory, men, women, and children, been driven from their homes in which they have lived for years by an armed minority. There was no justification in military necessity, or otherwise, for advising the expulsion of these poor people.

The cruelty of the manner of the expulsion surpassed the injustice of the Afrikander order. Not even tolerable provision was made by Messrs. Reitz and Smuts for the transport of the expelled refugees. I have seen women and children huddled in open cattle trucks and coal waggons, exposed to the rain and the night, while the rough Boer, accustomed to sleep in the open veldt, was sent by Afrikander order to first-class carriages. Curae leves loquuntur ; ingentes silent.

In one political move, the Young Afrikander signally failed. A long list of prescription had been compiled, containing the names of the Reform prisoners, of the leaders of the South African League, and of others, such as editors and staffs of the Uitlander journals, who had made themselves obnoxious to the Afrikander leaders. Warrants of State Attorney Smuts for the arrest of these Uitlanders as hostages, under a fictitious charge of treason, were prevented from being executed by the timely flight of those proscribed, many of whom have since marched into Pretoria in the Uitlander corps.

ment would formulate its own proposals to end an intolerable position, as meaning, "Wait until I get my pistol and I shall renew the discussion."

Here, again, I prefer not to rely on a minor, though perfectly legitimate, answer, that re-naming of towns hardly is consistent with taking up more defensive positions on alien territory—even by a pastoral peasant. But the true reply is, that if their Afrikander leaders had fulfilled the obligations of justice, and the pledged faith of their people, to give fair treatment to the Uitlanders, and had abandoned their project of ousting British power from South Africa, there would have been no prospect of their being attacked.

In one sense, of course, more especially since the tide of war has turned, the Boers have waged a war of defence. But, looking through mere phrases to the reality beyond, the defence they carried on was not of their independence, in the sense of autonomy, on the basis of justice, equality and liberty to civilised inhabitants, but of the right to dominate, as a privileged oligarchy. In that sense, the war waged by the Confederate States of America was a merely defensive war—to retain the right to keep negroes in slavery.

In any case it was, with the Afrikander leaders, only a question of time and season. There is too vast an accumulation of proofs—apart from those supplied by the annexations and rebellions which have marked the course of the war—that active aggression on British territory at a favourable moment has long been designed.

Dominating every thought and action of the militant Afrikander party was one idea—that the Boer had an inherent superior right to the land of South Africa, in the Cape, in the Transvaal, everywhere, "Ons Land." The intolerable injustice of this assumption has already been pointed out. A plain deduction is that the assertion of their right was only a question of finding a favourable moment, when the Empire was at war with another great Power. This, in that world, the most formative of action, that of ideas. What of deeds and declarations?

Colossal armaments—a world's wonder—have been revealed to the astonished Empire. These were ordered, be it remembered, before the fortunate excuse, the Jameson Raid of 1895, occurred. When have such enormous stores of arms been collected with no intention to use them? What purposes of legitimate defence would require an accumulation of rifles, estimated to number five for every burgher of the two Boer States? For what purpose could they have been procured—rifles, however expensive, become obsolete in a few years—except for distribution among the Cape Dutch? And lastly, as a writer in Switzerland inquires, What can a small State of 250,000 inhabitants want with a Secret Service Fund of £300,000 a year? * The Imperial Government has not one-fourth of that sum.

An anti-British campaign for twenty years—the Press, the Platform, the Pulpit, the School—took care that the ideal of Dutch domination and British exclusion should not grow dim. Was this to last for ever? Would words never be transmuted into deeds?

Let this war answer. It has presented us the spectacle of 15,000 rebels in arms against the authority of the Empire, led by members of the Cape Assembly who had taken the oath of allegiance.

These, indeed, are proofs that all the world now can see. But no one who knew the mind of the separatist Afrikander could help seeing it before the war, through all the veils of diplomacy.

So far, I have considered the Boer side. What of the British? There is one all-sufficient proof that the Imperial Government at the outbreak of the war had not abandoned the hope of peaceful remonstrance yet being sufficient, and that war, if it could be avoided, was not designed. It was pointed out some time ago in a speech by the Prime Minister of Canada, Sir Wilfred Laurier. The Empire was unprepared: only a handful of troops were in South Africa.

This consideration leads one to understand why, although the Afrikander leaders in Pretoria and Bloemfontein would

* Professor Edouard Naville, of the Geneva University, 'The Transvaal Question,' p. 36.

have preferred postponing the war until the Empire was involved in complications, yet they distinctly—though to their minds not to any great extent—incurred the risk of precipitating the war by sending the Boer commandoes to the Natal border.

In the first place, they believed that the Imperial Government would give way, and that the risk of war was no appreciable. But, if the improbable were to occur, they calculated that they had a fair chance, either of complete triumph or of substantial gain.

At the best, should foreign complications, through Russian action in China or India, or French interference in Egypt, cause war with the Empire, triumph would ensue, and the name of the South African Republic would become a literally correct description—the territory being expanded to include all South Africa.

State Secretary Reitz reveals his hopes in an interview published in a French newspaper, the *Echo de Paris*.

" At present, Great Britain is most gloriously isolated, and the British Empire itself runs considerable risk of being vanquished. France and Russia have never had a finer chance to get rid of a troublesome enemy. Does France mean to allow this opportunity—the last she will ever have, perhaps—to pass without taking her revenge on the British? No! I am sure you will not, for such conduct would be nothing less than criminal. It would mean your destruction. Make a bold attempt for Egypt then, and extend your possessions in Tripoli. Fight, I say, even at the very improbable risk of being beaten. Follow our example. As for Russia, anyone can see that it is to her interest to incite India to rebellion."

And, at the worst, what would happen? Substantial improvement in the position of the Boer States in the direction of shaking off Imperial control. The fact that the British were unprepared, and had only a handful of troops, was thoroughly well-known. Also, too, the " neutrality " of Bond members—of the loyal section; and the active assistance of thousands of rebels in the Cape and Natal—of the militant section. Their gigantic secret armaments were well known to themselves; and also that they were quite competent to use the large cannon—a fact of which the British

War Office apparently was not aware, although they knew of
the existence of the guns.

The Afrikander leaders, therefore, quite correctly counted
upon a series of initial British reverses, and, with fatal
reliance on the Colonial Office and British party precedents
of the past, expected that the Imperial Government, to save
further loss of blood and treasure, would assent to a weak
compromise, granting the Boer States a freer hand—with
which to prepare for a future war of extermination—and the
abolition of Imperial control over Transvaal foreign relations.

Fortunately for the Empire, the Afrikander leaders'
reliance on the paralysing of the Imperial arm, through
British party spirit, British humanitarianism, British altruism
(of the vicarious variety), and on the supposed want of
patriotism of British shopkeeper and workman, has failed
them for once, and the long tale of Imperial vacillation has
ended.*

From the purely military point of view, it is now agreed
on all sides that the Boer forces did not make the best of
their opportunities of immediate success, which were vastly
greater than even now is generally appreciated.   Military
men are agreed that if the Boer forces had moved on the
11th September instead of the 11th October, their army of
40,000 men could have swept through all Natal to the sea,
and occupied Durban, as the Indian reinforcements had not
arrived, and there were only a few thousand troops in all
Natal.   Or, even when they began the war, in October, † if

---

* An instance of Young Afrikander hopes which fell within my
personal experience will illustrate.   In Johannesburg, soon before the
Exodus of the Uitlanders, a member, though a not very convinced one, of
the separatist Afrikander party, who is a judge of the Transvaal, came to
see me about a legal question.   He expressed his regret that my pacific
counsels had not been adopted—the war party being too powerful, and
not having, until then, realised that it was mere " bluff " on the side of
the Imperial Government.   " However," he said, " we cannot help it
now ; we shall win at the beginning and for a long time, and then the
British will get so tired of the loss of lives and expense, that we shall get
better terms and a new Convention."   I replied, " You will get no Convention, and you will have no Republic."

† But for the foresight of the Premier, Colonel Hime, the Indian
reinforcements would not have been sent.

they had neglected Ladysmith and Kimberley—leaving a comparatively small force at the passes of Natal and at the diamond fields (where there were only 500 troops)—they could have seized the Hex River Mountain passes, and marched straight to Cape Town. There would have been from 50,000 to 100,000 rebels in arms in the Cape Colony— as it was there were 15,000—and there were no British troops to stop them.

The ultimate end, of course, would be the same, as the Imperial Government would have to reconquer the Cape, or the Empire would perish. But the magnitude of the task—the amount of time and lives and money would dwarf to insignificance the present war, heavy though the burthen has been.

CHAPTER XXV.

THE PRINCIPLES OF THE SETTLEMENT: MEASURES NECESSITATED BY THE WAR.

IT may be seen that, while the title of this book relates to the settlement after the war, hitherto I have dealt with the history of Boer and Briton in South Africa for the last century, the attitude of the Boer towards the Briton, the separatist Afrikander propaganda since Majuba Hill, and its fatal sequence in the action of the separatist Afrikander, lately in power in the Boer States.

My reason for approaching the subject of the re-settlement of South Africa in this manner is that it presented the only way of showing the crucial determinant of the immediate course of settlement necessitated by the war. I have endeavoured to present the mind of the Boer people, led and leaders, one, and the greatest, of the factors which must determine. The mind of our own people we know; as to that of the Kaffirs and other subject races we may form conjectures.

That the result of the present war will, if not at once, in the early future, modify the attitude of the Boer and lessen his depreciation of the Briton, we have reason to hope. But one campaign, however victorious, cannot obliterate a century's mistakes.

For some years to come, therefore, we must take as constant factors all those disruptive tendencies, in veldt Boer and separatist Afrikander, which I have described at length. The immediate and necessary conclusion, therefore, is that no separate existence outside the Empire can be left to the Boer States. Like causes would produce like effects in the future as in the present. Annexation of the territories must be absolute.

The same spirit exists in the Boer leaders—the militant Afrikanders, who even now ascribe their defeat to *force majeure* hostility to the Imperial Government; dislike and envy and jealousy of the unwarlike British-born colonist.* The same spirit still exists in the veldt Boer; their present defeats are only chastisings by the Lord, who will remember His people in good time and set them in strength again. They still are a slow and stubborn and patient people.

The recent annexation of the territory, lately the Free State, as the Orange River Colony may seem to some to render these reflections needless, in face of the *fait accompli ;* but that is not so. Unless the principles which direct annexation are clearly apprehended, there is danger, not so much of the annexation being reversed—although that occurred before in the Orange River Territory—but of hopes being entertained of a reversal; and, more serious still, of the internal reorganisation of the territories of the Boer States being conducted on lines which ignore the basic fact —the condition of the mind of the Boer people.

Intercourse, commerce, intermarriage, education, but, above all, time, must be waited for—until the growth of a local South African patriotism, common to all, of British or Dutch descent, and as loyal to the Empire as Australian or Canadian national feeling, has dispelled in its light the dark shadow of sixteenth-century tribal exclusiveness, which has wrought such evil in our day.

It is to be remembered also that, in view of the mental

---

* Mr. J. A. Hobson, in his book, 'The War in South Africa,', written from the standpoint of one favourably inclined towards the Boer side, states: "The able young judge put this point most impressively to me. . . . 'But conquered and humbled by Great Britain, our respect will turn to rancour; we shall submit only because we must, and so long as we must; the spirit of freedom will not die, and the Republics, which might have been in friendly alliance with Great Britain, will remain permanent centres of disaffection, waiting an opportunity to strike a blow.' "

attitude of the colonists of British descent in South Africa, Imperial statesmen cannot afford to make any more mistakes; enough has been made in the past to strain loyalty almost to breaking point. And never should it be forgotten what a menace would be the disaffection and scorn of the subject native races, consequent on any failure of their British rulers to see the facts of the hour which threaten the stability of the Imperial rule.

For the maintenance of that Imperial rule, charged with its share of the destined mission of the European race in the world; for the fusion of the European race in South Africa, a necessary means towards that end; for the good of Kaffir in Africa and India in our Eastern dominion; for the upholding of the confederation of the Empire, the most glorious instrument of justice which the world has seen—the menace to its heart, inherent in any persistence of an alien power, animated by racial antagonism in the midst of our South African dominion, must be removed; and not merely be removed, but must never be suffered to recur—never again.

Therefore must there be absolute and permanent annexation of these territories to the Empire; and obliteration of artificial barriers between races and territories marked out by the deeds of the past and the physical facts of the present, to be one.

The war has reaped a heavy harvest of the patriot dead, who flocked from lands of the snow and the sun, and laid down their lives for the Empire, and for the spread of justice, and liberty, and happiness to their fellow-men which the Empire means. The survivors, and the Government of the Empire, are trustees to posterity of the fruits of their heroic deeds. Canada, and Australia and New Zealand, as well as the Home Country, have paid their share of the toll. And South Africans as well: from the Helot of the Transvaal, who with the people of Natal—numbering in all less than an English town—bore the fiercest shock of invasion; to the British colonist in the Cape, distracted with doubts of once again being abandoned by the Imperial Power; to the loyalists of Dutch descent, who have undergone the bitterest test of all.

The two aspects of the problem of the settlement after the war relate, on the one hand, to what is palpably necessary—the territorial and constitutional settlement of the annexed territories ; and, on the other, to the reorganisation of the Imperial machinery of government, with a view to preventing those errors in the past which have borne such evil fruits ; a reorganisation, the necessity of which is not so palpable and inevitable, but yet is most urgently required, lest worse come.

As regards the settlement of the territory of the Boer States, the principles should first be clearly fixed on our minds.

The first is the conservation of the integrity of the Empire, and of the Imperial hold on South Africa. For this end other things and places will urgently require consideration ; but the question now is as regards the Boer territories.

To promote the fusion of the Dutch and British people, and to prevent the prospects of future war between British and Dutch, furnishes again a necessary principle.

And, again, the conciliation of Dutch sentiment towards the Imperial Government, as far as compatible with Imperial supremacy, must inevitably find its place. And, not at all to be forgotten, the conciliation of British sentiment in these territories.

Lastly, the promotion of the federation of South Africa— for the good of South Africa and of the Empire as well—to counteract and extinguish the separatist tendency.

Bearing these principles in mind, it becomes clear in the light of past and present dangers—of Boer and Afrikander sentiment and the danger of leaving it to be exploited by enemies of the Empire—the institution of Crown Colony government for some years to come is plainly inevitable. Any immediate institution of representative government, in which the Boer inhabitants were admitted to the suffrage, would mean transferring the fight from the kopjes to the ballot-box. An electoral system in which the Boer had no vote would mean erecting an Uitlander oligarchy ; and there is reason to fear an ideal kind of government would not be the result, besides the inevitable consequence of perpetuating race feeling.

It has been suggested that it might be well to consider the advisability of fixing a period within which Crown Colony government would come to an end. In this way two dangers would be avoided. Crown Colony government, like all kinds of government, including a Pretoria oligarchy, tends to perpetuate itself. Vested interests, family and personal influences, would rapidly cluster around it; and no one ever heard of the most minute, however patriotic, of German principalities consenting to be mediatised. If perpetuated, it would create an atmosphere alien to the freedom which is the breath of the Empire. It would ultimately diminish the strength of the territory as an integral portion of the Empire; and it would deter the most desirable class of British citizens, who have "reverence for the laws themselves have made," from immigrating. The second danger, which the fixing a period to Crown Colony government would avert, is that of premature agitation. If it is known at what period representation in a legislative assembly would be granted to the inhabitants of the new Colonies—assuming they are two, instead of one—then there would be no motive, unless the intermediate period were too long for agitation. But this is a matter calling for prolonged and careful investigation of the local conditions.*

---

* As well as the reasons based on the struggle between British and Boer, necessitating the postponement of the introduction of representative institutions, there are others arising from the character and composition of the population of the Witwatersrand.

In the first place, a very considerable section are non-British, and of these the majority come from a country like Russia, wherein there are no representative institutions, and, therefore, no experience of the principles on which they must be worked to be effective in producing good government.

In the next place, the feverish race for wealth has produced, even among the British to an appreciable extent, a type of character in England confined to the less reputable side of Stock Exchange business, versed in the circulation of unfounded rumours to bull and bear stock, and, by an easy transition, to injure inconvenient business or professional rivals. Able and unscrupulous intrigue of this kind applied to electoral institu-

As to the objection that the Imperial Government, after lengthy negotiation and insistence on the franchise being conferred on the Uitlander, then proceeds to give the franchise to no one, and institutes a Government consisting— as a Crown Colony Government does—of a Governor nominated by the Crown, and a Council also nominated, and so display inconsistency, there is a quite sufficient reply. What was aimed at by the demand for the franchise, as far as the Uitlander personally was affected, was simply a means

---

tions could only effect a regrettable reproduction of the less useful kind of American politics.

The following extract from Mr. J. A. Hobson's book, already referred to, is not without bearing on this aspect of the matter :—

" Mr. Winston Churchill's description of South Africa as a ' Land of Lies ' is not quite the reckless generalisation it sounds. Whether it be a subtle psychical reaction of certain deceptive qualities of the country, its illusive distances, mirages, the incalculable tricks of nature in this ' land of surprises,' or contact with ' the treacherous Kaffir,' or whether it be a ' natural selection ' leading to the survival of mendacity for use in speculative business, I am unable to decide.

" But about the fact there can be no doubt. There are liars and credulous folk in every land ; but for minute detailed mendacity and the wanton acceptance of the same, South Africa stands pre-eminent. It took me some time to adjust my inexperienced mind to this focus. For some time I was disposed to accept readily the circumstantial statements made, apparently in all good faith, by sober intelligent business and professional men. But I soon learned the need of severe scepticism. In the art of which I speak it is scarcely necessary to add that politicians were the greatest adepts, and when the business man becomes politician, he brings his business talent for detail into politics with marvellous results."

I will only say that it took me very much longer to adjust my mind to that focus; but I have done it now.

Lastly, there remains a reason for avoiding undue haste in the introduction of elective government—one which haunts the mind of the rank and file of the Johannesburgers like an evil dream—the danger that any elective government would consist of nominees of the great capitalist houses.

On this point the writer has some apposite reflections, pointing to a real danger ; but one which, I hope, Imperial Statesmen will be able to evert.

" The practical paramountcy exercised by financiers, the recognised leaders of whom are foreign Jews, over the economic interests of the Transvaal, extends also to the social and the recreative side of Johannesburg life. Many of the recognised leaders of society are Jewish. The newspapers of the 13th September contained the announcement: " There will be no performance at the Empire (Music-Hall) to-day, by reason of the Jewish Day of Atonement." The Stock Exchange was also closed upon that day.

to good Government—the only one possible means of attaining it without war. Since the war the circumstances are changed. The franchise is no longer necessary ; the sword has established the conditions of good government, which would now not be furthered by the franchise ; and, as well, has established that Imperial supremacy which was the greatest reason for demanding the franchise.

The usual powers of legislation and administration, of course, would vest in the new Crown Colony Government.

When the British arms have established firm order, this foreign host will return with enhanced numbers and increased power. During the distress of last autumn they bought up, often for a song, most of the property and businesses that were worth buying, and as soon as a settlement takes place they will start upon a greatly strengthened basis of possession.

It may be said, granting this story of a Jewish monopoly of the economic power is true, it does not justify the suggestion that the political power will pass into their hands, and that there will be established an oligarchy of German Jews at Pretoria.

But a little reflection shows that while this class of financiers has commonly abstained in other countries from active participation in politics, they will use politics in the Transvaal. They have found the need for controlling politics and legislation by bribery and other persuasive arts hitherto ; the same need and use will exist in the future. Politics to them will not merely mean free trade and good administration of just laws. Transvaal industry, particularly the mining industry, requires the constant and important aid of the State. The control of a large, cheap, regular, submissive supply of labour, the chief corner-stone of profitable business, will be a constant incentive to acquire political control ; railway rates, customs laws, and the all-important issues relating to mineral rights, will force them into politics, and they will apply to these the same qualities which have made them so successful in speculative industry In a word, they will simply and inevitably add to their other businesses the business of politics. The particular form of government which may be adopted will not matter very much. Government from Downing Street may, perhaps, hamper them a little more than the forms of popular representative government ; but the judicious control of the press, and the assistance of financial friends in high places, will enable them to establish and maintain a tolerably complete form of boss-rule in South Africa.

A consideration of these points throws a clear light upon the nature of the conflict in South Africa. We are fighting in order to place a small international oligarchy of mine-owners and speculators in power at Pretoria. Englishmen will surely do well to recognise that the economic and political destinies of South Africa are, and seem likely to remain, in the hands of men, most of whom are foreigners by origin, whose trade is finance, and whose trade interests are not chiefly British.

Above all things, in the control of the Imperial Governor, all arms, forts, and military equipment.

In the nomination of the Colonial Council to assist the Governor of the new colony of the Transvaal—and, of course, of the Orange River—special care should be taken to make it representative of all classes of the community. In view of popular interests—and prejudices as well—it should be made specially clear that there was no undue capitalist representation.*

In the appointing of officials the greatest care should be taken to avoid any appearance, not merely of undue weight being attached to the recommendations of the great capitalists, but to any appearance of race domination by the victorious British. It is to be remembered that thousands of loyalists of Dutch names and descent fought on the side of the Empire. In the late administration, especially in the Orange Free State, many useful officials can be found.†

On one point there should be no uncertainty. English should be the official language in every department of the administration, in the public offices and the Law Courts. It is not in the present crisis merely a question of permitting Dutch for the sake of convenience in the transaction of business. As a matter of fact, business is, and always has been transacted, even in Pretoria, in English. The fact is that the use of the Dutch language has been turned into a separatist propaganda. Its being permitted in the Cape Parliament in 1882 was openly declared as " the thin end

* Those who know Johannesburg do not require to be told that this feeling—one of fear of being " Kimberleyised," as they term it—exists among a very considerable section, many of whom have lived in Kimberley in former years. It was expressed to me quite recently by members of the Imperial Light Horse—an Uitlander corps—returned from being besieged in Ladysmith. In Kimberley, one great corporation, that of De Beers, not merely has a practical monopoly of the production of diamonds, but, by means of what is known as the " compound system," has the monopoly of the supply of goods to the natives working in the mines (the natives are confined to barracks, called " compounds ") with the result, of course, that there is no room for the ordinary trader.

† This fact has evidently been recognised and acted upon by Lord Roberts in the Orange River Colony.

of the wedge" towards ousting British rule; and its public use in the Transvaal and the Orange River Territory would be laid hold of as an incessant reminder of the intolerable claim to prior and superior right to the land in the Boers who fought the Matabele, over the British who subdued the Zulu.*

It is clear that an inquiry as to the measures necessary to be taken for the re-establishment of order and civil life will be required without delay. Possibly a General Commission, with subordinate sections, would present some advantages : as a co-ordination of results in some cases would be called for. The first and most necessary Commission of Inquiry would be to investigate the claims for compensation for losses suffered by the loyal Uitlanders in the Transvaal and the Orange River Territory as a result of their lawless expulsion and their being robbed of their property, under the guise of "commandeering," or even without show of form. A Finance Commission, to arrange for the completion of a State loan to meet these losses, and to contribute a reasonable share of the cost of the war to the Imperial Treasury, would obviously be required.

The assessment of the burthen of the necessary taxes for this purpose will be no easy task. Quite different considerations apply to the assessment of a war tax on the mines; on the property of the burghers in arms; on the property of their leaders—who, and not the burghers, are responsible for the beginning and the conduct of the war; on the property of burghers of British descent who abandoned their property rather than fight against the Empire; on the British Uitlanders : on the Uitlanders, subjects of neutral Powers.

A Commission of Inquiry on Law, and more especially, on Law Reform, is most urgently required. The present law must be taken as the basis of property rights until it is duly altered. The first step should be to appoint a competent body to select such laws as ought to be confirmed; but much more important is the selection of laws to be promptly

* See Chapter X.—"The Young Afrikander Propaganda."

repealed or modified. The Gold Laws, especially, require immediate modifications. As they already stand, they unduly tend to throw all the gold claims into the hands of the great capitalists, by requiring monthly licensing claims to be paid, whether the claims are being worked or not. The result is that, in times of depression, the smaller holders have to relinquish their claims, which are, of course, then taken up by the wealthy men.* Further, no new claims should be allowed to be taken up for a considerable time, for the same reason. Again, the Transvaal Government parted with many rights, which legitimately should have been retained by the State, under the guise of "Concessions." Special inquiry, at the most impartial hands not interested in any of the concessions, should be made as to the validity and real value of these claims.

Other matters of inquiry as to what, if any, modifications should be made in the existing law of the two territories relate to such difficult questions as the Kaffir laws : regulations as to Kaffirs being obliged to carry passes ; to remain indoors after dark—the Curfew Law ; not to walk on the footpath ; to pay a special tax ; and those relating to Asiatic immigration, which is totally prohibited in the Orange River Territory, and only permitted, under restrictions, in the Transvaal ; the Licensing Laws, dealing with the supply of alcohol to the natives, present questions of great difficulty, both of legislation and administration.

In addition to this work of inquiry, for which of course only temporary commissions will be required, all the branches already existing of the public service will require to be organised, and in some cases to be entirely reconstituted. Such are the departments of Justice, of the Railways, of the Treasury, of the Post Office, of the Mines, of the Land Registry, of the Surveyor-General, and of the Police.

The police, more especially, will require complete reconstruction. Urban police will be required for Johannesburg, Pretoria, and other towns, and in the mining centres in

* This process, I am informed by Johannesburgers, is called "freezing out."

especial, in very large numbers. In the country strong patrols of mounted police will be required for many years to come.

One new department should certainly be created, and large funds placed at its disposal in both territories—a Colonisation Department. The State-aided immigration of 1820 produced the only completely British district in the Cape Colony, the eastern province. The political effects of such immigration need not be dwelt upon. In the Transvaal especially, and also in the Orange River Territory, a very considerable proportion of land is still in the hands of the State, and would be immediately available. In addition to this, very large tracts are in the hands of various land companies, with which the new Government could directly deal. The New Zealand Land Acts would furnish useful precedents as to legislation, and their working a guide in carrying out the Acts. Agriculture, not cattle runs, would change the face of the two territories. State irrigation works are, however, an absolute necessity for agriculture as much as in India. No private individual could afford the enormous expense of adequate works ; and no merely commercial company, regarding dividends only, would expend its capital on what would bring in only a nominal return. To the State, on the contrary, and to the community, the return for irrigation works is not merely the actual interest paid yearly for the expenditure, but the total increased produce of the country ; an increase, which in some cases in India after returning yearly 7½ per cent. on the capital, is equivalent in one year to the total capital expended.* Parts of the Transvaal and the Orange River Territory are exceedingly fertile, and only require water to be converted into agricultural farms. In the Transvaal especially, a Forest Department would have a most favourable field. Trees of all kinds grow with wonderful rapidity.†

* Lord Curzon's speech at Lyallpur, October 1899.
† North of Johannesburg is an extensive wood, miles in circuit, called the Sachsenwald, which looks an ideal public park for the city, and which is only eight or nine years old. In England the same growth is said to require about thirty years.

Natal and the Cape Colony will, of course, be the scene of other measures necessitated immediately as the result of the war. A Natal Commission to investigate the losses of loyal colonists has been appointed for some time. A claim is also made for the cession to Natal of the remaining portion of Zululand, now annexed to the Transvaal, and for the annexation of Swaziland, now under the protectorate of the Transvaal. In the Cape, and Natal also, besides the question of compensation to loyalists, that of the punishment to be awarded to rebels is being considered, and of measures to be taken against seditious publications.*

It may be well here to notice much wider projects of readjustment of boundaries of the new territories published from time to time in the press. Suggestions have been made of the annexation of the Orange River territory to Natal, of Johannesburg and the Witwatersrand to Natal, of Johannesburg and the Witwatersrand to Bechuanaland, to form a new province, with the Gold Reef city as its capital.

The grounds on which these partitions are advocated are chiefly that they would obliterate the former lines of division, and with them the tradition of corporate unity. As to this I do not think there is much probability of the end in view being attained by such means, even supposing the course could be recommended on other grounds. The sentiment of unity among the Boers seems to rest on language and religion, and not territorial circumscription, the bounds of which—the late rebellion is a proof—race sentiment transcended. Another advantage claimed is that it would facilitate the restoration of civil government by putting a British majority in power. This also seems unfounded. It rests upon the assumption that an electoral body is going to be entrusted with legislative power, which, as I have pointed out, would be a rash experiment for several years. Again, the North-eastern Transvaal, almost completely inhabited by Boers, cut off by

---

* As I write, news has just been published of the resignation of the Bond Ministry, it is understood, owing to a party division over the first-named matter, and the annexation of the Republics.

any such operation as the last two-named, would become a focus of Afrikander propaganda. And, possibly, a gold reef may yet be found there, to be transmuted into rifles and cannon. But the greatest disadvantages of all are the delay and paralysis of industry, awaiting the return of civil life and law and order, pending the necessary inquiries as to population and boundaries, and, most of all, that it would be a complete leap in the dark as to the character and tendencies of any of the newly-formed communities.

CHAPTER XXVI.

THE IMPERIAL HOLD ON SOUTH AFRICA: REORGANISATION OF THE GENERAL GOVERNMENT.

To retain the hold of the Empire on South Africa—a hold essential to the continued existence of the Empire the world over—reorganisation of the whole political fabric in South Africa is essential.

The present crisis in the fate of the Empire, the present war, with all its terrible consequences to victors and vanquished alike, are directly traceable to the effect on the mind of a stubborn people of Imperial errors of a hundred years.

To strike at the root of the evil, profiting by the teachin of this war, we shall have to destroy and to create.

Destroy the causes of vacillation and ignorance of fact, which have characterised the Imperial Government at home ; destroy the causes of demoralisation and timidity of Imperial representatives in South Africa.

Create conditions of information with the Government at home ; create conditions of confidence and independence with the Imperial representative in South Africa.

The method recommended and endorsed by experience is plainly that of our most successful Government of India. There no attempt has been made since the Mutiny to shirk the Imperial burthen. Here, as Grey and Frere have in vain preached to a. people who would not heed, all the trouble has arisen by a series of vain endeavours to thrust the burthen of the Imperial people, now to a Griqua chief, now to a troublesome colony, now to rebels in arms.

The parallel between India and South Africa is not, it is true, very close. Here, as in India, there is a large subject population of non-European race. In India, however, the European population are loyal citizens of the Empire. In South Africa there is not merely the difficulty of a subject non-European people, but there is the difficulty, unknown in India, of a section of the European population, set for a generation past on ousting Imperial rule from the territory.

A little reflection will show that the analogies are greater than the discrepancies. In neither India nor Africa can mere counting of heads be sufficient to suffice for a rule of Government. The possession of the Cape is so all essential to the maintenance of the Empire that it is impossible to allow its inhabitants, of whatever race, to do as they please without regard to the higher interests and duties of the Empire as a whole. No more than the Orkneys—to which our original title is traceable to a pledge from Denmark as a security for a loan from Scotland four hundred years ago— no more than the Orkneys can be permitted to demand reunion to the Danish Crown, can Dutch-speaking citizens in South Africa be permitted to weaken or exclude the Imperial Power.

To follow the principle of our successful Government in India does not necessarily involve a servile copying of details. The creation of a Governor-General of South Africa, with an Advisory Council, the creation of an Under-Secretary in the Colonial Office at home, with an Advisory Council of South African experience, would reproduce the essential features characteristic of the Indian system. Of this last—the reorganisation of the South African section of the Colonial Office—no more need be said, as there are few difficulties in the way, except in the selection of persons.

Let us first consider the present system of Government in South Africa, which is chaos, and see what, on the Indian principles, should be substituted in its place. Evils, the immediate result of the present system, which is no system, we have had to repletion. If there had not been such chaos, a band of rash officers of a British territory would not have by a raid on a State with which we were at peace discredited the Imperial Government in the eyes of the world and tied its hands in negotiating for the redress of British grievances. Nor, again, would an attack by the most formidable Power in South Africa have found the Imperial forces utterly unprepared.

British experience in organising and administering dependencies and colonies in every part of the world has been as unique as it is renowned. In South Africa, nevertheless, there is no trace of any foresight in the organisation of the various territories. Everything has been left to hazard, to the accidental creation of a moment, to a temporary expedient to tide over a sudden difficulty. It is true, of course, that the constitution of the United Kingdom has grown, and not been carried out on a pre-arranged plan. There the parallel ends. In the United Kingdom the movement has been from diversity to unity, from warring provinces to a central Government, from the mid-Saxon folkmoot to the Imperial Parliament. In South Africa the ever-recurring desire on the part of the home Government to evade Imperial responsibility—really inseparable from the necessary retention of the Cape—instead of, as in India, in 1857, boldly facing it, has ended in a perfect mosaic of constitutions, heterogeneous in origin, jarring in action.

The constitution of Cape Colony is modelled on the ordinary type of the British Colony in Australia or Canada. It is self-governing, having a Governor nominated by the Imperial Crown, an Upper House of Parliament, the Legislative Council, and a Lower House, the Legislative Assembly, both elected; "responsible Government," that is to say, Government by Ministers responsible to the local Parliament, was introduced some years ago.

In Natal a similar system prevails. The Governor is appointed by the Crown. A Lower House is elected, but the Upper House, the Legislative Council, is nominated by the Governor in Council. Here, too, is "responsible Government." The Governor is also "Supreme Chief of the Native Tribes," Commander-in-Chief of Her Majesty's forces and

Vice-Admiral. Now, before proceeding to the second and third types of authority in this wonderful land of experiments, I may point out that the conditions which were so favourable for the working of local autonomy, and " responsible Government" in Australia, and almost to the same degree in Canada, were not, and are not, present in South Africa. In both Australia and Canada there is a subject native race, but it is relatively unimportant in numbers, and does not seem to increase. In South Africa the number of the native race south of the Zambesi is variously estimated; but all agree that it cannot be less than six to one of the white race—six millions to less than one million—and, more formidable still, it is rapidly increasing, owing, apparently, to their own custom of polygamy, and to the peace which is British. Imperial interests are, therefore, affected, and Imperial duties towards those races cannot be handed over to merely local governments.

Again, another difference, and equally important, at least for our time and generation. In Australia the population is homogeneous, and all are intensely British in spirit, all speaking English. In Canada, although there is a French-speaking province, the loyalty to the Empire of the French Canadians is as undoubted and as proved as that of the French-speaking folk of Guernsey and Jersey and the rest of the group of islands in the Gulf Stream. In South Africa the disaffection of a considerable section of the Dutch-speaking people has scarred deep traces in the history of the past century, and, while I write, is being proclaimed by the thunder of cannon on British soil.

Under such conditions it is not too much to say that the experiment of " responsible government " was somewhat rash.

The next form of authority we find is that of "the High Commissioner for South Africa and Protector of Native Tribes," Commander-in-Chief of Her Majesty's Forces, and Vice-Admiral of the Cape of Good Hope. There appears to be no precise definition of his powers, and no military force at his immediate disposal to enforce them, whatever they are. The High Commissioner communicates by despatch with the Colonial Secretary in London, but—apart from a sudden emergency, which has only once occurred, when in 1857 Sir George Grey despatched to quell the Indian Mutiny Imperial troops ordered elsewhere—he can only await instructions. As Commander-in-Chief he has under his orders only such portions of the Imperial troops as happen to be in Cape Colony—until the present war only a few thousand men. The Colonial troops are under the control of "responsible" Ministers. He has no authority over even the Imperial troops in the Colony of Natal, where the local Governor is Commander-in-Chief.

In the Native Reserves of Basutoland and Bechuanaland the High Commissioner holds the legislative power, his proclamations being law. The Resident of Basutoland and other officials represent his authority. From these territories white immigration is excluded.

Lastly, we come to Rhodesia. Here all the functions of State are partitioned. Originally, at the first occupation in 1890, all legislative and administrative power was vested in the British South Africa Company. Since the Jameson Raid the remainder of administrative power is still in the Company's hands, but the administration of justice and the control of the Mounted Police, the armed force, is in the hands of the Imperial authority, represented by a Deputy High Commissioner. Recently the legislative authority is shared with a newly-created Legislative Council.

This survey shows that it would surpass the wit of man to devise a more confusing maze of conflicting, overlapping, and clashing authority. And this in face of the fact that the whole white population from the Zambesi to Table Mountain, British and Dutch, are one community, inextricably interwoven by family and business relationships, and that the geographical conformation of the country makes the whole population, Dutch and British, dependent, up to the present, for their trade, import and export, on a few harbours, all, with one exception, in British hands.

To save trouble to the Home Government, an absurd

attempt has been made to constitute and deal with these
territories, as if they were different countries ; hence not so
much needless multiplication of authorities—for variations
of local authority to meet local needs can only be useful—
but the absence of any general scheme of government,
applying to the whole of South Africa, or indeed of any
reasoned scheme at all. If it wished to be consistent in its
inconsistency, why did not the Imperial Government erect
chains of fortresses all along the borders of these various
British territories, so as to imitate as closely as possible the
particularist Germany of *opera bouffe* ?

From the point of view of Imperial welfare the fatal omission has been to provide a means and method of co-ordination.
Imperial South Africa has been condemned to ataxia.

Both in war and in peace the hands of the Imperial
representative are tied. If, as we have seen, war be
threatened, the High Commissioner is liable to be impeded
at every turn by the self-governing power of Cape Colony,
of which he is Governor, in which he resides, and through
whose Ministers responsible to a local parliament he must
act. To use the Colonial forces, he must secure their
consent, consent which, one is told in South Africa, cannot
always be safely reckoned on. If Imperial troops use the
Colonial railways he may read of supporters in Parliament,
of the Ministry in power, murmuring at " Our Colonial
railways " being made use of by Imperial troops going to
kill " our kinsmen." Of course he can dismiss the Ministry,
and plunge a country at war into a general election, as Sir
Bartle Frere was intrepid enough to do, although that was
only war with natives, not with Dutch, and be proclaimed a
" prancing pro-Consul " by an eloquent Prime Minister in
England.

In peace, equally serious difficulties may arise. The
Protector of Natives may deem it expedient and just to
institute measures, within the self-governing Colony as well
as beyond its borders, which may not harmonise with the
beliefs or prejudices which regard " Zwart Schepsel " as
beings without rights.

In a word, co-ordination of the action of all South African States, when the safety of the whole Empire is concerned, must be provided for. Unless the necessity should become urgent, on account of developments which have not yet happened, it will not be necessary to suspend the experiment of self-government, already in operation in two of the Colonies. It will be quite sufficient to introduce certain modifications of the powers of the self-governing Colonies, which will give the Imperial representative in South Africa a free hand, in everything affecting Imperial welfare. The problem is too complex, the issues are too dangerous to be left altogether in local hands. The community, torn by racial Dutch and British dissensions, confronted everywhere by an overwhelming majority of Kaffir tribes; distracted by an anti-British propaganda, striving to expel the Imperial power; the centre, too, of operations of world finance, turning round the vast South African product of gold and diamonds, which, for the safety of the Empire, must not be allowed to come completely under the control of cosmopolitan capitalists; a community such as this is not one in which the welfare of the Empire can be with safety entrusted to local hands without Imperial guidance. A community, too, the protection of whose coasts the integrity of whose territory has lately been effected, once again, at the expenditure of tens of millions of Imperial treasure, and thousands of lives of Imperial soldiers.

To establish firmly the Imperial hold on South Africa, a complete re-organisation is therefore necessary of the office of High Commissioner, and such minor modifications of the local constitutions as may be required. Following the course marked out by our Indian experience the High Commissioner should become Governor-General of South Africa, with all powers needful for the protection of the integrity of the Empire, and the safety of South Africa as a whole; and for the discharge of duties incumbent on the Imperial Power towards the other great divisions of the Empire, which may not be delegated to local authority. The authority of the Governor-General should spring directly from the Imperial

Parliament, delegating to him power to annul acts of the Provincial administrations. In India the Governor-General in Council is charged "with the superintendence, direction and control of the whole civil and military government."

A Council, as in India, would be clearly necessary. In India, however, the appointment rests with the Crown, in South Africa, the precedent need not be so closely followed. Seeing that, unlike in India, there is a considerable European population endowed with self-government, a preferable method of appointing a certain proportion of members of the Council might well be from lists of alternative names, submitted by the local Administrations; the nomination to be by the Governor for the time being. In this way the Governor-General would be kept in touch with local views and experience; and at the same time the selection of the names of candidates would be less likely to degenerate into a party contest; while the power of selecting from different names submitted would facilitate the presence of members more likely to work in harmony with the particular Imperial representative in office. The remainder of the members of the Council could be appointed by direct nomination by the Governor-General from leading residents in South Africa, whether in or out of Parliament. The Commander-in-Chief of the Imperial troops in South Africa should be a member of the Council to advise on military affairs.

As in India the Council should be an advisory body, having no right to direct by their vote the action, legislative or administrative, of the Governor-General, but they should have the right of being consulted; and if the Governor-General decided to disregard the advice of the majority, it should be his duty to place his reasons on record. The Council should have the right of placing their opinions on record when they differed from those of the Governor, and of having their dissenting minutes forwarded to the Imperial Government.

The legislative powers of the Governor-General in Council should be defined. It would be found on investigation that they need not be unduly restrictive of local self-government. Nor would they be likely to be put to very extensive use, or even to lead to any material conflict with local legislation. The presence of these powers would nevitably tend to prevent local legislatures or administrations from taking any steps inimical to the interests of other provinces in South Africa, or of South Africa as a whole, or to the Imperial welfare. A general power of veto over local legislation or acts of administration in any of the three cases just enumerated, would probably be found sufficient, in conjunction with the power to legislate by ordinance—an extension of the present power of the High Commissioner to legislate by proclamation—with regard to military steps necessary for the safety of the Empire, the internal order of South Africa, the repression of rebellion, or of native risings; with regard to the native policy to be adopted by the Governor-General in his capacity of "Protector of Natives"; and with regard to matters affecting other Colonies or divisions of the Empire, such as the immigration of Indians.

A special Imperial force levied and equipped in South Africa—for which the present irregular corps would form an admirable nucleus—should, in addition to the ordinary Imperial troops, be under the direct command of the High Commissioner, to be despatched to any district of all South Africa.

In India, general control and supervision of finance is vested in the Governor-General in Council. In South Africa this power seems hardly required. Exception might be made, however, as regards a contribution to the military expenditure and to the navy expenditure of the Empire. A power to legislate by ordinance, as to the maintenance, by contributions from all the provinces of the whole organisation of the Governor-General's staff, of the Legislative Council, and of the special Imperial force, would be plainly desirable; the expense could be most conveniently assessed on the Customs duties. It would be highly inexpedient to leave the voting of such contributions to local authority. Further control over finance would hardly be necessary, as, in the only eventuality that might seem to require it—a tariff war between two or more provinces—the interposition of the veto of the Governor-General would prove a sufficient protection to general South African interests.

One word, in addition, as to the slight curtailment of the local authority of the self-governing colonies. It has been shown that it need not be considerable, urgently though it be required; it has been shown that the views of each province would be sure of representation at the Council of the Governor-General. The justice, however, of the Empire's claim, and that the claim is not a matter of favour, is clear when are considered the enormous loss and cost to the Empire of the present war—the direct result of the absence of a central authority to adequately represent the Imperial power in South Africa. And, again, when we consider that all the colonies and provinces rest immediately on the sea power for the protection of the coast, and immediately, too, on the Imperial troops, for defence against domestic rebellion and Kaffir attack.

These arguments, however, are hardly necessary. The loyalty of the loyal colonists of Natal and the Cape, which has stood the stress of battle, will not exaggerate the minor surrender of local privileges which the present war has shown the Empire to require. No such surrender of power and privilege is expected or is requisite as that which took place in India, when, after the Mutiny of 1857, the authority of the great company was transferred to the Imperial Crown.

CHAPTER XXVII.

POLICY OF THE GENERAL GOVERNMENT OF SOUTH AFRICA.

THE policy of the general Government of South Africa, carried out by its own immediate agency, or immediately through the local Government of the Provinces, should be initiated on clearly fixed principles, to ensure permanence in results and stability in purpose, although individuals may change. The melancholy record of South African history shows how the absence of any fixed scheme of Government, of any tenable or permanent ideal of policy, together with the absence of any real freedom of initiative or other than a merely precarious tenure of office in Imperial representation, have coloured the whole life and development of the composite people of European descent.

Vigour, initiative, security of power in the Imperial representative, having been rendered possible by the changes just now indicated, part of that necessary reorganisation must be the adoption as a fixed rule by the Colonial Office—the rule of the Council of the Secretary of State for India—to interefere as little as possible with the Governor-General n Council of South Africa.

The principles to be set steadily in view by the new general Government should be those which the mistakes of the past and the dangers of the present and future equally point out.

First must be a consistent repudiation of that unhappy ideal of tribal exclusiveness—that fatal heritage of isolation in the wilds—which has been the chief cause of the present war. The solidarity of the European race in South Africa must never be lost sight of, with its principles of justice, equality and liberty, sad though it may be, that the recognition of such an elementary truth should have to be enforced by the sword in the twentieth century. Equal rights for civilised men in South Africa, equal welcome for all, British or Dutch, Canadians, Australians or Americans, coming to South Africa to make it their home. To promote the growth of a new South African nationality, embracing all of European descent, and in active loyalty to the Empire of which it is a constituent part, must be the highest goal of Imperial statesmanship, while in any way consistent with the higher duty of preserving the integrity of the Empire, every consideration should be given to the sentiment of those citizens who are descendants from the earlier Colonists ; and care should be taken to show that the supremacy of the Empire does not mean the establishing of a racial oligarchy of any section of its citizens.

Another principle which past dissensions and present experience equally warn us is necessary, is that recognition should constantly be accorded to the truth, that not equality, social or political, but tutelage is the position which justice accords to the uncivilised natives of South Africa.

The principle should be recognised that, while the regulation of immigration from India and our other possessions is a matter of Imperial concern, there is a prior and superior claim of the Europeans—who in tropical lands can only exist as exotics—to immigrate and occupy temperate lands, such as South Africa, and that this right exists apart from the consideration that not Orientals, but Europeans, have colonised and civilised this land.

The measures necessary to be taken by the General Government for the establishing of secure prosperity for all inhabitants group themselves under various divisions. In some, the measures can only be taken—consistently with safety and efficiency—by the General Government. In others, while by instituting inquiry and affording guidance, the General Government may greatly contribute to the successful action of the subordinate governments, the actual carrying out of the measures may be left to local administration.

First, among the measures which can be efficiently carried out by the General Government alone, must be counted the placing of the whole European community in South Africa on a sound military basis.   The formation of a force of military police for the whole dominion is one of the first necessities of the hour.   Fortunately, as the war shows, there is no lack of material.

A sound economic basis is also essential, and some of the necessary measures could only, from their vastness, be adequately undertaken by the General Government.   A well organised scheme of irrigation works, carried out by the State would change the whole face of the country.   In view of its also changing the political complexion of large districts, by inducing greater British immigration of colonists, coming as agriculturists and not as cattle-ranchers, it is obviously a matter for the General Government.*

Land tenure is a matter with which, in view of the enormous tracts which are still Crown lands, the General Government should deal on a wide basis and with fixed principles.   A Commission to investigate and report on the New Zealand, Australian, and United States systems of opening up new lands would afford useful guidance, as the problems there are somewhat similar.   The growth of the class styled "Bijwoners" (tenants-at-will on another's farm) deserves speedy attention, as the class is rapidly developing into the most dangerous element in any society with a subject native race—the " Poor Whites."   With their recent military occupation taken from them, they will become an even greater menace.   Their origin seems largely to have arisen from the absence of enactments, like the United States Homestead Exemption Acts, to prevent farmers being quite expropriated for debt ; and partly from the subdivision of inheritances.

* One is assured on all sides that a steady opposition to any measures tending to favour British immigration has been pursued for years by those desirous of making South Africa all Dutch.

In other ways the General Government might deal with the question of improved land tenure. To abolish the class of " bye-dwellers," experiment might be made with village communal tenure—from which expropriation is impossible—instead of allotments. The prosperity of the Mir seems to be due to this characteristic rather than to the quality of the Russian villagers.*

To prevent the growth of a destitute class in the cities, and a further addition to the political danger of "poor Whites," the United States Acts—such as those of Pennsylvania, restricting legal process against poor debtors—should be adopted ; and similar protection should be given to workmen's earnings.

The General Government should regard the exploitation of minerals as primarily a fund for State purposes—the construction of State works, roads, railways, bridges, irrigation, harbours, schools ; and not for the creation of millionaires. The British legislation of the Klondyke Gold Fields seems to present a useful model for legislation.

The construction of means for communication through the length and breadth of South Africa is eminently a matter of Imperial concern, and should be in the hands of the general Government, from its political importance, quite as much as its relation to agricultural and trade. In the territory of the late Republics there are practically no roads or bridges, except in the suburbs of a few towns. New railways should belong to the general Government instead of local administrations.

Industrial education is also required as part of the means for furthering the economical development of the country.

Education of the ordinary type, and the diffusion of information, are also matters of Imperial and political concern. It would have been impossible for any propaganda

---

* It is not improbable that only for the action of a rashly-experimenting British Governor, Sir John Cradock, in 1812, nearly all the land in South Africa would have continued to belong to the State, as under Dutch-East India Company rule.

to have created such widespread distrust of Imperial policy and of British people if there were not a seed-plot of ignorance for tares of calumny to grow. Not, indeed, that wonders can be worked even by years of education, but it would help other agencies for dispelling race-hatred.

Legal administration would also be an appropriate subject for the concern of the general government. The establishing of a general Court of Appeal for South Africa, and the making uniform the conditions of admission to the practice of the law, are matters of great moment to the whole community. The necessary appeal to the Judicial Committee of the Privy Council will be a new link binding South Africa to the Empire.

This enumeration of measures which, in pursuance of fixed general principles of administration, would naturally fall to be dealt with, by way of enquiry or execution, by the general Government, is not meant to be exhaustive. It is only intended to show that many matters which, at first sight, might be looked upon as of merely local concern, are, in a vast undeveloped country, beset with complex problems of Imperial moment.

CHAPTER XXVIII.

IN THE COUNTERBALANCE: *VIDEANT CONSULES.*

In the counterbalance to the griefs and losses of this fateful war are many things to cheer all those who, in the darkest hour, never despaired of the Empire. That our people at home, in the United Kingdom, have shown their ancient spirit, and shown that mammon-worship has not killed patriotism, as so many had told us, is consolation indeed; that all the people have become conscious of the mighty heritage of the Empire, charged with the lot of bearing justice and happiness to so many hundred millions of the human race, is something to cheer the heart. All men now can see that the march of the Empire is no longer the step of the half-conscious giant, but follows clear purpose and steadfast resolve. The might of chaotic confusion, of crime, and misery, that fled from the sword of the Empire in India, is not to return; nor are the fires of triumphant barbarism that made Africa a hell in an earthly paradise, to flame anew, with the hoped-for failing of the Imperial people to realise their destiny and their duty.

The moving rally of our citizens from beyond the seas— from snowland and sunland, from Canada, from Australia and New Zealand—has set a seal to the unity of the Empire such as no parchments of confederation could bring. The world knows now, and the Chancelleries of Europe know, that the islands of the Northern Sea stand at the head of a world federation, in war as in peace. Not least has been gained by the dawning, slow but clear, over the mind of the people of that land of sorrow and renown, which has sent a victorious commander to lead the Empire's army of the sun of their Imperial duty, of their duty as co-heirs and joint rulers of the Empire which their valour in arms and their skill in administration have so greatly helped to create.

In South Africa, too, there is something to encourage, however dark be the immediate outlook. The valour of the despised helot of the Transvaal, the loyalty of the loyal Dutch, the tenacity and stubborn courage of the Boer in the field, the thrice-tried fidelity of the British Colonial in arms, the historic intrepidity of the Imperial troops, bring hope of common respect, which must lead, in later days, to that fusion which is the only way of salvation for the newer nationality now to grow up under the shield of the Empire.

For the Government of the Empire in South Africa there is something to be counted, in the new-born respect of the defeated foe—discarding the beliefs of a hundred years—for unlooked-for strength in arms and inflexibility of purpose. The hour came, and, all unexpectedly, the man.

Yet much remains to be done, that is worth the doing, and therein lies a field for the highest statesmanship, for men who lift up their hearts.

Videant Consules. Respect for Imperial strength and resolution is something; but much more is respect for justice, for liberty, for humanity; for all of which in truth, the Empire stands.

APPENDICES.

THE WAR AND ITS ISSUES: FROM VARIOUS STANDPOINTS.

APPENDIX I.

FROM THE STANDPOINT OF THE LOYAL CITIZEN OF DUTCH DESCENT.

THE YOUNG AFRICANDER.

The following is a report of a speech, delivered on the 6th June, 1900, at a meeting at the Paarl, Cape Colony, of the Guild of Loyal Women of South Africa, by Mr. Advocate Wessels, one of the leaders at the bar of Pretoria, who defended the Reform prisoners at the trial in Pretoria in 1896.

Sir Pieter Fauré (late Minister for Agriculture) introduced Mr. J. Wessels, himself an Africander, and well acquainted with Transvaal affairs.

The Mayor also introduced Mr. Wessels, paying a high tribute to that gentleman's past efforts in the Transvaal for South Africa's welfare.

Mr. Wessels said:—

I hardly thought when as a schoolboy I spent my holidays in your beautiful town I would one day be asked to address you on the subject of loyalty to the Crown. In those days there was little, if any, race hatred. One never heard of those visionaries who speak of an independent South Africa free from all British control. In those days everything was peace and happiness. Without peace there could be no happiness, and without happiness life was not worth living in any country. If I should be somewhat serious this morning, I feel sure the ladies will forgive me. The subject is such that it will not permit of any but serious treatment. I know that seriousness in a speaker is by many regarded as a great bore, but the subject will not bear much levity. As I understand the Guild, it was the intention of those that founded it that when the women of South Africa should influence their children in such a way that these would firmly understand that it was an honour and advantage to be a citizen of the British Empire. (Applause.) When I ask you to consider it an honour to belong to the British Empire, I would not for one moment suggest that it is a disgrace to be an Africander. On the contrary, I would ask you to be proud of the fact that you are Africanders, and never to attempt to pose as Englishwomen, for when we Africanders attempt this we only make ourselves contemptible. (Hear, hear.) There are two cardinal precepts that I would have you bear constantly in your minds. The first is that an Africander is every whit as good as an Englishman, and the second is that an Englishman is every whit as good as an Africander. (Applause.) I am an Africander, and I am proud of it. I am proud of the fact that I have Dutch, French, and German blood in my veins. This is just the very reason why I respect the Englishman's pride of birth. We have every right to be as proud of our ancestors as the English have to be proud of theirs. (Hear, hear.) There is, however, one bad quality which has become very prevalent amongst us Africanders, and that is the quality of conceit. It is especially noticeable in the rising generation of Africanders. I would not have you think for one moment that the Englishman is void of this vice, but I think that the young Africander is aggressively conceited where he has but little reason to be so. The young Africander reminds me of the fable of the frog that felt so confident that it could rival the bull in size, that it blew itself out until it burst. The young Africander states have tried to rival Great Britain as a military power, and like the old Greek's frog they have also burst. (Laughter and applause.) The young Africanders in the Transvaal and Free State gradually came to believe that they knew everything better and could do everything better than any Englishman. They thought that because they, or rather their fathers, could hit a bottle at 200 yards there was no limit to their capacities. Straight shooting became to them the be-all and end-all of virtue. (Laughter.) Education, culture, industry, commerce and skill in good government were as nothing compared with skill in hitting the bottle. (Renewed laughter.) To suggest to the young Africander that he was not omniscient and omnipotent was to be a traitor to one's race. To tell the Kruger oligarchy at Pretoria that it was quite impossible to prevent the active and intelligent majority of the community from obtaining a voice in the future government of the State, was enough to be jeered at and called a fool. They were strong enough to control that, and "om die Engelsche uit die land te schiet." To tell them that it was quite impossible for them to withstand the might of the Empire if they provoked the British so as to come to blows, was sufficient to show yourself a coward. To criticise the

Africander and show him that his inflated ideas were foolish was a natural offence. Yet that same class of Africander would listen with rapturous delight if Mr. Ernest Hargrove painted his own people as blood-thirsty tyrants. To hear an Englishman deny his countrymen and say that the Empire was going to ruin because it would not listen to the Bond, met with violent applause; but for an Africander, one of themselves, to point out their folly and to caution them that if they persisted in their foolish course, ruin would stare them in the face, was a sin that merited the contempt of every Africander. This conceit had brought ruin to many a Transvaal, Free State and Colonial home. I beg and pray of you to teach your children to be proud of their race and teach them that they are quite as good as others, but do not teach them that they are better. Conceit is born of ignorance, and ignorance is the best and surest guide to utter perdition. Widen the range of your children's knowledge and teach the young Africanders to look beyond the Limpopo to the broad world, where Anglo-Saxons, Germans, Frenchmen and Russians are in constant rivalry to civilise mankind. When he begins to realize what goes on in the wide world he will feel proud that he is a British subject—a subject of perhaps the greatest Empire the world has ever seen. (Hear, hear.) He will see that, go where he will, he may meet with the scowl of jealousy, the glare of hatred, but never with the shrug of contempt. (Loud applause.) Why is that? The complete answer is interesting but extremely complex. This great fact he will, however, quickly notice. Millions of British subjects are ruled in divers parts of the world with an army which compared with those of even the smaller European States is insignificant. If he be wise he will ask himself how is this huge Empire able to maintain itself with so small an army? How is it that over these large and populous tracts of country the Empire requires so small an army to maintain the Pax Britannica? In Germany and the other great States of Europe there are millions of soldiers to maintain the social order, and consequently militarism is rampant. In the British Isles and wherever there is British rule the social order is maintained by an almost insignificant army. The British Empire is thus not ruled by force, but by something else. What is that something else? There can be no doubt that this something else is the British love of freedom. (Applause.) Wherever the British flag floated there we find equality and tolerance. (Hear, hear.) No part of the Empire feels the goad of tyranny; there is therefore no inducement to break away; hence no large army is required to compel obedience and maintain the integrity of the Empire. On the contrary, so jealous is each State of the national honour, and so keen to secure the safety and integrity of the Empire, that directly one member is threatened we see the whole world in commotion, and we see citizens rushing to its aid from the icy regions of Canada to the sunny plains of Australia. The British Empire differs from the Empires of old and from those of to-day in that it has been built up not so much by conquest as by a peaceful, industrial and commercial expansion. No Alexander, no Cæsar, no Napoleon founded the British Empire. France, Spain, and Holland possessed not very long ago Empires nearly as great, if not as great, as the present British Empire. Where are their Empires now? How was it that Great Britain had maintained her Empire whilst the other nations had lost nearly all their vast extra-European possessions. The chief reason is because the British Empire had never been exploited for the benefit of a certain class or clique in Great Britain, but for the benefit of all. If to-day the noblest and wealthiest peer of the realm were to land in Table Bay, from the moment he set foot on Colonial soil he had no greater rights in this Colony than you or I. (Applause.) Each state or colony of the British Empire ruled itself, and was master of its own destinies within its own sphere. A Canadian had no right to interfere in the affairs of Australia; an Australian had nothing to say in the Cape Colony, and the Cape Colonist had the right to control the affairs of the Cape Colony. Beyond the borders of the Cape Colony he had no right of controlling the policy of the whole Empire. (Hear, hear.) Within the limits of this Colony the voice of the majority in the Legislature is the voice of the people for the time being. The Bond, for instance, is at present the ruling party in this Colony. Unfortunately, the Bond is not satisfied with having supreme power in this Colony, it desires to rule the whole of South Africa. Such is its conceit and ambition, that it deems this insufficient and seeks to rule not only South Africa, but the whole Empire. It is to my mind a curious phenomenon to hear the Bond shouting that the whole British Empire is going to ruin because Englishmen, Scotchmen, Irishmen, Canadians, Indians, Australians and the larger part of South Africa do not agree with their wild hallucinations. (Hear, hear.) Excuse this digression. I think you will agree with me that the British Empire is *sui generis*, that it does not hang together by force, that its watchword is Political Equality, Freedom of thought and Freedom of speech, and that under its wide shield every man is the master of his own destiny.

There is one other important fact. It is a fact very often overlooked but it is, nevertheless, to my mind, very important. The British Empire is composed of men of all nationalities. It is a Cosmopolitan Empire Men of French, Dutch, English, Scotch, Irish, and Asiatic descent are all embraced within its wide folds. Being, therefore, an agglomerate of nations and races there is no reason for any one to feel that his national pride is being trampled on. Everyone's language is respected and no one is interfered with in his religion, whilst every member has a voice in public affairs. (Applause.) Take Germany, Russia or any large European power, and what do we find? The Germans had conquered and partitioned Poland, they had annexed Schleswig-Holstein, and wrested from France Alsace and Lorraine. In all these conquered territories the inhabitants were compelled by order of the Kaiser to think and speak in German. You could not even dare to sell on the market a pound of butter in the Danish language. German alone is the language of the Parliament, the public offices, and the schools.

Most people wanted some material advantage for their loyalty. The subjects of the British Empire have the advantage of a ready protection wheresoever they might be. No region was so remote that the arm of the Empire could not reach it. Great Britain has so great a navy that she can always see that law and order is maintained and that no foreign nation dare trample on the rights of her subjects. *Ons Land* has this morning come out boldly with its policy. It wants the complete independence of South Africa. The British flag shall no longer protect its shores, or at the most it may obtain the voluntary concession of a right to protect. But do these people realize what the position of the Cape would be if it were not a portion of the British Empire ? Do they know that it would be exposed to the first naval power that came along, and that it is not impossible to conceive that the shrieking members of the Bond might become the subjects of some Asiatic sea power like Japan. (Laughter and applause.) It was therefore not only an honour, it was an advantage to be a member of the British Empire. Can you understand how anyone could wish to exchange his right of British citizenship for the privilege of being ruled over by President Kruger and his family ? Advisedly I add his family, for anyone intimate with political life in the Transvaal would know that the family of Paul Kruger had a greater influence there than the grandsons of the Queen have in the territories of the British Empire. To many there is a fascination in the word " Republic." They think you have but to baptise any form of government with the name " Republic," and then Freedom immediately sets her throne there. Unwise men ! If they will make themselves acquainted with the history of Venice and the Italian Republics they will soon find that the word " republic" does not always spell freedom. If by republic we mean political equality, freedom of thought, and freedom of language and religion, then the British Empire is verily the greatest Republic in the world, and its Sovereign its permanent president. (Applause.) But, ladies, if by Republic we mean a narrow and selfish oligarchy, then heaven defend us from Republics.

I do not wish to vex you with present-day politics, but one cannot help referring, though cursorily, to the controversial politics of the day. Had it not been for the conceit of the young Transvaaler and the young Free Stater—their ignorance, blindness, and obstinacy—we should not have seen South Africa bathed in blood, and we should not have seen two Republics cease to exist. You have heard how the members of the Bond Congress at Graaff-Reinet regret the war. I do not believe that they can regret the war more than I do. I did all in my power to persuade the oligarchy at Pretoria to cease to be a family party and to allow the Uitlander, who contributed so much to the State and whom they had to thank for their welfare, to have some voice in the government of the Republic, so that the Transvaal might cease to be an oligarchy and become a Republic in deed as well as in word. I begged them to give the Uitlander an honest and satisfactory five-year franchise, and so to satisfy the Uitlander's sense of justice. What was their reply? They called me a traitor to my race—a man whom his relations would not own. Thank God, this part of their prediction has not been fulfilled. I tried to persuade them that war with Great Britain was suicidal, and that when the first shot was fired the independence of both Republics would be gone. The *Volksstem*, the Government organ, told me that I was a fool, and that I knew nothing of the might of these young Republics. It was not only the Boer of the back country that thought the Africander invincible. A most intelligent man, a friend of mine, wrote to me from the Boer camp that they were sure of victory, and that many of them had vowed not to wash until they reached the Indian Ocean. Nay, he would even visit me in Cape Town. The worst feature of all this is that they really believed that their hopes would be fulfilled. Shortly before I left there was a feeling rampant in young Transvaal that they would sweep the British into the sea and compel the officials at Cape Town to speak Cape Dutch. Every young Africander was polishing his Mauser and openly boasting "dat hij gaat Engelsche schiet." He thought that as he could shoot straight—though many cannot even do this—he would soon be in Cape Town. (Laughter.) Was not the god of the Transvaal greater than the god of the British Empire? I have some relations and many friends fighting on the side of the Transvaal. I am sorry that their conceit and ignorance led them to take up arms, but I feel that they were misled by Kruger and that arch-fiend Leyds. (Hear, hear.) After the victory at Amajuba the young Transvaaler came to regard himself a far better man than an Englishman. The Hollander Leyds persuaded them that through his skill and cleverness as a diplomat the Transvaal had become the most important spot on the face of the globe. The German and French concessionaries were never weary of impressing upon the members of the Raad that England was an effete Power, and that they loved the Transvaal with more than brotherly love. All Europe would rush to the assistance of the young Republic directly it resolved to throw off the British yoke. They smiled at the unfortunate Boer and said, " aap wat is jy een mooie jongen." And yet when the war came what do we see? The German Emperor hastens to congratulate the Queen and tell her that his heart was always with the British Army. (Applause.) The people who in their conceit and ignorance thought they could shake the foundations of the British Empire, make it totter and fall, only succeed in overthrowing the independence of two Republics. The Bond regrets the loss of the Republics' independence. I, who lived in the Transvaal and knew it well, regret that loss far more than they. I know what happy, contented, and prosperous countries those two Republics could have been made under a Government with wide views imbued with a true feeling for freedom; under a Government that did not intrigue against British interests with Germany, France, and Holland; under a Government that honestly endeavoured to carry out the obligations of the Convention, and that did not try at every turn to circumvent British statesmen; under a Government that sought the friendship and did not do everything in its power to rouse the enmity of the British nation. Oh, what a country it might have been under a President like the late John Brand! Had the Transvaal recognised the fact that an Africander is as good as an Englishman, but no better, then the bitter race hatred would have disappeared, and the Republics would still have had their independence. This wretched idea that the Transvaal was a first class Power because they shot straight at Amajuba had spread even to the Cape Colony. Did not a member of your Parliament consider that 50,000 British soldiers were but a breakfast for the young giant. And because this feeling spread Cape Colonists were also anxious to take part in the onslaught against the tottering Empire. Now, ladies, though I regret the ignorance, blindness, and obstinacy that led the Transvaaler and Free Stater to declare war on Great Britain, I can understand and appreciate his aspiration to acquire for his country by his own right hand complete and full independence. I feel profoundly the misery that has been caused alike to South African and English mothers. Yet when I think of the battles that have been fought, though I feel bitterly sorry that ever a shot was fired, I feel proud that my countrymen are no cowards. (Applause.) As I respect the Englishman, so would I that the Englishman should respect the Africander. (Applause.) When, however, I come to think of the rebels in this Colony, I cannot understand how their leaders could have been guilty of such wrong and of such folly as to take up arms against the rest of South Africa. I feel indignant that these men could have led their misguided brothers into such misery. I feel no vindictiveness against the bulk of the rebels, for they were but the sheep that followed the goats. The victorious Transvaal would drive the English to the sea, and they too would join in the procession. Though they were guilty of a foolish crime, they at any rate came out boldly into the open light of day, risked their lives and took the consequences. But, ladies, when I come to think of that other crowd of Africanders who skulk in the twilight and whose courage is mere insolence, men who, secure in person and in property, sit behind the British lines of defence, and from there urge on the poor Transvaalers, Free Staters, and insurgents to continue the struggle for their own personal benefit, then words fail me to express my loathing and contempt. (Applause.) Their newspapers exaggerate British losses, sneer at British arms, cast grave doubts on

British successes in order to buoy up the Republican hopes; they exaggerate the spread of the flames of rebellion, and promise moral support with
an empty word. But would these men risk their lives? No. (Applause.)
At the most they will send a few scns across the borders and risk the
lives of a few children. Go teach your children to bewail and respect
those Africanders who fought and died for a hopeless cause, but to despise
and condemn those others who, secure under the aegis of British
protection, urged on their misguided brothers to die in the last ditch.
(Applause.) Why were these leaders so anxious to join the Republican
cause? Because they thought it would benefit them. If all South
Africa were one Dutch Republic, think of all the available government
billets. The glamour of the wealth and power of the Pretoria oligarchy
had crushed out their better reason.

Much as I dislike extension of empire by conquest or annexation, I feel
that the matter has gone so far that British sentiment could not be
appeased by anything short of annexation. Moreover, it seems to me
that the peace of South Africa would be in constant danger if the
Republics were allowed to carry on their former hostile existence. The
Bond at Graaff-Reinet says if you do annex there will also be evil. If,
then, this evil must and will prevail whether there is annexation or no,
then surely the better policy is to choose that evil which can most easily
be held under control—and that undoubtedly means annexation. If Sir
Alfred Milner should wish to justify his policy, he need but point to
the rebel districts and the Graaff-Reinet Congress. The speeches there
delivered will furnish Lord Salisbury with ample proof of the danger with
which the Republics threatened South Africa. The speeches of the
members of Parliament at that Congress transcended those of their
humbler brothers in idiocy, and offer the strongest possible plea for
annexation. These people say, if you annex the Republics, the whole of
South Africa will hate you; but they forget to say that they were all
standing on the tip-toe of expectation that the Republics would be
successful, and then they would have shouted Republicanism as loudly as
they now shriek out their fear that annexation spells ruin to the Empire.
They display a solicitude for the safety of the Empire one would never
nave given them credit for. (Laughter.) Did these men warn the
Republics after the Bloemfontein Conference that if they did not give the
five years' franchise the Republics might sacrifice their independence? I
never heard of that voice of warning. It was the old story of watching
the proverbial cat jump. Unfortunately the animal jumped on the wrong
side, and that is the reason for all this bluster and threatening and
gnashing of teeth.

Ladies, I will conclude by again asking you to teach your children to
be proud of their race, proud of their country, and proud of the fact that
they are members of the British Empire; but I will also ask you to teach

your children to loathe and despise those who sow the seeds of sedition, those who fan the flames of race hatred and who, to satisfy their envy and vindictiveness, their hatred and ambition, would wish to make of this fair country a veritable hell on earth. (Loud applause.)

In an introduction to the foregoing speech, which has been republished as a pamphlet, Mr. Wessels writes as follows:—

The Africanders in South Africa may be roughly divided into three political classes—1. The Africanders descended from English ancestors. These have a strong attachment to the Empire and no desire to break away from it.   2. Africanders descended from Dutch or Huguenot ancestors, who, like the English Africanders, are anxious that South Africa should form part of the Empire.   These may be shortly designated as loyal Dutch Africanders.   3. Africanders springing from Dutch and Huguenot forefathers, who are anxious to establish a United South Africa entirely free from British rule.   Many people identify the Bond party with this class, though I think this too sweeping a statement.   It is difficult to form an accurate estimate of the exact number of heads under each class, though I think that the combination of the English Africander and the Dutch loyal Africander considerably exceeds the disloyal portion. The disloyal portion clearly show through their newspapers that the liberty of the individual is no concern of theirs, and most assuredly no plank is their platform.   They hate with a bitter hatred everybody who is not of their way of thinking, and they would impose their rule upon their fellows, not by persuasion, but by brute force.   To them the Mauser is a holy symbol.   They have no desire to see South Africa a country peopled by free men.   Their aspirations are to pull down the British flag, to impose the Dutch language on all, and to establish a reign of barbaric terror.   They prate loudly of the liberty of the Press, but, judging by the past, they would suppress every anti-revolutionary paper.   They deprecate force, but rely for argument and conciliation on the Mauser and the Krupp gun.   They howl at the idea of British annexation, but would have freely annexed without a qualm of conscience any British territory that they were strong enough to hold.   They wail over the bloodshed which they themselves have caused, but openly gloat over the number of British soldiers they have slain and the number of South African homes they have made desolate.   They feed and batten on race hatred.   Their Christian Charity does not extend beyond their own narrow clique.   They abuse the liberty of English rule and make of that Liberty a licence.   We are therefore face to face with this problem.   Are we going to allow these people to prevail?   Are we going to allow them to cut us adrift from the Empire and expose South Africa to the attack of some other Power with which these people would readily conclude an alliance if it were only to wreak their vengeance against the British?

If we are going to allow this then we may bid Freedom farewell.

When one hears some of these people talk about their forefathers, one would imagine that the English took away their Freedom. They forget that the rule of the Dutch East India Company was a tyranny of no mean order and they forget that the Cape was handed over to Great Britain by solemn treaty.

It is high time, therefore, that English Africanders and Loyal Dutch Africanders stand together and oppose in solid phalanx the onslaught of those of our countrymen who long to establish over us a rule of Red Terror.

It was with the object of voicing the views of those Dutch Africanders who fear the threatened tyranny that I delivered the following address.

J. W. WESSELS.

APPENDIX II.

FROM THE STANDPOINT OF AN INTERNATIONAL LAWYER.

THE RECONSTITUTION OF SOUTH AFRICA.

The London *Times* publishes the following letter of the 10th March, 1900, from Professor Westlake of the University of Cambridge and of the Institute of International Law.

To the Editor.

Sir,—The nation appears to be practically agreed that the territories of the two Dutch Republics must become a part of the British Dominions, and that their inhabitants must enjoy the free institutions which have been found the best security for the loyalty of all races under the British flag. Whether those institutions shall be given to them as provinces of the same areas with the Republics, or there shall be a re-arrangement of areas in South Africa, whether they shall be enjoyed by each province separately or in federation with others, and what arrangements may be necessary in order that any part of the cost of the war may fall on the provinces on which it ought to fall—these are questions which it may not be premature to discuss, but which I do not propose to discuss to-day. I wish to draw attention to a preliminary point of which the importance may easily be overlooked—namely, the necessity of ending the war, when it comes to be ended, in such a manner as to leave no doubt that the Republics will have ceased to exist. To say that "their past system, which involved a large measure of political and military independence, will, of course, be materially modified as a result of the war" is probably to go as far as, at the present stage of the military operations, it would become the Government to go; but the public ought already to accustom itself to perceiving that, when the thing comes to be done, that will not be enough. If the Republics are left standing with a modified system they will continue to be separate States under restrictions extending, no doubt, to the franchise and to armaments, and, therefore, much more important than any to which they are not subject, but which, whatever they may be, must leave the situation open to the difficulty which uniformly dogs the attempt to maintain restrictions on any State acknowledged to be one. The right of Russia to emancipation from the Black Sea Clauses of the Treaty of Paris was put by many on the ground that restrictions on what a State may do to its own territory are contrary to nature, a contradiction in logic, and therefore never to be justified except for a temporary purpose. Those who remember 1848 will call to mind how, when tearing up the treaties of 1815, the satisfaction of the French in proclaiming themselves free to fortify Huningue seemed, at least, equal to that which they felt from claiming an increased liberty of action in Europe. So we may be sure that if the Republics continue to exist, it will not be long before they, with the support of their sympathisers in all parts of the world, will not only try, but will claim as of right, to shake off all fetters to which they may be subjected. And they will have the further support of those who, while unable to deny the attempts which the Transvaal has made from 1881, to shake off the successive Conventions, justify them on the ground that the independence taken from them in 1877 ought to have been fully restored. There are never wanting those who contend that a State is not prevented by its signature from re-opening the question whether the conditions which it signed were just, and their arguments will be backed by the fallacy that no permanent restrictions on a State can be just.

It may be said that it is forcing an open door to insist on its being made plain that the two territories are to be taken under the British flag. In answer, I would point to the bungling phases through which France, a country in which form is much more attended to than in England, arrived at her goal after her war in Madagascar ; the treaty of the 1st October, 1895, the unilateral declaration of the Queen of Madagascar on the 18th January, 1896, and the equally unilateral French law of the 6th to 8th August, 1896. In the words of the *Revue Générale de Droit International Public*, a very able periodical certainly not disposed to find France in the wrong, "these different documents gave rise to the most lively and confused controversies about the meaning of the words protectorate, annexation, sovereignty, and the consequences of the annexation of territories." If England, which has to face a widely-spread disposition to find her in the wrong, cannot arrive at her goal more simply than this, we shall not only incur the usual imputations of bad faith, but shall leave a real doubt to cloud the future. And our statesmen are, in such a matter, under the peculiar liability of being misled by our Indian experience. For reasons of policy, the reality of which I am far from disputing, we have built up in the Peninsula a system of our own, of which the result is that the relations between the United Kingdom and the native States cannot be expressed without contradiction in the terms of European international law. That does not matter, for there is no neighbour to take advantage of the circumstance, and it has been officially notified in the Indian Government *Gazette* of the 21st August, 1891, that "the principles of international law have no bearing upon the relations between the Government of India as representing the Queen-Empress on the one hand, and the native States, under the suzerainty of

Her Majesty, on the other." But in South Africa we dare not follow such precedents. If the evident mind of the nation is to be carried out it must be made clear to those who take their stand on European international law, that the Dutch States have ceased to exist, even as dependent ones.

This being so, it will be well that the public should begin to reflect on the way in which its intention of bringing all South Africa under the British flag can be fulfilled. A State may cede a part of its territory, but when the whole State disappears there can be no legal cession, because no constitution provides for such a case. Neither the Legislature, the Executive, nor any general has a commission to put an end to the State's existence. A general may conclude a military convention as to the terms in which he and his troops will lay down their arms, but there is this difficulty about inserting any political promises or holding out any political hopes in such a convention, that at that stage reconstruction cannot be far advanced, if indeed it has commenced, and in its progress it may be found impossible to carry out such promises or give effect to such hopes. The Treaty of Limerick is an instructive example of the difficulties which may follow from trying to make a military convention serve a political purpose. A moral sanction to the extinction of a State may be obtained from a popular vote, or from the resolution of an assembly specially elected to decide on the matter; and, since such sanction cannot in any case be a legal one, the voters summoned need not be only those who enjoyed the franchise before. The oligarchy hitherto governing has no moral claim to represent the South African Republic. But, as against third Powers with which a question may arise as to what has become of the rights and obligations of the annexed State, the only legal title which the annexing State can claim under international usage is the will of itself as conqueror sanctioned by time. And perhaps the annexing State will take the wisest course if it announces that will in the simplest way, by proclamation. For the moral justification which we all desire and expect, we must look to the co-operation, in working the system which we set up, of assemblies elected on a liberal franchise.

I will conclude with two warnings. First, in any reconstruction let the name " State " be avoided, even if the territories of the two Republics should be adopted without alteration of boundaries as colonies or provinces. In the case of the United States there was an original justification for the word, because the colonies became States by declaring and achieving their independence. But if, when they formed a true union, they had dropped that word with its misleading associations, it could not have been argued so plausibly that entrance into the union did not preclude eventual secession from it. The power of names is great, and not even England can afford to neglect accuracy in their use, and to rival Carlyle's " Emperor Sigismund super grammaticam."

Secondly, let the lesson of 1877 teach us the danger of delay in introducing the free institutions which we intend for these territories if and when conquered. There is no agrarian question and no religious question to fear. Since the Dutch language is sure to be admitted on equal terms with the English, as in the Cape Colony and Natal, and the exclusion of English cannot be again attempted without big guns, there will not even be a language question. Some persons talk of guerillas, but there can be no guerillas without a sympathising population from which to draw their supplies, and the small body of Boers cannot be at once guerillas in the mountains and farmers to supply them. And the non-Dutch vote will have the majority in the Transvaal, and our garrison will, for a considerable time, be large. If the new institutions are quickly got to work, we may rely, with Lord Loch, on the practical Teutonic minds of the Boers for settling down. The danger will be in the disaffection which delay in getting the new institutions to work may cause to spread from the Boers to those who are now Uitlanders.

Yours obediently,

J. WESTLAKE.

Chelsea, 10th March.

The *Times* comments as follows on the preceding letter:—

"Lord Salisbury refuses to be led into a discussion of the highly-contentious assertions made by the two Presidents. They move us as little as their pathetic reference to considerations which ought to have been present to their minds and to have held their hands when they prepared for and precipitated war and boasted that they would drive the English into the sea. The burden of blood and tears and of moral and economic ruin of which they talk is heavy, but it is on their shoulders and not on ours that the load must rest. It is enough for us that they deliberately made preparations for this contest for years on an enormous scale, and that when they thought they were ready they made war upon us and seduced numbers of our Dutch fellow-subjects from their allegiance. That is proof enough of the conspiracy, the existence of which is sometimes denied by their friends. It must be our business to abolish, as far as possible, any centre around which a similar conspiracy might hereafter re-form. Professor Westlake, who had some doubts about our legal position while the Conventions existed, writes us a weighty letter this morning on the situation which follows their abrogation by the war. He insists on the absolute necessity of doing in the most effectual way what the Government have now declared they mean to do. There must be no loophole for a doubt hereafter that the Republics have ceased to exist. To leave room for doubts is to leave room for aspirations and for intrigues which must be extinguished for ever if the peace and the security of South Africa are at last to be laid upon a solid and enduring foundation."

APPENDIX III.

FROM THE STANDPOINT OF THE CHURCHES.

THE NONCONFORMIST CLERGY AND THE WAR.—THE CONFIDENCE OF THE CHURCHES IN SIR ALFRED MILNER.

From "Cape Times," 18th June, 1900.

Yesterday, at noon, a large and influential body of Nonconformist clergy waited upon Sir Alfred Milner at Government House to present to His Excellency an address conveying the support of all the religious bodies in Cape Town and district in the Imperial policy towards the two Republics, and of confidence in His Excellency as the exponent of that policy. The deputation met the Governor in the drawing-room, where there were present: The Revs. J. J. McClure (convener), A. H. Hodges, H. Cotton, Ezra Nuttall, J. H. Gathercole, J. G. Locke, J. R. Saunders, B. E. Elderkin, W. S. Caldecott, R. Jenkin, Geo. Robson, Wesleyans; D. W. Drew, A. Pitt, Jas. Richardson, J. S. Moffatt, A. Vine Hall, and H. C. Newell, Congregationalists; W. E. Robertson, David Russell, and W. McIntosh, Presbyterians; A. E. Saxby and E. Baker, Baptists; and J. Tom Brown, London Missionary Society. The following ministers were unable for various reasons to attend: Revs. H. Tindall, J. le Pla, Jas. Fish, and W. Edwards.

THE ADDRESS.

On His Excellency entering the room,

The Rev. J. J. McClure said: Your Excellency, the address which I have the honour to present, with my brethren, to you this morning represents not only the respect and esteem in which you are held by the ministers of the Evangelical Churches of Cape Town and district, which are represented here, and also those who are not represented, but also a deep feeling of personal affection. We are here to-day to present this address to you convinced that the policy which you represent, and of which you have been such a distinguished exponent, has within it peace, prosperity, and abiding happiness for all the States and colonies of South

Africa. (Hear, hear.) Mr. McClure then read the address, which was in these terms :

To Sir Alfred Milner, G.C.M.G., etc.

May it please your Excellency,—We, the undersigned ministers of religion resident in Cape Town and the vicinity, feel impelled by a sense of duty to express our convictions on two or three important points involved in the present situation in South Africa.

1. We desire to express our entire confidence in Your Excellency's personal judgment, evidenced by the eminent fairness, justice and prudence you have displayed in the administration of South African affairs since you assumed the office of High Commissioner.

2. We emphatically approve of the general policy of which Your Excellency has been the exponent, and which you have unfalteringly and patiently pursued, in the face of much misrepresentation and antagonism.

3. We very distinctly hold the belief that the well-being of the whole of South Africa is dependent upon the indisputable establishment of British supremacy and sovereignty, and we do not hesitate to affirm that when the end is accomplished and the neighbouring territories are placed under a pure and wise government, in accordance with the policy that prevails in other provinces of the British Empire, disaffection will cease and the whole population, without distinction of race or language, will be welded into a peaceful and loyal community.—We are, Your Excellency's most obedient servants, (signed) Jas. le Pla, A. Pitt, D. W. Drew, H. C. W. Newell, J. Moffatt, J. Richardson, A. V. Hall, Ben Evans, J. Leipold, E. Baker, A. E. Saxby, J. Russell, J. R. Saunders, E. Nuttall, Wm. Flint, Hy. Cotton, A. H. Hodges, B. E. Elderkin, E. Mdolomba, J. E. Locke, R. Jenkin, W. Hewitt, G. Robertson, J. H. Gathercole, Jas. Fish, Henry Tindall, W. Edwards, J. W. Barns, W. J. Caldecott, W. E. Robertson, J. J. McClure, David Russell, S. J. Hamilton, C. E. Greenfield, W. McIntosh, J. M. Russell, J. M. Zahn, Hy. Tindall, Wm. Edwards, J. McMillan, H. H. G. Kreft, T. Weber, J. Rath, H. Kling.

The Wesleyans.

The Rev. Ezra Nuttall said they counted it a very high honour that they had been permitted to attend and present this address to His Excellency, who had many arduous and distracting duties to occupy his time. But they wished to say what was in their hearts. Were the matter under discussion one of mere parochial interest they would not have ventured to ask such an honour, but this Imperial and colossal question was very dear to them and to the Churches they represented.

They had come to speak as ministers of the Church, not so much in the name of the members of their churches, who had already had an opportunity of informing His Excellency as to their general views, but he might say for his brethren that they were in perfect accord with the resolutions that had already been passed at so many meetings. It had given them pain, when so often His Excellency's name and reputation had been attacked, and they recognised that the difficulties of his exalted position actually debarred him from answering, as he might so easily do, such sophistries, he need not say slanders. (Applause.) Would His Excellency accept from them this expression of their kindly feelings, very deep respect and esteem, and their expression of trust that under God his administration might be carried to a successful issue. (Applause.)

THE CONGREGATIONALISTS.

The Rev. J. S. Moffatt, speaking on behalf of his own denomination, said they perfectly understood each other. (Hear, hear.) They had come with a profound conviction, one shared by every man there, that they could do a great deal for His Excellency and for the Empire, of which they were proud to be the subjects, in one way. There were more things wrought in heaven and earth than man knew of by the power of prayer, and His Excellency might rest assured there were prayers going up, earnest prayers, day by day, that he might be supported in his present responsible and heavy work, and in the end attain the objects set forth in that petition. They wished fervently that His Excellency might come successfully out of this crisis, such a one as had never before occurred in this country. (Applause.)

THE PRESBYTERIANS.

The Rev. W. McIntosh said he was a Presbyterian, and until recently a Transvaal uitlander, and he had come to say that they, the uitlanders, felt confidence and strength when His Excellency took up this matter so recently. They felt that now the power of the King was going to be made manifest in this land. And, being here, he felt that he could do no less than stand forward and express the feeling they had towards His Excellency. (Hear, hear.) The men who were bred under the banner of the Queen should be with His Excellency in these trying times. (Hear, hear.) They had come as Christian men to say that they believed the Kingdom of our Lord was a Kingdom of righteousness, and that that Kingdom would be advanced when liberty which was not licence reigned throughout this land. They felt that His Excellency's policy was on the lines of that great Providence in which they believed, and so they came to-day to give what little courage and confidence and strength His Excellency might get from their support. (Applause.)

The Baptists.

The Rev. E. Baker said his church unfortunately had not had an opportunity of giving expression to its opinion on the great subject, although that was not due to any want of conviction, but he hoped to forward to His Excellency their resolution in a few days. He was only too glad to be there to assist in giving a wider echo to the chorus of approval that had come to His Excellency that morning, and which he hoped would strenthen His Excellency's hands. He had also pleasure in testifying to the statesmanship His Excellency had displayed during the troublous months through which we were passing. (Applause.)

Sir A. Milner's Reply.

His Excellency, after accepting the address, said: I thank you for coming here to-day to present me with this address. Emanating as it does from a body of men so representative, and whose deliberate opinion on a question of the highest public importance is entitled to so much weight, I cannot but feel it is an event of unusual importance. You represent, I think, all the great Nonconformist religious bodies of this town and neighbourhood. Your attitude is typical of the unequalled unanimity and strength of conviction which exists among the Nonconformists of South Africa with regard to the great struggle at present convulsing this country. The men whom I see here to-day, and their fellow ministers throughout South Africa, are not in the habit of obtruding their opinions on political questions. (Hear, hear.) It is a unique crisis which has brought them into the arena, and the exceptional character of their intervention lends additional weight to the temperate, but strong and clear, statement of their position which has just been placed before me.

A Victim of Mendacity.

As regards myself personally, I cannot but feel it is a great source of strength at a trying time to be assured of the confidence and approval of the men I see before me, and of all whom they represent. You refer to my having to encounter misrepresentation and antagonism. I do not wish to make too much of that. I have no doubt been exposed to much criticism and some abuse. There has, I sometimes think, been an exceptional display of mendacity at my expense. (Laughter.) But this is the fate of every public man who is forced by circumstances into a somewhat prominent position in a great crisis. And after all praise and blame have a wonderful way of balancing one another if you only give them time.

Balancing Eulogy and Abuse.

I remember when I left England for South Africa three years ago, it was amidst a chorus of eulogy so excessive that it made me feel thoroughly uncomfortable. (Laughter.) To protest would have been useless; it would only have looked like affectation. So I just placed the surplus praise to my credit, so to speak (laughter) as something to live on in the days which I surely knew must come sooner or later, if I did my duty, when I would meet with undeserved censure. And certainly I have had to draw on that account rather heavily during the last nine months. (Laughter.) But there is still a balance on the right side which, thanks to you and others, is now once more increasing. (Applause.) So I cannot pose as a martyr, and what is more important, I cannot complain of any want of support. No man, placed as I have been in a position of singular embarrassment, exposed to bitter attacks to which he could not reply, and unable to explain his conduct even to his own friends (hear, hear) has ever had more compensation to be thankful for than I have had in the constant, devoted, forbearing support and confidence of all those South Africans, whether in this colony, in Natal, or in the Republics, whose sympathy is with the British Empire. (Applause.)

A Settlement of "Never Again."

In the concluding paragraph of your address you refer in weighty and well-considered language to the conditions which you deem necessary for the future peace and prosperity of South Africa, and for the ultimate harmony and fusion of its white races. I can only say that I entirely agree with the views expressed in that paragraph. The longer the struggle lasts, the greater the sacrifices which it involves, the stronger must surely be the determination of all of us to achieve a settlement which will render the repetition of this terrible scourge impossible. (Applause.) "Never again" must be the motto of all thinking, of all humane men. It is for that reason, not from any lust of conquest, not from any desire to trample on a gallant, if misguided, enemy, that we desire that the settlement shall be

No Patchwork and no Compromise;

that it shall leave no room for misunderstanding, no opportunity for intrigue, for the revival of impossible ambitions, or the accumulation of enormous armaments. (Applause.) President Kruger had said that he wants no more Conventions, and I entirely agree with him. (Laughter.) A compromise of that sort is unfair to everybody. If there is one thing of which, after recent experiences, I am absolutely convinced, it is that the vital interests of all those who live in South Africa, of our present enemies as much as of those who are on our side, demand that there should not be two dissimilar and antagonistic political systems in that which nature and history have irrevocably decided must be one country. (Applause.) To agree to a compromise which would leave any ambiguity on that point would not be magnanimity, it would be weakness, ingratitude, and cruelty; ingratitude to the heroic dead, and cruelty to the unborn generations.

THE TRUE MAGNANIMITY.

But when I say that, do not think that I wish to join in the outcry, at present so prevalent, against the fine old virtue of magnanimity. I believe in it as much as ever I did, and there is plenty of room for it in the South Africa of to-day. We can show it by a frank recognition of what is great and admirable in the character of our enemies; by not maligning them as a body because of the sins of the few, or perhaps even of many individuals. We can show it by not crowing excessively over our victories, and by not thinking evil of everyone who, for one reason or another, is unable to join in our legitimate rejoicings. We can show it by striving to take care that our treatment of those who have been guilty of rebellion, while characterised by a just severity towards the really guilty parties, should be devoid of any spirit of vindictiveness, or of race-prejudice. (Hear, hear.) We can show it, above all, when this dire struggle is over, by proving by our acts that they libelled us who said that we fought for gold or any material advantage, and that the rights and privileges which we have resolutely claimed for ourselves we are prepared freely to extend to others, even to those who have fought against us, whenever they are prepared loyally to accept them. (Applause.)

His Excellency conversed for a while with the members of the deputation, who, with an expression of thanks for the interview, then retired.

DESPATCH BY A CONGREGATIONAL MINISTER.

The Rev. R. J. Campbell has been writing a series of letters to the *Daily News* on the subject of the war, its causes and its probable effects. The most recent of these letters appears in the issue of 11th May; a few extracts are appended.

In a former communication I endeavoured to show that in the judgment of many Colonials whose experience gives them a right to speak, the present war is a conflict of forces rather than of individuals, and that its principal causes lie much further back than the Conventions of 1881 or 1884, much less the Jameson Raid or Uitlander grievances. Nevertheless, it goes without saying that the course of South African history would have been altogether different but for the 1877–81 policies; and the struggle in which we are now engaged would have taken another form, and yielded another result than now seems likely to be the case, but for the Raid and the Kruger policy towards the Uitlanders.

By the working out of the effects of the 1877 to 1881 policies in the Transvaal, assisted by the Krugerite and the Bond propaganda, quite another situation arose, which it is instructive to trace.

The first effect was the impression created of the bad faith, inconsistency, and weakness of the British Government. Had the Beaconsfield Cabinet kept its promise of the grant of free institutions to the Transvaal, and avoided the blunder of setting up a military Government instead, it is possible, though by no means certain, that the Boers would have given up their aspirations after independence. Upon this no one can speak positively, as the event would have depended upon so many contingencies; but when it is taken into account that Mr. Kruger himself held a post under the British Government, and only resigned because he was refused an increase of salary, it is at least reasonable to assume that given self-government and a fair measure of prosperity, the Boers would speedily have acquiesced in British ascondency, and that the insurrection would never have taken place. But once it did take place the Gladstone policy, a policy in which Mr. Chamberlain had a voice, was certain to lead to further complications, and even its immediate effects were felt throughout the whole of South Africa. It not only injured British prestige both with whites and natives, but inflicted heavy damage upon British interests of a material kind.

Previous to the war of independence the race feeling did not exist, or, if so, was very far from being a political danger. The retrocession woke it into activity. The Englishman sank a step; the Dutch Africander rose. In Cape Colony appeared the Bond, whose political objects have gradually become more clearly defined, but whose attitude from the first was anti-British. Africanderism became a force with a centrifugal tendency. In the mouth of a Dutchman the word was associated with the achievements of his brethren in the Transvaal, and the thought began to shape itself that the victory of the Boer farmers might be the prelude to a greater consummation, when Anglo-Saxon should be exchanged for Dutch supremacy in the Cape itself. There is plenty of evidence that this aspiration was not ill-founded, as those who read the words of the Rev. S. J. du Toit, written nearly twenty years ago, and now translated, may discover for themselves.

In Paul Kruger Dutch Africanderism has found its focus, partly by force of circumstances, but chiefly by the character and ability of the man. The President of the South African Republic is a typical Boer, the embodiment and exponent of all that is most characteristic of his race. Narrow, ignorant, forceful, unscrupulous and cunning, in his own way religious, and perfectly fearless in carrying out his aims, he is the head and centre of the South African problem. So far not another man has shown a tithe of his ability, and little as it might suit the more refined Africander political malcontents of Cape Colony to see such a man at the head of affairs, in the event of a thorough-going federal success they could never have dispensed with him. Boer sympathisers in England utterly mistake Paul Kruger. For twenty years he has consistently worked towards one ideal, a United States of South Africa, an Africander Republic with himself as George Washington. It is not so absurd as it seems, and assuredly not so impossible as we far-off islanders in our complacent self-confidence have imagined. Every act of his career since Majuba Day fits in with the supposition that his objective was Cape Town, though his policy was such that if the larger scheme failed the smaller might succeed, and Pretoria become the capital of a sovereign international State, which should absorb its smaller neighbour on the South, and force its way to the sea on the East.

The President is a millionaire, thanks to the British, and enormous sums have been paid to consolidate and render subservient the Kruger party in the State. Nor was this Kruger party confined to the Transvaal. Vast sums found their way across the border. At the last General Election the Bond party defeated Sir Gordon Sprigg with Transvaal gold. Transvaal emissaries found their way to every part of South Africa stirring up disaffection and race feeling. Why was this done? or, at any rate, why was the money spent? The only reasonable explanation is that Mr. Kruger's policy was not simply defensive, but offensive.

Once only did it seem to strain Africander sentiment too far, and that was when the closing of the Vaaldrifts was attempted. But here the policy was not really changed. Dutch Africander hopes were centred upon the power and importance of the official clique in the Transvaal, and it was worth risking something to further that end, which in this instance, happened to be served by the success of the Netherlands Railway Company.

The whole thing has been worked with marvellous cleverness. No one can prove a "conspiracy" to oust British authority; Mr. Kruger and the Bond have been too wary for that. But if for "conspiracy" we read "understanding," then we can safely affirm that Africanderism has long known its own mind. To the world it looks as though the two Republics armed for their own defence. At the worst the Federals believed that European intervention would save them from extinction, while at the best, well, the Powers might have to recognise a *de facto* sovereignty, the result of a spontaneous Africander uprising from the Zambesi to Cape Town. All the afore-mentioned measures have been means to an end; the very name South African Republic instead of as formerly Transvaal State is not without significance, as is also the annexation of British territory at the commencement of the war. It may be that this fact has been overlooked by philo-Boers at home, but Colonials are under no mis-apprehension as to its meaning. It is a portion of the price that England has had to pay for "acquiescing in the existence of the two Republics." That the price has not been greater is due, first and foremost, to Sir Alfred Milner, and after him to the splendid loyalty of the Colonial Volunteers.

It was not the Transvaal but the Empire which was menaced at the commencement of the present struggle. If this be an unrighteous war the responsibility for it does not rest at the door of the British Government. England did not make it; Africanderism made it, and intended to make it, though not so soon as has actually been the case. To the end of time no doubt it will be denied that a conspiracy against British power ever existed at all. Good hard lying has always been part of it, and it takes a good deal to open the eyes of the British public to the fact. Perhaps when the pacification comes sufficient black and white evidence will be forthcoming to establish beyond all doubt the fact which every loyal British subject here well knows—that we have had a very narrow escape. Will the Nonconformist irreconcilables at home ponder the evidence that is forthcoming even now? I cannot be surprised that they should be slow in believing it, but let them do justice to Colonial testi-mony, and they will exactly reverse their present notion that the war is on our part one of aggression, and on the part of the Boers one of defence. It is not so. We are the attacked, and if our policy of self-defence involves the annexation of the defeated aggressors it cannot be helped.

One cannot but be sorry for the Boer rank and file. The untutored farmer of the veldt has been the dupe of a clique, which has never perhaps numbered more than a hundred individuals. If it can be proved up to the hilt that this clique had some of its representatives in Cape Town as well as Pretoria and Bloemfontein, sharp punishment should be meted out. It is no light thing to juggle with men's lives. The Boers, as well as we, are paying in blood for the ambitious schemes of President Kruger and his familiars. Perhaps they may some day discover, if prejudice will let them, that they have been misled. We must see to it that British victory shall mean for them the very liberty they love, and for the sake of which they are found willing to die.

When the reckoning comes let the loyalists have their due. There is a surprising uneasiness abroad in regard to the possible action of the British Government. At first I found it difficult to understand, but now I am getting used to it. When one speaks of the firmness and determination of Ministers and the British people generally that this time the settlement shall be thorough, and of such a nature that the work will never need to be done over again, Colonials laugh. "We have heard all that before," they say. "We know the sort of firmness to expect from the British Government." This is rather humiliating, but true. Nor is it all.

There is a grimmer note sounded. The loyal inhabitants of Cape Colony and Natal are determined that upon the policy to be pursued by Great Britain in the forthcoming settlement they will adjust their own future attitude to the Motherland. " Barring sentiment," they declare, " what have we to gain by inclusion in the British Empire? We cannot stand another twenty years like the last. Either there must be a real settlement, or we shall make terms for ourselves and cut the cable." This kind of loyalty savours of disloyalty, but it is not really so : it is sentiment overcome by indignation. Are our statesmen alive to the danger ?

I ought here to remark that it is well understood both in Cape Colony and Natal that in any event the Free State was bound to lose independence. Part of the declared purpose of some of the Transvaalers was the early absorption of their smaller neighbour. There are, of course, some even amongst Colonials of British origin who regret the position of the Free State much more than that of the Transvaal. Amongst such are men like Mr. Henry Beard, one of the most respected citizens of Cape Town, and a member of the Legislative Assembly. Mr. Beard is one of the few who refuse to believe in the reality of an Africander conspiracy to drive the English into the sea. In particular he regrets the fate of the Orange Free State, concerning which he has held an opinion approximating to that of Mr. Bryce. He is dubbed pro-Boer, as so many moderate men are just now, both here and at home. Yet it were well if such as he were listened to. While disbelieving in the inevitableness of the present war, he regards annexation as the only possible settlement in the state of public feeling. Indeed, I understood him to say that he regarded it as the best policy under the circumstances, but pleads that it should be of such a nature that the Free State burghers should scarcely know of the change. Autonomy without independence seems the clear line for the future. This, one is glad to say, is also the course approved of by Sir Alfred Milner, who shared Mr. Beard's sympathy with the Free State. Sir Gordon Sprigg's recommendation, that self-government should only be conceded when the Home Government is satisfied that a majority of the burghers are willing to accept British supremacy, is more drastic than probably Sir Alfred would recommend. Besides, is it English ? The vanquished must not be crushed. If we have fought for equal rights let us concede them as soon as law and order can be restored in the conquered territories.

The Rev. W. Tees, Presbyterian Minister in Durban, furnished me with a surprising piece of first-hand evidence of the Africander conspiracy. In his congregation there is, or was, a gentleman who was formerly Attorney-General in the Free State, and who is of avowed pro-Boer proclivities When the war broke out, and the Boer success made it seem probable that Natal would be overrun, this gentleman made no pretence of concealing his satisfaction. Mr. Tees, in conversation with him, referred to the general consternation at the thorough preparedness of the Republics for the struggle. "Yes," was the calm rejoinder, "Great Britain has been completely taken by surprise. Sir, this has been preparing since 1884."

"In both States?" "Yes, in both, and in the Colony also. The Transvaal has been the arsenal, but those in the know in the Free State and the Colony have worked in unison with Kruger."

"And the object was to oust the British from South Africa?" "Precisely, but it was not intended to do it all at once. The first step was the consolidation of the two Republics as a sovereign international state, and later on an Africander rising at the right moment."

"Then do you mean to say that when President Kruger attended the Bloemfontein Conference he knew perfectly well that the proceedings were a farce, and that he really meant to fight?" "Yes."

"And President Steyn's announcement that the Free State had never thought of war was made in the full knowledge that war had long been prepared for?" "Yes."

"But, sir, that was most blasphemous lying, for he called upon the name of God at the time he made the statement."

"Well, I suppose it was—diplomatic lying, diplomatic lying, you know."

This kind of thing is slowly coming to light. Englishmen find it difficult to understand the deliberate falsehood and long-sustained insincerity of the Africander policy in this land of lies, as Mr. Winston Churchill calls it.

One thing I cannot omit to mention—the splendid, touching loyalty to the Queen which is shown on every hand. At home we take such loyalty for granted; here it means perhaps a little more, because it cannot be taken for granted. Just think of it! Seven thousand miles from Old England in a territory which Her Majesty has never visited, and the majority of whose inhabitants have never seen her, the sound of her name is greeted with a reverence, affection, and enthusiasm that I have rarely heard equalled. I saw men in Greenmarket-square, at Cape Town sing the National Anthem with a solemn feeling and emotional earnestness that were irresistible. It stirred the fibres of the most stolid.

THE CHURCH OF ENGLAND.

The following is the copy of a letter addressed by the Archbishop of Cape Town on the 21st April, 1900, to the High Commissioner:—

Sir,—I feel that the absence of any official expression of opinion on the part of members of the English Church during the present crisis, at a time when other religious bodies have combined in addressing Your Excellency, is likely to lead to an erroneous inference as to that Church's attitude in respect of the future of South Africa. I therefore hope that I may be permitted to express to Your Excellency my firm conviction

that no enduring peace can be secured to this country so long as the
Northern Republics are allowed to retain their independence and to
remain outside the limits of the Queen's sovereignty. I believe that the
cause of freedom, righteousness, and progress, as well as of justice to the
native races depends upon the establishment of British rule throughout
South Africa.

In saying this I feel no doubt whatever that I am expressing the
decided and deliberate views of an overwhelming majority of those over
whom I have the honour to preside as Metropolitan, and that they, like
myself, entertain the fullest confidence in Your Excellency's prudence,
wisdom, and courage in dealing with the momentous issues now at stake.

I remain, sir, your faithful and obedient servant,

(Signed) W. W. CAPETOWN.

THE ROMAN CATHOLIC CHURCH.

The Rev. Dr. McCarthy, whose speech in support of the High Commissioner's policy, appears in the report of the meeting of Irish Colonists,
writes :—

The Roman Catholic clergy at the Cape are almost unanimous in their
support of Sir Alfred Milner's policy; but their abstention from public
utterances may have left a false impression. One of them, Dr. Kolbé, of
Colonial birth and editor of the *South African Catholic Magazine*, was
strongly opposed to it; and the emphasis of his expression may have
caused some to think that he voiced the opinion of his fellows in the faith.
This was so far from being the case that public opinion compelled him to
resign the editorship of the magazine. With the toleration characteristic
of the Boer advocates he, after months of undisturbed monopoly in
expressing his views, complained that he was denied liberty of speech;
merely because his Bishop had attended a meeting opposed to the Boer
policy.

THE DUTCH REFORMED CHURCH AND THE KAFFIR.

The Rev. J. S. Moffatt writes :—

One of the most remarkable statements that has appeared is in the
manifesto signed by a body of the most influential ministers and theo-
logical professors of the Dutch Reformed Church. They contend not
only that there is a better understanding between Boer and Black Man
than there is between Black and British, but that the Dutch Reformed
has always been a missionary church in South Africa, and is so at the
present time in a greater degree than any other. It is out of the question
to attribute to these Reverend Fathers any wilful intention to mislead by
saying the thing that is not, the only other supposition possible is, that
they are profoundly ignorant of the past history of South Africa and of
things as they are at the present moment.

Take a case in point—the relative position of the natives in the Cape Colony, and in the Transvaal. The Reverend Charles Phillips, formerly of Graaff-Reinet, now a refugee from Johannesburg, has stated the case so concisely and yet so clearly that I make no apology for taking over the whole passage. "To come to the fundamental policy of the two Governments, the essential principles as embodied in their laws, which regulate their relations to their coloured subjects, no one dare affirm that the natives are not treated worse in the Transvaal than in Cape Colony. The difference begins with the 'Grondwet,' or Constitution itself:—

"In its ninth article it is affirmed that there shall be absolutely 'no equality, either in Church or State, between white and coloured.' The natives are the 'zwart goed,' black goods or property, the schepsels, mere creatures, the Gibeonites, to be used as the 'hewers of wood and drawers of water' for the white people.

"Till two years ago there never was such a thing as a legal marriage among coloured people. When it was granted, lest it should be thought that there was the shade of equality at the hymeneal altar, the preamble introduces the 9th Article of the Grondwet, quoted above. It then insisted upon a fee of £3 to the Government, and so hedged it round with other restrictions as to put a premium on immorality, insomuch that all branches of the Christian Church sent deputations to Pretoria, and worked desperately for its abolition, preferring the old condition of things."

The reverend authors of the manifesto tell us that the Dutch Reformed Church is not, and never has been, unwilling to give the Gospel to the black man. Yes and No! Certainly not so far as these particular ministers are personally concerned. They have given an honourable example struggling successfully as they have done to rouse in their own church missionary zeal. They have worked hard and well, and they have done good work. No one will grudge them that testimony who is a well-wisher to the native. But it would seem as if while absorbed in this effort, and in the joy of its success within the range of their own observation, they had quite forgotten what is the real attitude of the vast majority of the adherents of the Dutch Reformed Church. That can only be understood by those in such regions as the Transvaal and its borders, who in their missionary efforts have found their path crossed, their labours retarded, their successes crushed by the undying hostility of the Boer. There are many Boers, good Christian men, who are zealous and willing to give their native dependants a sort of Christian teaching, but it is doubtful whether even these would allow that teaching to take a direction which would give progressive advancement to the native in status and education. Yet these are some of the results without which the missionary's work remains incomplete.

We need not go beyond the Cape Colony to know how bitterly the Boer resents the education of the black man. It was only lately and within sight of Table Mountain that I listened to a Dutch lady who laid down with almost vehement conviction the following exposition of her views : "Education of the coloured people was no use, it only spoiled them. There ought to be a law made, that every coloured person should be compelled to apprentice his children for three years to the service of some white man. That is what they were made for." Yet this lady belongs to the inner circle of revived religion in the Dutch Reformed Church. In another house I had to sit in meekness under a wild tempest of words in which were set forth the injustice of a Government which assisted the black man to educate his children, whilst the white people could not afford to spare theirs from the work of the farm to go to school : yet these people were landowners on the northern slope of the Paarl mountain who drove in to church every Sunday with a well set-up equipage and a pair of spanking horses. Travelling through the karroo by train some years ago, I was approached by a Dutch Reformed minister, who with an incredulous yet deeply serious air, inquired if I really believed that these black people had any receptive faculty for divine things, and whether it were any use preaching the Gospel to them. I answered him in the spirit of gentleness, for I saw that he meant no harm, and that he was a sincere seeker after truth.

To go back to the Transvaal—that there are many missionary stations there is true enough. The missionary is tolerated and looked down upon as belonging to an inferior order of clerics. He must be discreet—he must teach his flock to be submissive to their superiors and contented with that state of life in which it has pleased Providence to place them.

Resolutions supporting the policy of the Imperial Government, declaring that the present war is the result of a long prepared design to drive out the British Government from South Africa, and to substitute a Dutch-speaking dominion as the result of a war of aggression and conquest ; and affirming their confidence in the High Commissioner has also been passed by—

1. The Baptist Church of South Africa.
2. The Cape Town and District Congregational Association.
3. The Congregational Union of Natal.
4. The Durban Church Council.
5. The Maritzburg Church Council.
6. The Evangelical Church Council of Port Elizabeth.
7. The Evangelical Ministers of Kimberley.
8. The Lovedale Missionary Institution of the Free Church of Scotland.
9. The Cape Town Presbytery of the Presbyterian Church.
10. The King William's Town Presbytery of the Presbyterian Church.
11. The Natal Presbytery of the Presbyterian Church.
12. The Adelaide Presbytery of the Presbyterian Church.

13. The Kaffrarian Presbytery of the Free Church of Scotland.

14. The Kaffrarian Presbytery of the Presbyterian Church of South Africa.

15. The Cape of Good Hope Synod of the Wesleyan Methodist Church of South Africa.

16. The Clarkebury Synod (Native) of the Wesleyan Methodist Church of South Africa.

17. The Queenstown Synod (Native) of the Wesleyan Methodist Church of South Africa.

18. The Conference of the Wesleyan Methodist Church of South Africa.

APPENDIX IV.

FROM THE STANDPOINT OF AN IMPERIALIST.

Sir Alfred Milner on Local Patriotism and Citizenship of the Empire.

The following speech by Sir Alfred Milner, High Commissioner for South Africa, was delivered to a deputation of the Guild of Loyal Women of South Africa, attending to present an address to the Queen. The report is taken from the *Cape Argus* of 25th April, 1900.

It is hardly necessary for me to assure you that it will give me great pleasure to send home this address for submission to Her Majesty. I venture to think, though perhaps I go beyond my province in saying so, that among the innumerable demonstrations of loyalty and affection, of which she is the recipient, this address will possess a peculiar interest and value, because it comes from South Africa, because it comes from the women of South Africa, and because it springs directly out of the great crisis through which South Africa is at present passing. I have been looking back to see when it was that I first heard of the movement which has resulted in the formation of this Guild, and I find it was just before Lord Roberts left Cape Town, before the operations which led to the relief of Kimberley and Ladysmith, at the moment when

The Tide of Rebellion

in this Colony had reached high water mark, and the hopes of the enemy were at their highest. They are no fair weather friends, the Loyal Women of South Africa (cheers), neither are they, I fancy, in the ordinary course, much of politicians. But there are crises in the history of every State when the latent reserves of strength in those sections of society which are usually the least political, naturally and rightly show exceptional activity. It is such an impulse, a generous and spontaneous impulse, which has led you, women of South Africa, in one of the gravest crises which has ever threatened Her Majesty's Throne and Empire, to

Rally Round your Sovereign,

herself a woman, the most august and venerable figure on the world's stage. But when I say that, do not suppose that I think that your movement begins and ends with an expression of personal devotion, however deep. What I specially welcome about the statement of principles contained in your address is its wide outlook, its appreciation of what is meant by citizenship of the British Empire. That is what we all need so greatly, not only in the Cape Colony, or in the Colonies generally, but quite as much in Great Britain itself.

THE WIDER PATRIOTISM.

Do not think it is inconsistent with local patriotism. Quite the reverse. The latest political red herring is an attempt to confuse the minds of men about the real issue at the bottom of the present struggle, which is simply whether this country shall be inside or outside the British Empire, by representing it as a struggle between those who think first of the good of South Africa, and those whose interests and sympathies lie outside. In future we are told that we are only to have two parties here—South Africans and Uitlanders (laughter), but the difficulty of this ingenious idea is, that it takes two to make a fight. Before you can get two bodies of men to engage in combat, they must both exist, and, as it happens, there is no such thing in existence, either here or in Great Britain, as an Uitlander Party, if that means a party which wishes to see South Africans governed in any other interest but its own (cheers). I am, I believe, supposed to be a typical Imperialist (hear, hear). Speaking as an Imperialist, I can only say that it is not only consistent with my political creed, but it is an essential part of it, that South Africans should be governed in the interest, and by the agency, of the people whose lives are bound in it (cheers), who feel for it, and who work for it, as their home. But the

SPIRIT OF LOCAL PATRIOTISM,

which I for one desire to see strengthened, not weakened, is liable to two aberrations. It is a mistake to think that such patriotism can only be found, or only exist in full measure, in born South Africans. Nothing can be more unwise in a young country than to make distinctions between those who are born in it, and those who have come from outside, provided they are equally attached to it, equally prepared to serve it as their home (cheers). And it is even a greater and more vital mistake to regard a devotion to South Africa as inconsistent with, much more as antagonistic to a devotion to the British Empire. If there is one thing of which I am absolutely convinced, it is that the highest interests of South Africa itself make for its inclusion in that great association of free and self-governing communities which is known as the British Empire— (cheers)—and the existence of which as a unit of invincible power, is essential to the maintenance of the political ideals which these communities have in common; and which mean so much for the whole future of humanity. It is its highest merit in my eyes that the body, whose members I am addressing, recognize that fact, and that their object is to spread its recognition. And this leads me to make one remark with regard to your critics. I do not refer to hostile critics whose attacks are an honour and should be encouragement—(laughter and cheers)—but critics of your own household who at heart are at one with you, and with whom you would wish to avoid even the shadow of a misunderstanding. I can sympathise with some whose loyalty to the Throne and Empire is quite undoubted, and who say: "What need is there that we should profess our loyalty, or form an association to demonstrate it?" And certainly no one would dream of pressing those who have that feeling, to join in any public movement if that method of contributing their quota to the stock of common effort is uncongenial to them. But I fancy they somewhat misconceive the object of those who are present here to-day. That object is not to demonstrate their own loyalty, which is quite unnecessary, but to help to spread and strengthen throughout the community a sense of what loyalty in its true sense really means (cheers). Can any one say that in this country, at this time, that is a work of supererogation? That is one criticism. But then there is another, and again from friendly quarters. I hear there are some who think that you are not sufficiently exclusive, that this Guild is drawing to itself adherents from among those who do not feel, or have not at all times felt, as strongly as some of us do, the honour and privilege of citizenship of the British Empire, or who do not agree in all respects with every aspect of Imperial policy. But if that is true, it seems to me to be a reason for satisfaction rather than the contrary, and shows that

The Guild

is already doing good work, by uniting those who, despite minor, and perhaps serious differences, are prepared to take their stand on one broad platform of Imperial patriotism. I don't care what the differences may be in other respects. If any one is able to subscribe heartily to the principles laid down in your programme, it is good enough for me. In conclusion, I wish to say one word on a personal matter, though I am sorry to introduce the personal note at all on an occasion of this kind. It is one of the principles of this guild to loyally strengthen the hands of the Imperial Government and of Her Majesty's representative in this land, and in handing me your address you have been kind enough to speak in very strong terms—in terms which I feel to be too strong, though I am grateful for the kind feeling which prompted them—of the action and services of Her Majesty's present representative in this Colony. Now, I see a very great difference between the cordial support of Her Majesty's representative as her representative—especially at a time of great national danger, and when he has his hands full, and more than full, in upholding her lawful authority in this country (cheers), and the approval of the particular methods and acts by which he may strive, however conscientiously, to fulfil that duty. Certainly he may claim that great allowance should be made for him, that his actions should be judged generously and as a whole. But God forbid that he should claim to be exempt from criticism, even at a time like this. It is a favourite allegation of the enemy that people are liable to be accused of being disloyal because they criticise the action of the Governor. I do not believe that this is so, but if it were so, it would, frankly speaking, be absurd. I deprecate any attempt to invest the Governor with a sacrosanct character, as I deprecate the intolerant spirit, the mania of suspicion, at present abroad in some quarters, which would even ostracise people whose essential loyalty is not open to question, because on this, that, or the other point of a widely involved controversy, they may not agree with the opinion of the majority of loyalists. From that suspicious, that intolerant spirit, I believe the Guild of the Loyal Women of South Africa to be entirely free (cheers), and that is one of the many reasons why I welcome it and look forward hopefully to its future. Faithful to the Sovereign, faithful to South Africa, and faithful to the Empire, its members have

A Great Work

before them in the coming days, not only the remaining days of what is still a critical struggle, during which all our energies must be centered on ensuring the triumph of our cause (cheers), but in the subsequent period of reconstruction and development on new and broader lines. For that we indeed require the strenuous, the unselfish, the patient efforts of all loyal men and women, working in a spirit of generosity and comprehensiveness in order to place this country for ever beyond the danger of a renewal of intestine strife, to make it a strength, and not a weakness, to the Empire, and a happier place to live in, for those of every race, than it has been in the immediate past (loud cheers).

APPENDIX V.

FROM THE STANDPOINT OF THE TRADER.

Trade and the Issue of the War.

A leading trade journal—the *British and South African Export Gazette*—contains in a recent number an able article, from which are extracted the following useful reflections on the issue of the war in its bearing on the commercial interests of the world; and on the settlement after the war from the same point of view.

The New " Progress and Poverty."

The parties in the field represent the opposing forces of progress and reaction. Those who fight under the banner of "Africa for the Afrikanders" are fighting to make South Africa a close preserve for themselves and their descendants. They are deaf to all appeals for enlightened advance; they care nothing about utilising the resources of the country so long as they can live in their traditional sloth. They simply desire not to be bothered with agricultural improvements nor commercial activities. The busybody from Europe would have no place in their commonwealth except as the helot to work mineral deposits for their benefit, or develop other native industries on a percentage to the State. The Afrikander Republic would be a Republic of prohibitive import dues, of enslaved native labour, of oppressive land tenure, of cheap brandy and dear bread, of few railways, of a scanty white population living in patriarchal ease upon a tributary working community, white and black. The twentieth century, which is being welcomed by the rest of the world, would never enter South Africa if by any possibility the Boers should prove victorious in the present campaign. For it must not be forgotten that though we are only fighting the burghers of the two Republics, the ideas which animate them are held just as ardently by the Dutch population of the Cape Colony and Natal. The fight is to settle whether South Africa is to be made a second China or to be thrown open to the capital and enterprise of the world.

A Policy of Open Markets.

The British spirit in South Africa, as opposed to the Dutch, is for the fullest and freest possible expansion of the sub-Continent's resources, for utilising the free labour of the black, for abolishing all taxes that hamper trade and industry. These are all objects which bear immediate relation to commerce, and commerce in South Africa accordingly has had to play the part of a vigorous political combatant. To read the resolutions of the South African Chambers of Commerce, and compare them with the proceedings of the Dutch political organisations, would make one believe that both pronouncements were equally the issues of a vigorous party propaganda. But commerce has fought in vain for most of the reforms she has asked for. The Dutch have been the predominant power, and they have set themselves with the most unintelligent doggedness to resist any proposal which might interfere with their narrow conception of their own interests.

A New Trade Epoch.

Now, however, at the dreadful cost of a desperate war, commerce is to gain a voice of authority. The task of reconstituting the shattered fabric of South African politics will devolve upon Great Britain, and we can feel the utmost confidence that her object will be to ensure the fullest freedom for the economic development of the country. The conversion of the two Boer Republics into British territories will mean an enormous change in the political tendencies of the Cape Colony. The secret Pan-Afrikander ambitions of the past few years will have to be abandoned, and the continued maintenance of many abuses which recently seemed impregnable will have ceased to be within the limits of practical politics. Then Natal, which is refreshingly British and vigorously commercial, will be given a stronger position in the making of South Africa than it has hitherto enjoyed. No doubt the winning of the war and the pacification of the two Republics are tolerably arduous preliminaries to the general reconstitution of government. But the subject is of such vast importance and intricacy that one cannot very well be premature in discussing it.

The "Dominion of South Africa."

There is a great deal to be said, for example, for and against the projected Dominion of South Africa. Whether the war will leave the country in such a condition that the fragments of old institutions can be pieced into this whole of political federation is a question which only a bold man will attempt to answer. But, whatever the prospects of political unity may be, the conditions are already prepared for commercial unity. It will be for the trading interests of the country to see that both in the remodelling of the Boer Governments and in the formulation of the larger scheme of South African administration as a whole, every means are adopted to relieve commerce of the many absurd and injurious restrictions which at present retard her progress. In the successful construction of a new commercial system everything depends upon a clear recognition of the force and effect of existing conflicting tendencies and interests. It seems to us, therefore, worth while to point out, even during the progress of the great struggle between Briton and Boer, the abuses which are at present complained of in the commercial conditions of the country and the remedies which are most likely to prove successful in dealing with them. British manufacturers know how enormous has been the recent advance in the value of South African trade despite these abuses. Who can place any limit to its growth if these abuses were removed and the magnificent resources of the sub-Continent were thrown open to the enterprise and capital of the outside world ?

Free Trade versus Protection.

To some extent the economic position of South Africa resembles that of Great Britain at the time of the great Corn Law agitation. The fiscal system has been designed entirely in the interests of the producer as against those of the consumer. That the import tariff has not been constructed on a frankly prohibitive basis is due to the fact that the producer is so poor a hand at production as to be of sheer necessity a heavy consumer too. But the spirit of the country's fiscal policy is unequivocally exposed, beyond any dispute, by the clapping on of extra duties to meat and breadstuffs when these commodities began to be largely imported from Australia and America. Where the position in South Africa differs from that in England in the thirties and forties is in the fact that no party in the State is quite prepared to advocate unadulterated Free Trade. This, of course, is explained by the fact that there is no huge industrial population in South Africa, as there was in England, to whom cheap food means the possibility of a tolerable existence. Besides, it is generally recognised in South Africa that the development of the soil is really a prime necessity of a prosperous development, and the consuming portion of the community is quite ready to make some reasonable sacrifices in order to stimulate the growth of flocks and herds. But even amongst the town populations in the Cape Colony and Natal, and far more strongly amongst the mining communities of the Transvaal and Rhodesia, there is spreading the bitterest indignation against a policy which imposes fresh duties on oversea food supplies while the native production is far below even the present proportions of a continually growing demand.

Commercial Union.

It follows from these facts that commercial union for British South Africa cannot come, as it has been hoped in the past it would come, from the universal adoption of the Customs Union tariff, although with the abolition of the special tariff of the Transvaal it will be the only fiscal scheme in actual operation. It is true that Natal has lately subscribed assent to that very anomalous tariff. But she entered the Union grudgingly, and mainly because she was anxious to avoid any cut-throat competition for the Transvaal trade. As to Rhodesia, the acceptance of the Cape Colony tariff is one of the keenest grievances of the people against their administration. Indeed, one cannot expect it to stand as a permanent principle of taxation that miners in one country should pay unnecessarily dearly for their food and drink in order to support the farmers and distillers in another. So far as British manufacturers are concerned, they have hardly anything to complain of in the Customs Union tariff, beyond a few anomalies and stupidities such as are to be found in all tariffs. The dead-set of the South-African protectionist is not against manfactures but against foodstuffs. If, however, the war is to result in any scheme of fiscal federation for the sub-Continent, the Imperial authorities who have made such a measure possible will certainly have a right to demand that it shall be made a measure of assistance to Imperial trade.

FISCAL FEDERATION OF THE EMPIRE.

The idea of special favouring tariffs within the Empire has made huge progress since the days when Mr. Rhodes was snubbed for a tentative attempt to put it into practice. The new tariff of a United South Africa might very well give British (or, rather, Imperial) goods an advantage over Continental and other foreign merchandise. The country is a large importer from Australasia and India as well as from Great Britain, and it has practically no trade interests that are worth conserving with any foreign Power. The only objection which can be raised to this proposal is its effect upon revenue, but it is probable that any diminution in customs receipts would be more than compensated for by an all-round expansion of trade.

INTER-SOUTH AFRICAN FREE TRADE.

The "free interchange of South African products" is the one principle of the Customs Union which the reorganisers of the fiscal system, to include the Transvaal, could most heartily and emphatically endorse. The stupid and vindictive policy of the Transvaal—which has shut out Cape tobacco while it has let in Delagoa Bay spirit—has undoubtedly proved a severe handicap upon the producing industries of South Africa. With the old barriers removed, and with the fresh influx of capital and enterprise which will follow upon British control, there ought to be an extraordinary growth in the farming, fruit-growing, and viticultural activities. The oldest-fashioned Dutch landowner will have to recognise that he is face to face with new conditions after the war, and the soil of South Africa will cease to be an example of how it is possible to make nothing of the gifts of nature. There will no longer be that artificial inflation of produce prices which in the past has so largely reduced the necessity for agricultural exertion. And in the Transvaal the distressed burgher will no longer be able to draw a subvention from the public funds because he has no mind to cultivate his farm.

RAILWAY REFORM.

With a universal import tariff, and with the abolition of excessive duties on imported foodstuffs, the principal evils of which the South African trader has had to complain would be removed. Such matters as postal and telegraph anomalies are only matters of detail. There remains, however, the great question of the railways. In the past, unfortunately, the railways have been much too largely used as political instruments. The British Colonies cannot be held guiltless of exploiting the resources of the interior for the benefit of revenue, nor of making one branch of traffic bear the burden of others less profitable. In the Cape Colony there has been followed a cheese-paring policy of building local lines out of through traffic earnings, when at once the bold and the wise course would have been to float a new railway loan and to enter upon a big scheme of extension. These heresies are nothing, however, to the petty malevolence with which the Netherlands Railway Company of the Transvaal has been employed by the Transvaal Government to forward its pet scheme of crushing out British commercial supremacy within its territories. When the Imperial authorities take over the functions of Mr. Kruger's Government, they will, of course, assume its obligations towards the railway companies. They may be depended upon to establish a more equitable system of through rates from the ports, abandoning the foolish policy of placing obstacles in the way of trade's development along the line of least resistance. It will not be long, probably, before the Transvaal railway system becomes the property of the State. It will then only be reasonable to expect that the transport of goods for the up-country mining industries will, for the first time, be placed upon a thoroughly sound economic basis. There are, too, many details in the local working of the Netherlands Railway, of which both the mines and the merchants have the strongest reason to complain. One of the grievances of importers is the frequent impossibility of putting the responsibility for loss and damage in transit upon any one of the several railway authorities, and the freighter's consequent inability to obtain any redress. There is no doubt that the general adjustment of rates might be made on the Netherlands system with very great advantage to freighters. The small instalment of reforms which was granted a couple of years ago by no means exhausted the capabilities of concession in this direction.

TRANSVAAL MERCHANTS' GRIEVANCES.

The questions of tariffs and of railways are questions in which under the promised federation the whole of South Africa will be dealt with.

But before federation is considered the Imperial authorities will have to carry out the important and difficult preliminary of reorganising the administration of the two Republics. There are no commercial problems in particular to be dealt with in the Orange Free State, but almost the whole body of the Uitlanders' grievances in the Transvaal is made up of oppressions and exactions upon trade. It is needless to point out how intimately the interests of merchants and storekeepers are bound up with the prosperity of the mines, and with the widespread movement in mining enterprise which is certain to follow upon the establishment of British control. But it may be pointed out that the wholesale evasion of the native Liquor Law has meant an enormous drain upon the native demand for all other commodities. Then there is the question of the treatment of Asiatics. Mr. Kruger's proposal was to insist upon the confinement of Asiatics, both for trading and residence, in locations. Against this proposal the Imperial Government protested on the ground that it was a breach of the Convention. Probably the majority of wholesale traders in the Transvaal would prefer the maintenance of the present freedom for Asiatics, with a stricter enforcement of sanitary regulations, and they would certainly object to any legislation which would favour their further increase. Another matter of almost equal consequence to both mining and commerce is the question of native labour supply. Something like free trade should be established in this traffic in place of the ill-advised pass regulations which have served only as encouragements to the flagrant dishonesty of Boer officials. It is not too much to say that a native labour supply at once plentiful and sober would mean the beginning of a new industrial era in South Africa. The effect upon the community's consuming power of lower import dues and railway rates need not be dwelt upon. Nor is it necessary to discuss such minor matters as trading licenses, police protection, and municipal administration. It may be worth pointing out, however, that the theory of Transvaal jurisprudence, as established by the autocrat Kruger, gave positively no security of title to property ; and it will be readily understood what sort of an influence this fact exerted upon commercial enterprise in the last days of the Republic. It is impossible to say what the aggregate benefit to British manufacturers of a healthy condition of things in the Transvaal would be. Probably it would amount to several millions of additional purchases annually. But what is certain is that after this war, Johannesburg will follow in its old courses and once more " beggar expectation."

THE ECONOMIC IDEAL.

It is perfectly obvious, therefore, that commerce has a very substantial concern in the lamentable struggle now proceeding in South Africa, and that it will have much to say in the reorganisation of affairs which will follow upon the conclusion of hostilities. In many of its contentions trade will run counter to the views of other interests, though we believe that the policy we have formulated would be found to benefit in the long run every class of the community. It is well, therefore, that the representatives of commerce should determine upon the attitude they will adopt, and that they should be prepared to prevent any perpetuation of the anachronisms and anomalies which have hindered the economic development of South Africa. It would be a thousand pities if the effusion of blood and the sacrifice of life which the settlement of pending questions by war has involved should leave unaltered any of these abuses. Many of them are local in their working and must be left to the gradual operation of local opinion. But the whole trend and tone of opinion in South Africa will depend upon the wisdom and breadth of view of the men who are entrusted with the task of setting up a new scheme of administration in the conquered Republics, and with the greater task of federating the several territories into one free, prosperous and progressive commonwealth.

APPENDIX VI.

FROM THE STANDPOINT OF A PROGRESSIVE BURGHER OF THE ORANGE FREE STATE.

The Orange Free State and President Kruger's Policy.

The Special Correspondent of the London *Times* at Bloemfontein sends an interesting despatch, dated 25th April, 1900, from which the following extracts are taken. They contain the views of a Progressive burgher of the Free State, the party lately led by Mr. J. G. Fraser, who, to the loss of all South Africa, was defeated in the Presidential election of 1896.

Few chapters in the history of the development of that anti-British movement which finally culminated in the present war in South Africa could be more interesting than that dealing with the political relations between the Orange Free State and the Transvaal.

Both Republics had their origin in the Great Trek. But, though both sprang from that movement of discontent with British rule, such as it was in the thirties, there was a great difference in the degree of the discontent. A large section of the emigrant farmers was composed of men of adventurous nomadic habits, impatient of all control, and bitterly hostile to all those elements of modern civilisation which British influence represented. It was these who, when in 1848 direct sovereignty over the country between the Orange and Vaal rivers was resumed by Sir Harry Smith, decided to cross over into the then almost unknown regions beyond the latter river, and founded various turbulent little States carved out of territories conquered from the natives. These ultimately coalesced into a single republic, which assumed to itself the ambitious title of the South African Republic. Those, on the other hand, whose grievances had been largely temporary and local, and who realised the advantages of some form of stable government, remained in the fertile country south of the Vaal, and, being joined by many immigrants, Dutch, English, and German, became the fathers of the Free Staters of the present generation. Thus there was from the very first a great difference of character between the two Republics, and for many years after the retrocession of the Free State intercourse between it and Cape Colony was much closer than between it and the Transvaal. There grew up in South Africa during the sixties and seventies a Dutch nationalist aspiration, aiming at the ultimate creation of an united Dutch South Africa from which English rule should be eliminated. This aspiration was chiefly fostered by foreign immigrants, Hollanders and Germans, who came to seek their fortunes in the Republics, and by some of the more educated among the Cape Dutch who had studied in Europe, and there imbibed the views about nationalism which were in fashion with the generation that followed the half-nationalist, half-liberal movement of 1848. Conspicuous among these were men like Carl Borckenhagen, a talented, ambitious and unscrupulous German, who, through the medium of his journal, the *Bloemfontein Express*, and still more through the enormous secret influence he exercised over President Reitz and his successor Steyn, devoted all his powers to the propagation of the nationalist idea of hatred of England; F. W. Reitz, a rising advocate in Cape Colony, who afterwards rose to become Chief Justice and President of the Free State, and is now State Secretary of the Transvaal; the Rev. S. J. du Toit, editor of the *Patriot*—since converted to a sounder appreciation of what the future welfare of South Africa demands. It was these three men who, in 1882, founded the Afrikander Bond. In President Burgers, too, with his magnificent plans for the future development of the South African Republic, these views found a typical representative.

It was the revolt of 1881, the series of defeats inflicted on British regulars by a handful of Afrikander farmers, and the short-sighted and unexpected surrender of Mr. Gladstone's Government, that gave the nationalist aspiration a chapter in history, a new hope, and—in Paul Kruger—a leader.

During the war of 1881 large numbers of Free Staters and colonials flocked to the Transvaal to join their kinsfolk. In the Free State many petitions were signed and addressed to President Brand expressing sympathy with the Boers and asking the President's intervention. On 7th February, 1881, Kruger sent from Heidelberg a long appeal for intervention or assistance to President Brand, ending with a passage which may well be quoted as summing up the object of Kruger's policy from that day to this: "Freedom shall rise in South Africa, as the sun from the morning clouds, as freedom rose in the United States of America. Then shall it be, from the Zambesi to Simon's Bay, Africa for the Afrikander." Brand offered his mediation, which the British Government, glad to get out of the scrape as best it could, eagerly accepted. At the Newcastle conference Brand practically dictated the terms to which both parties were to submit. But, though Brand's sympathies inclined towards the revolted burghers of the Transvaal, he still remained a friend to Great Britain. He was far too sagacious to be led astray by the nationalist delirium which the war awakened among the Dutch all over South Africa. He did all in his power to discountenance the Bond advocated by Borckenhagen and Reitz as only calculated to cause future mischief. His sane, far-seeing policy was guided by a sincere patriotism which looked not only to the Orange Free State, but to the whole of

South Africa. He looked on the British power as a friendly factor—a factor essential to the development of those portions of South Africa which it had retained under its control. Brand's comparatively early death in 1888 was one of the greatest misfortunes that ever befell South Africa, as it left the field clear for Paul Kruger. From the very first Kruger was determined not to rest content with the settlement secured for the Transvaal by President Brand. Through the weakness of Lord Derby he secured its modification by peaceful means in 1884. But the reaction which followed in England and which led to the despatch of the Warren expedition in the following year convinced him that he had now got as much out of Great Britain as he was ever likely to get by peaceful request, and that henceforward he must look to political intrigue and physical force to help him in his further plans. For a time the poverty of the country, internal dissensions, and the task of maintaining himself in power—an object which in his eyes has always ranked above all else, above even the destruction of the British power in South Africa—kept him quiet. In 1886 came the discovery of the Witwatersrand with its promise of immeasurable wealth, to be used not only to keep the President in office, but also to carry out by the practical instruments of armed force and lavish intrigue the vague ambitions once cherished by President Burgers. The Delagoa Bay railway scheme initiated by Burgers was now taken in hand by Kruger with characteristic determination and unscrupulousness, and as an essential preliminary the Portuguese Government was driven into breaking its faith with the English company which had got the concession for the railway to the Transvaal border. The objects Kruger kept before his eyes in those years were twofold. On the one hand, his aim was to connect the Transvaal with the sea, not only through Delagoa Bay, but by the actual extension of its territory to the coast through Zululand or Amatongaland, so that it should have its own harbour and become economically free both of Portugal and the British colonies, and be able to enter into more direct relations with European Powers which might support it against England; and, on the other hand, to arm his own burghers and render the Free State economically and politically so completely dependent on the Transvaal that, when the time should come either for throwing off the London Convention or for annexing some piece of disputed territory necessary for his schemes, he should have at his back a military Power with which no British Government, such as British Governments then were, would dare to try the issue of war.

In 1887 two secret conferences took place between the Transvaal and the Orange Free State, dealing with various economical and political questions. Nothing could give a clearer idea of Kruger's policy towards the Free State than some brief account of these meetings. The first conference took place in President Kruger's house at Pretoria on 31st May and the next two days. There were present on the one side President

Kruger with his State Secretary and State Attorney, Messrs. Bok and Leyds, and a commission of the Transvaal Volksraad consisting of Messrs. F. Wolmarans, Klopper, Taljaard, Lombaard, and Spies, and on the other side a deputation from the Free State Volksraad composed of Messrs. Fraser, Klynveld, and Myburgh. The Transvaal representatives are very typical. Above them all stands out the President, who practically leads the whole conference; knowing exactly what he wants, indifferent to argument, returning again and again to the same point, however often refuted; incapable of conviction, though ready as a last resort to lower his demands step by step and claim that he has made a great concession —the same Kruger as twelve years later at Bloemfontein, only here not on the defensive against a superior intellect and a will as strong as his own, but active, persuasive, impassioned, speaking among men more capable of submitting to his influence. At his side is the smooth plausible young Hollander Leyds, taking no part in the debate, but making his influence discernible in almost every argument. The commission represents Kruger's stalwarts in the Volksraad, the men chosen for their unquestioning fidelity to the hand that has fed them and kept them in their places, for their narrow religious and political prejudices and for their genuine hatred of England. Just as the Transvaal representatives for most purposes mean President Kruger, so the Free Staters mean Mr. J. G. Fraser. Son of one of those Scotch Presbyterian clergymen who came out to South Africa in the middle of the century to supply the intellectual deficiencies of the Dutch Reformed Church, Mr. Fraser entered the Free State as a young man, and threw in his lot unreservedly with the country of his adoption, rapidly attracting President Brand's attention and becoming his right-hand man, his political *alter ego*, in which capacity he came on this occasion to Pretoria. After Brand's death Mr. Fraser resolutely continued the tradition of Brand's policy, but unfortunately, as year by year the influence of the noisier and extremer party led by Reitz and Borckenhagen, and afterwards by Steyn, prevailed, his own hold grew weaker. In vain Mr. Fraser for years prophesied the inevitable result of following the mischievous policy of the Transvaal. The mass of the burghers, swayed by sentiment and deluded by their belief in England's weakness, refused to heed his warnings. And now Mr. Fraser has lived to see the little State with which he has so long been identified, and which owes so much to him, throw away its independence in defence of an unworthy and hopeless cause.

The object with which the Free State deputies had come was a single and straightforward one—to arrange for a general treaty of amity and commerce which should bring the two kindred States closer together, and more especially to come to some agreement with regard to the scheme of building a railway across the Free State from Cape Colony to join on to a proposed Transvaal railway from the Vaal to the Witwatersrand and

Pretoria. Another suggestion the deputation had come to urge upon the Transvaal was that of joining a general South African Customs Union. Both these suggestions met with Kruger's strongest disapproval. They meant bringing South Africa together, linking the Free State in closer commercial, social, and political relationship with the British possessions, instead of bringing it into completer dependence on the Transvaal. More than that, it meant English commerce and English immigration on the Rand, and threatened to swamp his carefully-fostered schemes for the Delagoa Railway and for German and Hollander immigration. Throughout the whole series of discussions at the conference the contrast between the attitude of Kruger and the Free State Deputies is very striking. The latter have come to discuss in a straightforward matter of fact way certain economical matters of vital interest to both Republics. For Kruger and his commissioners these are all questions of high politics, to be judged according as they fit in, or clash with, a certain mysterious secret policy to which allusions are constantly dropped. In fact, while the Free Staters talk like business politicians, the Transvaalers talk like stage conspirators. On the railway question Kruger insists that the Free State shall not construct, or even sanction, its railway, or, at any rate, the part connecting Bloemfontein with Cape Colony, before the Delagoa Railway is completed. Delagoa Bay must be the port for the Free State, and not an English port which would let in English trade and bring English influences into the land. For in Kruger's eyes English trade is the worst form of ruin. It must be kept out of the Republics at all costs. To quote his own metaphorical language :—" For the little sheep my door is open ; but the wolf I mean to keep out." Or, as another member of his commission puts it :—" What need have we of the Colony and its importation ? The trade they represent to us as life and prosperity is our death. We Republics are strong enough; let us go together." Against such arguments it is useless for the Free Staters to plead that the line is an urgent necessity for them, and that there is no sign of the Delagoa Railway being completed for years to come, or to ask whether the Transvaal is quite indifferent to Free State interests, as long as it can get the Free State under its control. Kruger entreats them to wait, vows that railways are a delusion and a snare, that for the present the Free State is much better without one, that to join with Cape Colony now wil ruin the Delagoa Railway or any railway he may wish to build to a harbour yet to be acquired. In time, he promises them, they shall have a great railway system radiating all over South Africa from Pretoria, but not before the Transvaal has made itself absolutely independent of English political influence and English trade.

Delagoa is a life and death question for us. Help us! If you hook on to the colony you cut our throat. . . . . How can our State exist without the Delagoa Railway ? . . . . Keep free ! We shall help you, even with a contribution if necessary. I wish to share with you, but if you refuse, go! We shall build, if it takes us ten years. The Lord rules! If the Free State will not work with us, we shall make our own harbour on our own borders. . . . . If you build your line I will not let it join mine.

As for the Customs Union, Kruger declares that the Transvaal could never enter it unless it had its own harbour and was free of its dependence on the convention. As things are the English will only use their position to swindle the Transvaal of its proper share in the receipts. He entreats the Free State to keep clear of such a union.

No Customs union! Customs unions are made between equal States with equal access to harbours, but where one is master and the other dependent there can be no union. We are striving to settle the question of our own harbour peacefully.

Mr. Fraser sceptically remarks that a harbour requires forts and ships and soldiers and sailors to man them, or else it would be at the mercy of the first passing gunboat. Kruger, somewhat nettled, replies that, once the Transvaal has a harbour, foreign Powers can intervene in its affairs. The Transvaal must get into touch with foreign Powers in view of eventualities.

The strength of our position lies in our making the British Government understand that the Republics hold together. Then we can be sure that we will be taken into account. . . . . Let us speak frankly. We are not going to be dependent on England. Take no railway union—remain without a railway. That is better than to take their money. The future will provide greater blessings if you work with us. Let them keep their money. Let them not bind you. The Lord reigns—none other—the deliverance is near at hand.

So, too, Mr. F. Wolmarans :—

We must look at the matter from the political standpoint of our independence. We have had much experience of Her Majesty's Government, and we will and must shake ourselves free and become independent. We are still insufficiently prepared (*ongerust*). We wish to get to the sea, more especially with an eye to future complications. Let us first get to the sea and achieve our independence. Wait a few years. Why are we to-day worried at Delagoa? English influence! They wish to keep us in bonds and dependence; that is what we struggle against. . . . . You know our secret policy. We cannot treat the colony as we would treat you. The colony would destroy us. It is not the Dutch there that we are fighting against. Time shall show what we mean to do with them; for the present we must keep them off.

These extracts give some idea of the hopes and fears that animated President Kruger and his followers in 1887. They hardly suggest the theory so common among those whose knowledge of South African affairs begins with New Year's Day, 1896, that Kruger bore no ill-will to England or the English, before the bitter disillusionment of the Jameson raid.

The result of the conference was that Kruger retired beaten, Brand having made it quite clear that he would not let the Free State be dragged into Kruger's policy or give up his power of independent action as regards either the railway or a customs union.

In the following year Brand died, and was succeeded by Reitz. For a while Brand's influence in the Volksraad was strong enough to act as a check on Reitz's desire to subordinate Free State interests to Transvaal ambitions. Transvaal maladministration and the exclusive policy adopted towards the Uitlanders, many of whom were Free Staters, offended a large section among the more thoughtful people in the Free State. Nevertheless, in 1889 Reitz succeeded in concluding a conditional defensive alliance with Kruger at Potchefstroom; and as Brand's influence died away the doctrines of Pan-Afrikanderdom, as expounded by the new President and still more eloquently confirmed by the growing wealth and power of the Transvaal, found ready acceptance. How far this change of sentiment had gone by the autumn of 1895, when Reitz resigned owing to mental breakdown, is shown by the fact that in the preliminary selection in the Volksraad of candidates for the Presidency only nineteen votes were given to Mr. Fraser as against forty-one given to Mr. Steyn, an out-and-out follower of the extreme Afrikander doctrine as preached by Reitz and Borckenhagen. In the interval between this selection and the actual election came the Jameson raid. Fraser, who had for years condemned Kruger's policy towards the Uitlanders, and could not, therefore, enter into the denunciation of the raid with the same unqualified fervour of invective as Steyn, was disastrously beaten. Transvaal money is believed to have played no small part in the expenses of that election. Immediately after the raid the Free State Volksraad passed a resolution setting aside the Potchefstroom treaty and declaring that the Free State burghers should be at the disposal of the Transvaal if its independence were endangered from without or within. In the following year Steyn went to Pretoria, where he was received with tremendous enthusiasm and welcomed as the destined President of the United Republics. A definite treaty of offensive and defensive alliance was now concluded—the treaty under the terms of which the Free State declared war upon Great Britain two years later. It was in vain that the moderate party, headed by Fraser, protested and declared that there could be only one outcome of a policy whose whole object was to strengthen the Transvaal in its resolve to suppress the Uitlanders and defy the British Government— namely, war and the destruction of the Republics. In a speech to his constituents on 17th March, 1898, Mr. Fraser condemned in the strongest language the misrule and corruption in the Transvaal, and, reviewing the whole history of the relations between the two Republics, denounced President Steyn for having sacrificed to a spurious sentiment the proud and independent position won for the Free State by President Brand, and for having reduced the Free State to be a vassal of the South African Republic, enjoying the extreme privilege of fighting its enemies and policing its citizens without having a voice in its affairs. The alliance was a sham which was destined to ruin both States.

Mr. Fraser's protests fell on deaf ears. President Kruger and his agents at Bloemfontein had completely persuaded the people of the Free State that no British Government would dare to challenge the combined forces of the two Republics to the issue of war, and that beyond diplomatic protests there would be no interference with Kruger's policy as long as the Republics held closely together.

The Bloemfontein conference made some pretence at reviving the old mediating policy of President Brand. But it was only a pretence. There was no attempt at impartiality; still less could the Free State, bound hand and foot as it was by treaty, bring any real pressure to bear on its ally. Mr. Abraham Fischer, a plausible, ambitious lawyer, attended the sittings of the conference professedly as interpreter, really in order to mislead the Free State Volksraad as to what passed. It was upon his account of the proceedings that the Volksraad voted its resolution expressing its complete satisfaction at Kruger's first proposals. In the subsequent negotiations Fischer, while actively engaged on peace missions, did no little to make peace impossible. It was he who, in August, went to Pretoria and urged Kruger to refuse the proposal for a joint commission as an unwarrantable interference with his independence. Undoubtedly it was the attitude of Messrs. Steyn and Fischer, and of the Volksraad which they swayed, that more than anything else strengthened President Kruger in his resolve to resist the British demands. The history of the last few months, the secret session of the Free State Volksraad, where President Steyn openly accused the British agent at Pretoria of having deceived and misled Mr. Smuts, the correspondence with Sir A. Milner ordering him to withdraw British troops from the Republican frontiers, the wholesale annexation of British territory and commandeering of British subjects to fight against their allegiance are too recent and well known to require fuller treatment. Never in history has the independence of a small, prosperous, and well-governed State been more wantonly and light-heartedly thrown away by its rulers than in the case of the Orange Free State.

APPENDIX VII.

FROM THE STANDPOINT OF IRISH COLONISTS IN SOUTH AFRICA.

From the *Cape Times* of the 16th March, 1900.

IRELAND FOR EVER.

An Enthusiastic Meeting—The National Sentiment—Irish Regiment of Guards—His Excellency's Policy.

A representative meeting of Irishmen resident in Cape Town was held at the International Hotel last night, under the presidency of the Deputy-Mayor (Mr. T. J. O'Reilly). There was a large attendance, including the Rev. Dr. McCarthy, the Rev. Father Moran, the Rev. Father O'Reilly, the Rev. J. J. McClure, Dr. Farrelly, Messrs. J. C. O'Riley, F. L. St. Leger, Burke, Ford, Wallace, J. Gabriel, Chadwick, W. Black, Ryan, J. E. Wood, and many others, the hall being well filled, and the proceedings throughout of an enthusiastic character.

The Chairman, in opening the proceedings, said that the present was a most opportune time for the Irishmen to come together and pass resolutions of the nature which would be submitted to them that night, especially considering the amount of valour which had been shown by the Irish troops now in this country (cheers). Probably such another occasion would never come again during their lifetime, and it would be seen from the resolutions that the Irishmen of the army and navy were to be allowed to wear the national emblem, the shamrock, on St. Patrick's day (cheers). And further, the valour of the Irish troops was going to be marked by the formation of an Irish regiment of Guards, and when they had heard the resolutions which would be spoken to he had no doubt that they would be carried unanimously (cheers).

St. Patrick's Day and the Shamrock.

Dr. Farrelly moved the first resolution in the following terms: "That we Irishmen, in public meeting assembled, recognise that our countrymen in Her Majesty's service have added fresh laurels to the national honour, and thank Her Majesty for acknowledging their merit by her order to wear the shamrock on St. Patrick's Day, and of her intention of forming an Irish regiment of Guards, and of paying a visit to our country, where a loyal and enthusiastic welcome awaits her. And that this resolution be handed by the chairman to His Excellency Sir Alfred Milner for transmission to

Her Majesty." Speaking to the resolution, Dr. Farrelly said that the present occasion marked the beginning of happier times which were in store for them. He thought that after many centuries Englishmen, Irishmen, Scotchmen, and Welshmen had learnt to appreciate one another's qualities. The Queen's action in regard to the shamrock, everyone must admit to be a most graceful recognition of the national sentiment, a recognition of the Irish as a constituent force, and not as a disruptive element of the Empire which ruled the greater part of the civilised world. It sealed the union of the scattered units of the Empire, and tended greatly to heal those wounds inflicted by dead and gone dissension—(cheers)—far off things of long ago. That those were not altogether ended, of course they all knew, and it certainly marked an event which could have only one result, and that was to lead Irishmen to understand not merely their national, but their Imperial responsibility. The formation of the Irish regiment of Guards was also a step taken by Her Majesty which must commend itself to Irishmen. It was a most fitting recognition of the valour of their countrymen in the field, and of the skill of Irish generals (cheers). Her Majesty's visit to Ireland was also a mark of a clearer understanding among the constituent peoples of the United Kingdom. They had not made their own destiny; it had been imposed on them, and they were linked together for ever, English, Irish, Scotch, and Welsh, and he thought it was a most fortunate omen for the future of the Empire, which they all had to administer, that Her Majesty should have proposed to pay a visit to Ireland.

CONTINENTAL CRITICISM.

He had noticed a very curious misapprehension of the attitude of the Irish towards the Empire on the part of the foreign critics. There were many subjects of dispute and misunderstanding between English and Irish, but very few of the foreign writers had noticed that their attitude was that of disputants in a family quarrel. They were prepared to discuss, even with unnecessary heat at times, their respective sides of the quarrel, but on the intervention of one whom they conceived to be outside the circle of the Empire, their attitude changed. That was one of the greatest lessons which the present state of affairs in South Africa impressed upon them, and the effect itself was emphasised by Her Majesty's recent action. Another thing which their foreign critics had failed to see was the position of the English towards the Irish themselves. One could not have lived for many years in England without perceiving the extreme good-nature, the absolute absence of jealousy, and the readiness to appreciate public service on the part of the English towards the Irish, and most foreigners absolutely failed to grasp that fact. He thought there lay a heavy burden on them not to be behind in reciprocating that feeling, and to recognise that however much they might dispute on minor issues, on the greater

issues which affected the safety of the Empire they were one with their
English friends (loud cheers). The Imperial sentiment amongst the Irish
was usually described by continental critics as non-existent, but he thought
that was a complete failure to appreciate the facts, for they must remember
that at all great crises of the Empire's fate—from Waterloo to Delhi, from
Kandahar to Alexandria, from Khartoum to Paardeberg, Irish skill and
Irish valour in the field had helped to create the Empire. In the more
peaceful field of the law, of administration, and of diplomacy, Irish service
had constituted our people co-heirs of a great inheritance (loud cheers).

Mr. Wood, in seconding the motion, said that never would an order have
been so gladly obeyed as the order for the wearing of the shamrock on
St. Patrick's Day, and he was sure that Her Majesty would have no more
loyal and devoted Guardsmen than the Irish Guards (cheers).

The resolution was carried by acclamation.

LORD ROBERTS.

Dr. Marius Wilson moved the second resolution as follows: " That this
meeting of Irishmen wishes to convey to Lord Roberts their high appreciation of the great services he has rendered to the British Empire, and, as
brother Irishmen, to congratulate him and the troops under his command
on the great successes which they have achieved. They hope and trust
that the great work which he has still in hand may be brought ere long to
a successful issue, so that the British flag may triumphantly fly from Cape
Point to the Zambesi. As Irishmen we drink your health and our
brother countrymen's on this St. Patrick's Day." He observed that Lord
Roberts had come out to take the command of the forces in South Africa
at a time when he was mourning the death of a son who had laid down
his life in the service of his country, and since his lordship had been out
here he had carried matters on in a way they all liked (hear, hear). For
years past everyone had looked forward to a United South Africa; the
only difference in the point of view was that one section of the community
wanted it under one flag, whilst they wanted it under the flag under which
they were born, and under which they lived (cheers).

Mr. J. C. O'Riley seconded the resolution, and said that for the last fifty
years he had been a resident of this Colony, and he had witnessed the
arrival of every general since the days of Sir Harry Smith in 1851. He
also mentioned that he had served through the Kaffir War of 1851, at a
time when he was scarcely bigger than the gun he carried (cheers).

The motion was passed with unanimous enthusiasm and hearty
cheering.

A SCANDAL TO CIVILISATION.

The Rev. Dr. McCarthy then moved the next resolution, which read as
follows : " That this meeting of Irish colonists records its profound convic-

tion that in the present war the Empire is fighting for justice and peace, and tenders to the High Commissioner its absolute confidence and respectful sympathy in his grave anxieties." He said that personally he held that the war was just simply because it was unavoidable, and he took it that the Empire was quite justified in forcing the Transvaal to remove the state of oppression which existed, even by the employment of force. Both legally and morally Great Britain was fully justified in taking such steps as should remove what had been for a long time a scandal to civilisation and an insult to their brethren, which they all felt (hear, hear). He might also point out the necessarily bad effect which the Transvaal had upon the Dutch in the Cape Colony. He had lived in the country too long to say that the Dutch were disloyal. There were disloyal Dutch no doubt, but the tendency of things was such that the prevalence of the Africander ideal in the Transvaal meant a war for the existence of the British flag, or else the reduction of all men except the burghers to the level of the population of Johannesburg. So he was firmly convinced that the Empire was fighting for justice and for peace, because if they had hesitated now they would have had to fight later on. It was not the Empire that had broken the peace; it was those men who, by their irreconcilable attitude, had shown that their anxiety was to govern the whole of South Africa.

THE HIGH COMMISSIONER.

He would ask them to recollect, moreover, if they had ever heard of a nation piling up arms which they did not intend to use; and while they piled up arms in the Transvaal, the Transvaal emissaries had invaded the Colony, and while he was perfectly ready to acquit the majority of the Dutchmen of the Colony of disloyalty, he was perfectly sure that there was a conspiracy to seduce them, and that it had succeeded only too well. In conclusion, it only remained for him to ask them to tender to His Excellency Sir Alfred Milner their absolute confidence (loud cheers). He regretted greatly to learn that under the recent strain His Excellency's health had suffered during the past few weeks, but he would have the sympathy of all honest Irishmen—(cheers)—and when his term of office expired they would show him how much they admired the courage and wisdom which His Excellency had shown in spite of domestic treason, insult, and contumely (renewed cheers).

The Rev. J. J. McClure, in seconding the resolution, paid an eloquent tribute to the manner in which Sir Alfred Milner had conducted the affairs of the Empire in South Africa, and observed that they must all feel proud of the part which their country had played in this great struggle.

The resolution was carried with much enthusiasm.

On the motion of the Rev. Father O'Reilly, a vote of thanks was passed to Lady Roberts for the great work she has done in aiding the families of

Irish soldiers, and the proceedings came to a close with the singing of the National Anthem.

The Queen's Reply to the resolution moved by Dr. Farrelly addressed to Her Majesty was transmitted by cable and forwarded through the hands of the High Commissioner.

Copy of message dated London, 17th March, 1900 :—" The Queen sincerely thanks the Irishmen in Cape Town for their loyal message, unanimously agreed upon at a public meeting and transmitted through the High Commissioner. The sentiments which it expressed have greatly touched Her Majesty. The Queen has always felt confident that the same spirit of courage and allegiance which has distinguished her Irish soldiers in the face of the enemy would be shared by their brethren in the Colony in support of the authority of Her Government."

(*Cape Times*, 19th March, 1900.)

APPENDIX VIII.

FROM THE STANDPOINT OF A MINISTER OF THE CROWN
IN CAPE COLONY.

A Speech by the Hon. T. Lynedoch Graham, Q.C., M.L.C., now
Colonial Secretary in the Present Cabinet.

The speech was delivered at a meeting in support of the policy of the
Imperial Government, held at Claremont, Cape Town, on 30th March,
1900, and is reported in the *Cape Times* of 31st March.

"A Governor with a Backbone."

The Hon. T. L. Graham, Q.C., M.L.C., who was received with loud and
prolonged cheers, moved: "That this meeting desires to place on record
its high appreciation of the conduct of Her Majesty's High Commissioner
throughout his tenure of office, and its complete confidence in the policy
of Her Majesty's Government, as administered by him." (Loud cheers.)
Mr. Graham said, "I find some difficulty in adequately expressing myself
in moving the resolution, because I feel that few, if any, of the distinguished individuals who have occupied the onerous and responsible
position of High Commissioner of this Colony so rapidly gained the
lasting affection of the loyal inhabitants of this country as Sir Alfred
Milner—(loud cheers)—and this in spite of the fact that to the vast
majority of the inhabitants of South Africa when Sir Alfred Milner
accepted that responsible position his figure was an unfamiliar one. We
knew him as an able scholar. We knew him as a brilliant writer, but
we had yet to learn of those high qualities of statesmanship and administration which we have now learned by personal experience. (Cheers,
and a Voice: He's too sharp for Kruger.) I well remember when the
question of a successor to Lord Rosmead was first mooted how eagerly
we scanned the cables from England to see who was coming out as High
Commissioner. I well remember the critical period of His Excellency's
appointment. I recollect early in February, shortly after Sir Alfred's
appointment was promulgated, an article had been published in the *Daily
Chronicle* of London, then under its old régime, and edited by a man
whose sympathies were strongly pro-Boer, and in that article it was
pointed out that Sir Alfred Milner was coming to the Cape at one of the
most critical periods of its history, and the writer wound up his article,

which created a considerable sensation at the time, by pointing out that the time would be considered even more critical were it not for the full trust and confidence reposed in Sir Alfred Milner's fairness and honour. And the editor of the *Chronicle* was not the only person who had been prepared to eulogise our new High Commissioner, because we found at a public function men of almost every shade of political opinion united in wishing our High Commissioner God-speed, and in congratulating the Government upon the excellence of their appointment. We found men like Sir William Harcourt, John Morley, Lord Rosebery, combining with Mr. Asquith, Mr. Balfour, and Mr. Goschen in their congratulations, and we waited expectantly, and we have not been disappointed. (Cheers.) We, however, soon found that in Sir Alfred Milner we had a man of iron will—(cheers)—and fearless courage—(renewed cheers)—and what was more, a man who intended to do what he considered was best in the interests of the Empire, entirely regardless of the consequences. (Cheers.) I remember well having a conversation with your member (Mr. Innes), whose eloquent and interesting speech we have heard with such pleasure to-night, very shortly after Sir Alfred Milner's arrival in this colony, Perhaps Mr. Innes will not mind my mentioning it. We were discussing. as everybody was at the time, the High Commissioner, and I asked Mr. Innes what his opinion was of the new High Commissioner. Mr. Innes said—I shall never forget his words—" Well, of one thing I am perfectly certain. He has got a backbone like a lightning conductor." (Loud and prolonged cheers.) And if there was one thing that South Africa wanted at that time it was a man with a backbone, and within a very short time we have all been only too eager and anxious to join in the chorus of praise with which Sir Alfred Milner had left the shores of England. (Hear, hear.)

THE ATTACKS ON SIR ALFRED MILNER.

Now in what I have said I have been specially referring to the circumstances surrounding His Excellency's early appointment, for this reason, because lately we have seen political parties in this country and in England—(Voice: "Rebels," and cheers)—people perhaps who eagerly and by all kinds of means, underhand and otherwise, endeavouring to prove that Sir Alfred Milner was a firebrand, sent out here by Mr. Chamberlain with the deliberate object of plunging Great Britain into an unjust war with the Transvaal. (Cries of "Shame.") We know that that was absolutely untrue. (Loud cheers.) We know that when Sir Alfred Milner arrived here his sympathy with the Dutch was a matter of regard. In June, shortly after his arrival, with the cheers of the Jubilee still ringing in his ears, he wrote a despatch to Mr. Chamberlain in which he stated that notwithstanding racial difficulties in South Africa, so far as he could observe, they had no effect on the loyalty of any section of the inhabitants. (Cheers.) What was it that made him change his mind? It was the inexorable logic of facts. It was that that had changed his mind, and now we find him attacked by those persons whom he had referred to, and I have been endeavouring to ascertain on what grounds they based their attacks. First of all, so far as I can learn, they said that Sir Alfred Milner had rushed this country into an unjust war. ("No.") Well, I would say, let them refer to the despatches; let them refer to the prolonged negotiations which preceded the ultimatum that was sent by the Transvaal Republic, and I would ask, could any negotiations have been carried on with more patience, and with greater tact than those conducted by Sir Alfred Milner? (Loud cheers.) When one came to read those despatches and follow the train of events that led up to the war, it was clear that if there was one thing that the British Government desired it was peace, and if there was one thing that the British Government desired to avoid it was war, at all costs, saving the loss of British supremacy in South Africa. (Loud cheers.) And then another charge that has been hurled against Sir Alfred Milner was that he made reflections upon the loyalty of a certain section of the inhabitants. It was a charge which was seriously advanced in the columns of certain papers appearing both here and in England. It certainly did sound comical in the light of events, when we see a large section of the inhabitants of this Colony who have broken out into open rebellion. We have got to look not only at the rank and file. We have beyond the mere rank and file professional men, field-cornets, justices of the peace galore. (Laughter and cheers.) We have ministers of religion and members of Parliament. (Loud groans.)

TRAITORS IN PARLIAMENT.

Yes, we have members of Parliament, and I will give them one or two little particulars with regard to these latter gentry. (Cheers.) First of all, let us take the case of Vryburg. If you will take the map you will find that in every district into which a Boer commando entered the inhabitants of Dutch descent have risen with open arms to receive them, not all of them, but the vast majority who took Vryburg. Seventy-five per cent. of the inhabitants were now either squatting round Mafeking, endeavouring to subdue the indomitable Baden-Powell—(loud and prolonged cheers)—or else they were engaged in the more congenial occupation of looting loyalists' farms. And, as I have said before, it was not only the rank and file, but we have a fair sprinkling of members of Parliament. What happened at Burghersdorp? There was a patriotic gentleman, named Joubert. (Laughter.) He is at present, I believe, member for the district of Albert. When the Boer commando entered Burghersdorp, of course this gentleman was there. One of the very first things done was to raise a commando of rebels, and a considerable force was got together, which was captained by a well-known field-cornet, also a Justice of the Peace—(laughter)—and a rebel commando consisting almost entirely of Dutch Colonists. What did this patriotic gentleman, Mr. Joubert, do? On the market square at Burghersdorp he presented the gallant commandant with a Free State flag, beautifully embroidered, and expressed the pious hope that he would carry it with the force with honour and glory to victory. (Loud groans and cries of "Traitor" and "Hang him.") That patriotic gentleman is still at large. And then there is another gentleman, well known to all members of Parliament, whose speeches were read by all with the very greatest attention. That gentleman is Mr. Van der Walt. (Groans and laughter.) I believe Mr. Van der Walt has been a member of Parliament since the year 1884, or even longer. What has this gentleman done? He is one of the most loquacious members in the House. He makes lengthy speeches on almost every conceivable subject; but never was he so eloquent as when he was protesting the loyalty of the Dutch-speaking inhabitants of this country. (Loud laughter and cheers.) Now, what has Mr. Van der Walt done? When the commando arrived at Colesberg he had welcomed them, and had made a speech. That was not surprising. (Laughter.) And he told them, that as an old member of the Cape Parliament, the time had arrived when every Afrikander should work shoulder to shoulder. That gentleman is also still at large. Then they came to a somewhat painful subject. That is, the colleague of the Treasurer-General. I will not say anything about him—(A Voice: " Do ")—because he was in durance vile. (Laughter.) Last, and perhaps not least, we have that reverend patriot, Mr. Schroder, of Upington. Until very recently he was the Landdrost of Upington, and at the same time he never knew when he might be called upon to take his seat in the Cape Parliament. In the face of all this, can we not say that Sir Alfred Milner was perfectly right in making aspersions upon the loyalty of certain inhabitants of this colony? And we have only to look close at hand and read the speeches which many of the members who attend these so-called Christian meetings make, and we will find violent treason in a very large number of them. (Hear, hear.)

THE GRAVITY OF THE SITUATION.

It is a significant fact that the military authorities had found it necessary to place tens of thousands of men on the lines of communication between this and Bloemfontein. (Cheers.) I will go farther, and say that it was Sir Alfred Milner's duty to draw the attention of the English people to the state of affairs which existed in this colony. Fortunately, not only the people of Great Britain, but the people of Greater Britain over the sea, had recognised the gravity of the situation, and had made up their minds that such a state of affairs should never exist again in

South Africa. (Loud cheers.) They sent some of their best men, many of whom had given up their lives fighting for the old flag. In the words of one of their most eloquent colonial Premiers, " Every bullet that finds its way to the heart of our colonial soldiers is an irresistible rivet in the links of that chain which welds together the different parts of the British Empire." (Loud cheers.) I will just briefly refer to another series of charges against His Excellency. It has been said that Sir Alfred Milner had disregarded the advice of his constitutional ministers. (Laughter and a Voice: All rebels.) Well, he certainly declined to jettison the Uitlander. He certainly put his foot down when large quantities of ammunition were being sent over our railways to the Free State at the time when those extraordinary expressions of neutrality were being made by the Prime Minister of this colony; the doctrine that an integral part of the British Empire could remain neutral in the struggle. I think you will agree with me that His Excellency was right. (Loud cheers.)

SLANDERING THE HIGH COMMISSIONER.

But I can hardly believe that these charges were levelled against the head of the High Commissioner and the Governor of this colony. If it is true that the Governor had a serious disagreement with his ministers, they had a constitutional course open to them, which perhaps they might have adopted. Of course this remedy involved retirement; but I do not think that the representatives of a party who had the monopoly of that "righteousness which exalteth a nation" would consider such a question on such a vital point. (Laughter.) They had their constitutional remedy. They had not chosen to take it, but had remained in office. I think that was the strongest argument in favour of the suggestion that there could not be any very large amount of disagreement between the Governor and his constitutional advisers. (Hear, hear.) It has been said by my friend Mr. Innes that, after all, was there any necessity at the present moment to raise any agitation, when the bulk of thinking people in England were with us, when the bulk of the colonies were with us, was there any reason why we should not sit absolutely quiet and allow matters to take their course? I feel that in 1881 and 1882, if the truth had been known to the Empire, then war might never have been raised. (Hear, hear.) Consequently, I would echo the wish that has been expressed by the last speaker, and urge upon you to roll up at the meeting which has been organised by the Vigilance Committee, and I will go one step farther, and ask you to put your names down on the Vigilance Committee. Its sole object is to carry out the motion which you have just enthusiastically passed. (Loud cheers.)

APPENDIX IX.

FROM THE STANDPOINT OF A LOYAL WOMAN IN SOUTH AFRICA.

An Open Letter from Mrs. T. Lynedoch Graham.

The *Cape Times* of 12th July contains the following open letter :—

To Mrs. Cronwright-Schreiner.

Wynberg Hill, July 10.

Sir,—Can you find space in your paper for this open letter to Mrs. Cronwright-Schreiner?—I am, etc.,

A. Graham.

July 10, 1900.

Dear Mrs. Schreiner,—As only sympathisers with the views of your own party were invited to the meeting in Cape Town yesterday afternoon, I could not, of course, be present, but your speech is reported in this morning's paper, so though we might not hear there is evidently no objection to our reading it, and I should like to make a few remarks upon it.

Unfortunately we women on the other side have no Olive Schreiner to voice our sentiments on public platforms, so mass meetings are not much in our line. But do not imagine that because we are silent, we do not exist, or that because we make no noise we are in the minority. The women of South Africa who believe in the justice of the British cause are in a great majority, and their feelings on the rights and wrongs of the war are deep if silent.

You say you have received letters from Canada, Australia, New Zealand, and other English colonies, condemning the war and the proposal to annex the Republics. Doubtless you have. There are cranks in every community. But shall I tell you what we have received? Not letters, but men, men who have flocked to the Imperial standard and gladly given their blood to fight for the cause that they believe to be just. Men in hundreds have voluntarily come from all those very places from which it is your boast to say that you have received letters. The cause for which men will die is more likely to be fundamentally right than the one for which they will only write letters.

You dare to accuse us of a "Hideous crime against justice and humanity;" the "hideous crime against justice and humanity" lies at the door of the Republics. The war was none of our making. They made long and careful preparations, they spent millions on armaments; they launched the ultimatum, they invaded our territories, and finding us unprepared, in the first dark days of the war, they slew the flower of our manhood by hundreds. To plead in justification that they did all this in self-defence, on account of Great Britain's threatening attitude, is a poor argument. I wonder how much excuse your friends would find for me if I met you some day and killed you, because I fancied you looked ferocious and might be meaning murder? Over and over again we have given blood and treasure to save these same Boers from extinction by the native tribes that swarm around them; we ignored the shameful defeat of Majuba, although our troops, ready to wipe it out, were actually in Table Bay; and this, because the conscience of the British people thought the Boers had some right on their side. And what was the return we got? Hardly were our backs turned than some of the people of this colony, thinking they scented weakness in our treatment of the Transvaal, began to conspire to turn us out of South Africa altogether. As far back as 1882 (which was before the Jameson Raid, you know) this dream of a United South Africa for the Afrikanders, under a Dutch flag, was first dreamt of and plotted for; and this scheming and plotting has never ceased since. Read the articles under the title "De Transvaalsche Oorlog" which appeared in *De Patriot* in 1882, and deny it if you can.

Your parallel of a surgical operation is good, but it fits us better than it does you. We all know a serious surgical operation is not undertaken for fun, neither is a great war undertaken for the benefit of a few capitalists, as you pretend to think. We tried a surgical operation in 1881, and we were both stupid and careless—we left some of the instruments of discord in the wound; we gave the Transvaal a badly-worded Convention and the right to arm itself to the teeth, although every child knew the only Power those guns and cannon were to be used against was Great Britain. We have suffered long, and now we are going through another surgical operation. This time, please God, we will be more careful, and leave no instruments inside to cause a festering sore in the future. We should be fools indeed if we did not profit by experience; if we left the Transvaal and the Free State the independence they have so grossly abused, so that they might again have the satisfaction of invading our territories and oppressing our subjects as soon as the khaki backs of our soldiers were turned. The Republics have made a bid for Empire, and played us for a great stake, and in a fair fight they have been beaten; if the peace you talk so much about is dear to your heart, now is the time to show it. Bid them pay their stakes like honourable men, then bury the hachet and shake hands; that is the only way to promote peace. What would you say of a man, who having lost his game, went whimpering round to his friends asking them to try and get him let off paying his stakes—his debts of honour? You would say he was a mean, dishonourable cur, that no decent man would speak to. What is dishonourable in an individual is dishonourable in a nation.

You talk glibly of the "loftiest traditions of English morality"; would you not be serving your country better if you tried to inculcate some of this lofty morality into your own countrymen and country-women, instead of insisting that there shall be no peace, because your wish is father to your thought, and you have not got your own way about the war?

My dear lady, under all that political bias and personal bitterness, I think your heart is really tender. Think a little sometimes of our desolate homes and the dear ones we, too, have lost, and give up egging on an unfortunate people to shed more blood in a lost cause. The game has been played, and lost and won; to go on killing now is surely murder in the sight of God. It is His decree that the British arms should be victorious, and after all is said and done, there might certainly be a worse fate than to become citizens of the greatest Empire the world has ever seen.—I am, etc.,

A. GRAHAM.